Keeping
Their Place

Library Learning Information

To renew this item call:

020 7364 4332

or visit

www.ideastore.co.uk

TOWER HAMLETS

Created and managed by Tower Hamlets Council

Keeping Their Place

DOMESTIC SERVICE IN THE COUNTRY HOUSE

PAMELA SAMBROOK

This book was first published in 2005 by
Sutton Publishing Limited

Paperback edition first published in 2007

Reprinted in 2009 by
The History Press
The Mill, Brimscombe Port,
Stroud, Gloucestershire, GL5 2QG
www.thehistorypress.co.uk

British Library Cataloguing in Publication Data
A catalogue record for this book is available from the British
Library.

ISBN 978 0 7509 3560 9

Typeset in 10.5/13pt Photin.
Typesetting and origination by
Sutton Publishing Limited.
Printed and bound in Great Britain.

Contents

Acknowledgements

I am greatly indebted to the archivists and searchroom assistants of all the record offices, libraries and museums used. Their staff not only suggested sources but also helped with reproduction and permissions. Internet systems are gradually making collections more accessible, but the painstaking and time-consuming work of cataloguing still requires the human brain, and the personal touch is invaluable.

I am grateful also to the many depositors of archival collections used, to whom copyright is reserved. Specifically, archival extracts and illustrative material are reproduced by permission of the following: Bedfordshire and Luton Archive Service and their depositors; Berkshire Record Office; Birmingham Central Library; Cambridgeshire Archives, Cambridge, together with the County Record Office, Huntingdon, Cambridgeshire; Cheshire Record Office; Derbyshire Record Office and the depositors of the following archives: Harpur Crewe of Calke; FitzHerbert of Tissington; Annie Norman of Repton; Durham Record Office and Captain G.M. Salvin, the Earl of Strathmore, the Marquess of Londonderry and Miss L. Hodgkin; Enville Hall Archives and Peter Williams; Kelmarsh Hall; Arthur Inch; John Rylands Library, Manchester University; Gillian Jones; Hampshire Record Office; Leeds Central Library; Leicestershire Record Office; Manchester Central Library; Mary Evans Picture Library; National Trust, Lyme Park; National Trust Photo Library; Northamptonshire Record Office and their depositors; Nottinghamshire Archives and Derek Adlam, Curator of the Portland Collection; Staffordshire Arts and Museum Service, Shugborough; Staffordshire Record

Office and Lord Stafford, Lady Bagot, Mr Richard Dyott, and the Countess of Sutherland; Surrey History Service; Warwickshire Record Office and Lord Daventry; West Sussex Record Office, Lord Egremont, and the Goodwood Estate Co. Ltd and the University of Illinois Library at Urbana-Champaign. Extracts from *Backstairs Life in a Country House* (David and Charles, 1982) appear by kind permission of the publishers.

All reasonable efforts have been made to trace copyright holders of material reproduced in this book. Any untraced claimant of copyright should contact the publisher or myself.

I would like to thank also the following individuals for their help: Jessica Gerard, Claire Bissell, Chris Copp and Andrew Dobraszczyc. For their sustaining interest and advice I am hugely in debt to my friends and colleagues in Staffordshire, especially Rose Wheat and, of course, the staff at Sutton Publishing, Jaqueline Mitchell, Alison Miles and Jane Entrican.

Abbreviations

Within the text, each reference to an extract is given in a short form. Full details of printed sources can be found in Sources and Select Bibliography. Abbreviations used in archive sources are listed here.

BLARS	Bedfordshire and Luton Archives and Records Service
BRO	Berkshire Record Office
CCRO	Cambridgeshire County Record Office, Cambridge
CRO	Cheshire Record Office
CRoH	Cambridgeshire County Record Office, Huntingdon
DeRO	Derbyshire Record Office
DRO	Durham Record Office
EA	Enville Archives, Enville Hall, Staffordshire
HRO	Hampshire Record Office
JRL	John Rylands Library, University of Manchester
KH	Kelmarsh Hall
LCL	Leeds Central Library
LRO	Leicestershire Record Office
NA	Nottinghamshire Archives
NRO	Northamptonshire Record Office
SHC	Surrey History Centre
SRO	Staffordshire Record Office
WCRO	Warwickshire County Record Office
WSRO	West Sussex Record Office

Introduction

What was it like to be a domestic servant in a country house? The question is still a valid one, despite a large body of literature about domestic service. Though much has been published in recent years, the written word of the servant, rather than that of the master, is rarely seen. The aim of this book, therefore, is to give a sample, necessarily highly restricted, personal and therefore biased, of servants' writing – their letters, diaries and autobiography. Editorial comment has been strictly limited, aimed at making sense of a wide range of subject matter rather than providing a closely argued analytical discussion. Above all, it is intended that the writers speak for themselves.

When friends were told of this enterprise, the invariable question was: 'Is there enough material?' The answer is a decided positive. Servants of the country house were, of course, working people of largely restricted education. Many of them began their careers with limited writing abilities, but many won promotion to higher levels of service where competence in literacy and numeracy was essential. Academic research has shown that literacy was more widespread among the working population than previously believed, but in any case the great country houses ran on paper.[1] Enormous numbers of household records were kept, largely by servants themselves – accounts, wages books, bills, memoranda, reports and letters. Add to this the admittedly rare diaries and slightly more numerous autobiographies written by servants at the end of their careers, and there emerges a rich field to choose from indeed the difficulty has been in eliminating material, not finding it.

For this reason, a number of arbitrary choices have had to be made. The majority of extracts included in this collection were written or generated by servants, but not exclusively so. It would be perverse to exclude all letters written to or about servants by their masters, where these throw light upon particular circumstances. So some letters from employers have been included, especially in the chapter dealing with recruitment. Also included are individual examples of official documents such as articles of agreement, quarter-session depositions and employers' or servants' wills. All the diaries and autobiographies, however, were written by servants, not masters.

The decision has also been made to exclude oral history records. Collected over the last few decades, there is now in existence a large body of evidence recorded by servants, too large and disparate to include here, and certainly justifying a separate collection. This is not as distinct a category as might be thought, however; the line between oral history and assisted autobiography is sometimes hazy.

The time frame runs from the eighteenth to the early decades of the twentieth century. Few extracts have been included from the first half of the eighteenth century and most date from the nineteenth, in many ways the high-point of the country-house servant. It is difficult to pinpoint exactly the date of the last extracts as the writers of autobiography were often imprecise about timings, but few have been included later than the 1920s. This wide time frame covers a period when many changes took place in domestic service. Positions and duties changed: the traditional posts of house steward, usher of the hall and groom of the chambers became restricted to only the very richest households, replaced more usually by butler, housekeeper and parlourmaid. There was a general tendency to replace menservants by women. Conditions of employment, frequency of payment, time off, personal freedom, mobility, deference – all these features evolved or declined. Such developments over time may well be under-emphasised in a collection which is arranged according to topic rather than chronology, but it is hoped that the overall pattern of change emerges, albeit subtly.

Drawing clear-cut boundaries is always difficult. The concept of the country house itself is an elastic one. Jessica Gerard defined a country house 'by its owner rather than by its size or grandeur', and went on to debate the inclusion of the lesser or 'parish gentry'.[2] Yet all shared a common culture based on land ownership and tenantry, similar values and the exercise of local or national power. This means that a country-house servant could experience service in establishments which varied widely in size but usually provided a continuity of ethos, skill and tradition.

In addition, country-house servants were mobile in several senses. Many started their careers at a low social level, working as single-handed servants in urban or rural contexts, but their early employment was part of their overall experience and coloured many of their attitudes later in life when they had moved on into the country-house world proper. For these reasons an occasional extract from a single-handed footman or housemaid has been included, where this seems particularly apposite. At the other end of the scale, contributions from senior staff such as stewards have also been included, though whether these are more accurately described as 'servants' or 'managers' is a moot point. In the eighteenth century and earlier they may well have originated from fairly well-to-do families themselves, but by the nineteenth century house stewards had usually worked their way up the employment ladder.

Personal servants such as footmen and lady's maids were mobile in a different sense, moving around with their employers from house to house and taking in the London season. One of the Sutherlands' footmen, for example, spent much of 1838–9 dividing his time between the Leveson-

Gowers' house at West Hill, south of the Thames and still semi-rural, and their main town house, Stafford House in St James's.[3] Yet it would be absurd to include one and not the other. What has been clearly excluded, however, is the experience of the long-term urban working-class or middle-class servant.[4] Even though these made up the vast majority of servants, theirs is a different story.

Domestic service as a whole employed a wide variety of servant types, but within the restricted world of the nineteenth-century country house Jessica Gerard has identified four categories: the career servant, whose whole working life was spent in service; the lifestyle servant, for whom service provided a useful stage, a traineeship before going on to something else, usually marriage; the impoverished genteel servant, often governesses or housekeepers who had come down in the world; and labourers, usually locally based, casual or outdoor workers.[5] This categorisation is far from exhaustive, excluding as it does the highly skilled outdoor craftsmen such as gardeners or carpenters and the well-to-do stewards. The relevant point here is that this collection includes all of the above categories where they worked mainly indoors. In deciding to restrict the scope of the collection to indoor servants only, outdoor staff, including gamekeepers, gardeners and many other skilled workers, are necessarily excluded.

SOURCES

Some of the great family archive collections contain thousands of letters. Most are of personal, family, social or political content, but some relate to aspects of household management. The peripatetic nature of many wealthy families required frequent and detailed contact between houses. Family members would move between their own town and country establishments, visit friends or stay in London for the season, leaving behind a skeleton staff to care for their own house in the country. The servants were divided therefore into what were often called the 'residents' (staff who stayed in the same house all year) and the 'travellers' (who moved around the country with the family).[6] The most numerous household letters to survive, therefore, are instructional or reporting letters, exchanged between members of the family and the resident person left in charge of the house. This last might ultimately be a steward who had responsibility for both house and estate matters, but it was more usual to leave the house in the charge of a female housekeeper. She would head a resident indoor staff which was largely female – a few housemaids, perhaps one or two laundry maids, a dairymaid, plus perhaps a brewer, carpenter and porter.

Given a regular annual routine of absence, some family archives contain long runs of instructional letters. One such is the collection of the Fitzwilliam family of Milton in Northamptonshire, a collection covering much of the seventeenth century and well into the eighteenth. The letters contain mainly estate-related material, but there are also ongoing sagas relating to brewing, a recalcitrant smoking kitchen chimney which seemed to afflict the household for decades, and difficulties with recruiting servants.[7] In another case, the FitzHerberts of Tissington, the housekeeping contact was an old and trusted nanny who lived in a house in the park.[8] The other side of this relationship, of course, is represented by letters from senior servants reporting progress, disaster or gossip. Letters from agents reporting on estate and farming progress are fairly common; much rarer are reports of internal household affairs.

Very different in style and content are 'nanny' letters, correspondence from old servants to their grown-up charges. These are very affectionate in manner, sometimes reproachful, evidence of the close and long-lasting bond that could develop between mistress or master and servant. Occasionally long-serving housekeepers had similar relationships and wrote similar nanny-type letters.

Different again are 'begging' letters, written by ex-servants to ex-employers, asking for help of various sorts, be it money, work or patronage (help in obtaining a position elsewhere). These tend to be addressed to mistresses since many are from women fallen on hard times, and it was the women of the family who seemed to deal with this side of the household administration. The 3rd Duchess of Sutherland, for example, seems to have received many such letters from contacts on the family's vast estates throughout England and Scotland.[9]

Servants of course also wrote letters to their own families and friends, though these are much less likely to survive as they were not deposited in a large archive. Many families, however, had a long tradition of high-level domestic service and there are occasional survivals of treasured letters, such as those kept by the Inch family.[10] An unusual survival is the Spendlove collection in Northampton Record Office – letters from Ruth Barrow, a girl living in service in Leicester to the man who later became her husband.[11]

Perhaps the most numerous relevant correspondence is that relating to the whole issue of recruiting staff. In many families this was a thorny problem and there is no shortage of letters complaining of the quality of servants and the difficulty of finding suitable staff. The aristocratic network of kin and friends was the most favoured means of recruitment by the incumbents of country houses. After scouring the immediate neighbourhood for likely candidates, the next recourse was to write to contacts asking them to do likewise in their area and to generally 'put word out', sometimes enclosing very specific requirements. Some households – the Harpur Crewes for example – had a tradition of using local employment agencies to make such searches and this was usually conducted by letter, at least in the country. Mr Palmer, the Harpur Crewe's steward in the mid-nineteenth century, kept even failed job applications from servants.[12] Generally records of servants' 'characters' or references survive in great number. Given the rapid turnover of servants, especially lower-ranking staff, writing and receiving characters must have been a major domestic chore, even though most employers adopted a fairly standardised format.

Within most family and estate archives, formal household management records are much more numerous than personal records of servants. The elaborate structure of vouchers (bills or receipts), house books, collected accounts, inventories and so on are evidence of the extent to which the country house needed paper records, and they have been used extensively in studies of households and domestic service.[13] Most of these records were, of course, written by middle- or senior-ranking servants, and as such speak volumes about servant literacy and numeracy. Such records can, however, be obstinately silent about individual servants and their experience of work. As it is that missing personal quality which is the target of this search, only a few short extracts of this type of record have been included where relevant.

Servants' diaries are unfortunately fairly rare, and this collection contains extracts from six, two of which are in published form. Some senior servants kept what was called a memorandum book. This was a record of daily events, but ordered alphabetically rather than chronologically. It seems an odd record to modern eyes, but alphabetical records of various descriptions were fairly common in the eighteenth century. One such extract has been included in this collection, the alphabetical record kept by a footman in the service of the 6th Earl of Stamford.[14] The book does not carry the name of its writer, only the initials WT. As the earliest retrospective entry is the record of the deaths of Mary and John Torry (under T), and other records of the Stamford servants reveal the existence of a William Torry who became footman, later promoted to butler, the record is referred to here as the memorandum book of William Torry.

One of the published diaries is by William Tayler, the only manservant of a wealthy widow, who kept a diary in 1837.[15]

Although much of his experience during that year was in an urban environment, a few extracts have been used to shed light upon the lot of footmen, who played such an important role in the life of the country house. Tayler's record forms an interesting comparison with that of Thomas, the footman in the service of the Duke of Sutherland, from whose manuscript diary a single year, 1838–9, has survived in Staffordshire Record Office.[16] Use has also been made of a diary written most unusually by a young housemaid in the service of the family of one of the staff of Repton School in Derbyshire, dated 1914.[17] Again it is hardly representative of true country-house service, but her experience in a restricted rural world was comparable. Single extracts have been included from the famous diaries of Hannah Cullwick, whose experience of country-house service was limited; of Harriet Messenger, a nanny/governess who accompanied Mr and Mrs Leveson-Gower of Limpsfield in their European travels in the 1880s and 1890s, and of Sarah Wells, housekeeper at Uppark in 1892.[18]

Servant autobiographies are more common than diaries, though many of the printed ones are of a late date, published in the mid-twentieth century.[19] Some of them, however, reach back in memory into the late nineteenth century, the 1860s and 1870s, and even in one case to the mid-eighteenth century. They give a very colourful picture of life in the domestic offices of great houses. Retrospective records such as these have to be viewed with great care, of course. Memoirs are usually written by people who have a particular point to make – recording a rise from poverty and degradation to respectability and relative wealth, for example. With the best will in the world, memory plays tricks and some plainly bear the imprint of a strong editorial hand. For example, the servants' memoirs which were collected together by Rosina Harrison sometimes read uncannily like Rosina's own separately published autobiography.[20]

Servants' testimonies appear in more official forms, such as wills and sworn witness statements to events, sometimes criminal, which took place inside the domestic environment. In particular, county quarter-session records contain numerous witness statements made by servants, as victims, perpetrators, or eye witnesses, but most are outside the limits of this collection as belonging to middle-class, working or urban environments. A single example of a witness statement has been included here to complete the selection.

SERVANTS' LITERACY

The issue of the extent of servants' literacy is an interesting one. The quality of writing in servants' letters varies greatly, both over time and according to status. Many senior servants in the eighteenth century were well-educated sons of well-to-do families and could write highly literate, beautifully penned letters. Other examples are more idiosyncratic. Some, like the housekeeper of Lady Mordaunt writing in the early 1700s, are examples of almost phonetic spelling, what has been called 'oral writing', but none the less lucid for that.[21] Punctuation is often non-existent, even in highly literate letters. For the purposes of presentation to a modern readership unused to such streams of consciousness, an occasional comma has been inserted, but only where the sense is difficult to follow without it. Otherwise transcripts are as exact as possible. Abbreviations and superscripts have been kept where the meaning is obvious and spelling is original.

Why did servants keep diaries or other personal records? William Tayler tells us he did it to improve himself, in which task he felt he was unsuccessful: 'I am got quite tired of this writing as I do not improve as I expected I should, but I neglect writeing for two or three days sometimes, then I take up my pen and hurrey it over anyhow. I am a regular dunce and allways shall be. I was born a dunce, I live a dunce and I shall die a dunce. . . .'[22] Yet he also clearly wrote for an outside readership, to explain what a servant's life was like. Thomas the footman seems to have written his entries mostly at night as he went to bed, remarkably regularly. His diary was a personal record of a time when he was experiencing work in one of the richest households in the country. He tried hard to keep in touch with his father, a Cheshire farmer, and his brother, also in service; they were obviously interested in his life and he bought newspapers and court magazines to save for them and presumably the diary would serve him as an *aide-mémoire*.

On the whole, employers needed literate servants. A Mrs Boon sacked her footman for not being able to read and write and Mrs Wrigley found an employer who helped her with her lessons.[23] Annie Norman's mistress gave her a present of ink, so she probably knew about her diary writing.[24] Some letters, however, are clearly written by someone else more literate. We can see this in the case of Mary and Elizabeth Brook, two sisters who wrote to the Lucas family asking for help – letters from two separate people but with the same handwriting.[25]

Finally the point has to be reiterated. The country-house archival collections in our record offices are enormous; what appears here is but a tiny selection, taken almost at random. The choice of archives examined has been dictated largely by the practical considerations of travel and access. Diaries and autobiographies apart, any number of collections could have been made of entirely different material and featuring entirely different archives. The present selection is therefore a product of partial and personal choice, a coloured and, I hope, colourful glimpse of the real people who walked the corridors and kitchens of our great country houses.

ONE

'I am perfectly master of my work'
– the recruitment of servants

Contemporary sources can show us something of the problems of recruitment experienced by both sides – the master or mistress trying to find the right servant and the servant trying to find a good place. Most writers on country-house service agree that there was a self-contained circulating system of employment at this level. Youngsters were brought into the house from the local rural areas. They were often the children of estate workers or tenants, some of them, girls especially, having gone through a first stage of training at a 'petty place', perhaps working for the local vicar or doctor or as a part-time child-minder. They might then be passed around the circuit.

The attributes of servants, particularly their vices, were a favourite topic of conversation among country-house families and their guests. Descriptions of servants as 'wastfull and exstravagant' are common in correspondence.[1] Details of their characters and interviews are often casually buried among general friendly gossip in letters. At other times the writer might exude a touch of serious desperation in their need for a servant. Friends sometimes acted as recruiting agents on a regular basis. Some writers, such as Kenelm Digby and Richard Huddlestone who enjoyed a correspondence lasting many years, showed a general interest in placing servants and a genuine care for their welfare, acting as patrons in the better sense of the word.[2]

Rosina Harrison's autobiography described an equivalent network among servants, a '"Who's Who" and a "What's What" below stairs . . . also a blacklist and woe betide anyone who got on it'.[3] Many country-house servants, especially those with a personal element to their work such as footmen or ladies' maids, were highly mobile within their jobs. They moved around with their employers throughout the social season, visiting other country houses in the late summer and winter or London during the spring and early summer. At this level servants kept in touch with friends made during previous employment. The servants' hall and steward's room must have been the venues for lively gossip about employers and their idiosyncrasies.

Yet the existence of such country-house systems did not preclude the use of external means of recruitment. In the eighteenth century isolated country houses used the traditional venues of hiring fairs to find employees, and as the nineteenth century progressed more and more use was made of newspapers and agencies. Advertisements in local papers are usually for work at large farms rather than country houses, and quality households preferred to reply to adverts rather than place them, searching newspapers such as *The Times* and *The Morning Post* as well as magazines such as *The Field* and *The Lady*. Agencies appear from the mid-eighteenth century onwards and some households made no bones about using them. Reliable local firms and national companies such as Mrs Massey's and Mrs Hunt's specialised in the country-house market and could save a deal of trouble in tracking down and sifting through likely candidates. For the servant, working through an agency could save many a wasted journey.

The one critical feature when finding a new place or servant was the 'character'. This was a written reference from a previous employer and was essential for any decent servant. On leaving an employer the servant had to ask them to provide a character when approached by the next employer. Usually, the servant would not see what had been written. Theoretically, an employer could be asked to supply a character once only, and this could cause problems if the new situation did not work out well. By the nineteenth century this had become a standardised system and many characters have a similar format – short and formal, even brusque.

Country-house service showed a high turnover of staff in the lower and middle levels. Individuals moved on for more money and more experience, for promotion and to meet new people and possible marriage partners. The character system would reveal this very quickly, and the ambitious servant had to balance the advantages of moving on to a better job with the problem of gaining a reputation for being 'short-charactered'. Ernest King reckoned a servant ought to stay in each place for at least two years in order to obtain the 'precious passport' of a good reference.[4] Job mobility declined among senior servants and varied, too, from house to house. Some, like Welbeck, promoted internally whereas others made it a policy not to do so. Some families, such as the Rushouts of Northwick, had a tradition of keeping their servants for twenty, thirty or even forty years and thus had limited experience of recruiting staff.[5]

Widows with a known track record before marriage would be welcomed back into service. With this exception, servants who had been out of work for some time could find it difficult to get back into the system. This was partly because of the need for an up-to-date character and partly because of exclusion from the internal networks. But servants' private lives could be complex, and among the most pathetic survivals within country-house records are letters from would-be servants begging for work. Asking for patronage in this way required some sort of connection between the supplicant and the patron. This could be real or tenuous, sometimes involving a degree of ingenuity. Such letters reveal the difficult and sometimes tragic circumstances of many servants' lives.

FINDING THE RIGHT SERVANT

Away from home, families kept in touch with their estates by letter. In the 1700s, during his absences in London, Lord Fitzwilliam wrote weekly to Francis Guybon, his steward at Milton, Northamptonshire. Most of his letters were taken up with instructions about tenantry, brewing, the culling of deer and general gossip, but a continuing theme is the need to find good servants.

Lord Fitzwilliam to Francis Guybon, 9 May 1700.

> . . . Pray make it your business to get us some servants against we come downe. There must be a fellow to look after the Gelds, to make Cleane the House, heate the Ovens, & so do the other drudging work about the House. There must be Two Maids, One for the Kittchin wh: can roast & boile meale clearly, & do the other work in the Kittchin: and the other Maide must make cleane the House, & Wash the Wash Bucks and do any other business that is to be done about the House fitt for a Maide . . . Pray gett Mrs Bull to help you to these maids, or any body else that you thinke can do it: & do not neglect to do this, thinking Goody Buttler may serve for one: we will not have it so, she must go home, & will have work enough to do to wash for the family . . .
>
> Your loving Friend
> W Fitzwilliam

Same, 16 May 1700

> My wife is very earnest that you & Mrs Bull should help her to Two working Maids, one for the Kittchin & the other for the House for this summer, for we must be in Towne againe the latter end of October. Neither will the Maids in this Towne do such sort of Worke, they are too fine fingered for country business . . .

Same, 5 September 1702

> . . . we are sorry we can't have the man Mrs Bull mention'd to us, because she thought he was so fitt for us: so pray lett there

be another hired for us. We should be glad you could help us to good Cooke Maids because they are all here such Slutts or Whores or Thieves or Druncken Beasts, that we dare hardly bring any of them downe

(NRO, Fitzwilliam, F(M)C 1125–6, 1230)

Robert Smith, house steward to the 5th Duke of Richmond at Goodwood, was also given responsibility for servant recruitment.

Robert Smith to Dr Archibald Hair, secretary to the Duke, 19 May 1858

. . . I have not left a thing undone that I could do about getting a Still Room Maid both Publick & Private but I can find nothing Likely to suit at all – Mrs Sanders would like her to be 30 years of Age and to know Something of cooking and the Wages 10-10-0 every body tells me there is nothing of the kind to be had in London.

Same, 23 June 1859

. . . I walked from their to Chelsea where I was Likewise unsuccessful – but having called on A Friend in Grosvenor Square I was recommended to call on Lord De La War's Butler and I think I have got hold of a capital man he lived three years with Lord De La War as Under Butler and three years before that with Lord Macclesfield in the same situation and bears an excellent character from both Places I enclose Lord De La War's Recommendation and the Butler Said ask me whatever you like I can only give you this Answer he is (A Perfect Servant) Particularly Sober Honest Clean Truthful Active & Obliging and not Scrupleous about doing anything that does not Exactly belong to the Under Butler department he is single & 32 years of age . . . their are plenty of under Butlers out of Place just now but nearly all Short Characters and A Something behind that does not bear Searching into . . .

(WSRO, Goodwood, MS 1830 f. 1607; 1841 f. 1742)

Another option was to ask friends or family for help. Here the daughter of Dr Percy, Bishop of Dromore, writes to a family friend on her mother's behalf.

Barbara Percy to Mrs Mary Orlebar, 13 January 1738

Carlisle

My dear Madam,

My Mother would esteem herself greatly obliged to you Ladies if you would have the goodness to make inquiries in your neighbourhood for a Housekeeper for her, and also a maid to wait on herself; her present servant in those capacities does not suit her well enough to carry her with her into Ireland and she cannot meet with any in this part of the world. She wishes to have a careful steady Person to act as Cook and Housekeeper (with a Kitchenmaid under her) one who thoroughly understands every branch of her business and will take upon her the Management of the other servants. She must have lived in genteel Families or she will not do for us as it will be necessary to give handsome entertainments in the Country where we are going to . . . My Mother likewise begs the favour of you to inquire for a Maid to wait on herself, one who understands Hair Dressing, Millinery and the getting up of fine Linen. She would wish to have a quiet steady young woman. Should you hear of Persons in these capacities who you think will suit her she begs you will be so good as to send her all particulars and what wages will be expected . . .

I remain Dear Madam very
sincerely
Y^r obliged Friend
Barbara Percy

(BLARS, Orlebar, OR 2071/315)

Recommendations of individuals appear in many letters from friends.

Lady Blount to Francis Fortescue Turvile at Bosworth Hall, Welford, Northamptonshire, 3 May 1804

Clifton

. . . I beg you to give my love to Mrs Turvile & tell her if she is not yet provided with a House & Laundry maid there is a very good one to be had who was bred up by Lady Clifford when a younger brother's Wife & when she went to Igbrooke took with her as under nursery maid where she lived till within these two years, she had a regard for her – & at her recommendation served Lady Southwell in the capacity Mrs Turvile wants to fill, when Housekeeping was broke up at Swinnerton she was of course discharged but had given great satisfaction, from thence went to Stonor where I understand they have lately parted from many servants & her amongst the rest. You might know from thence any particulars you want. George has hired the servant who lived with your son. His whom I mentioned to you would now be glad of your place, and wear a Livery. I before said all I knew about him & I believe mentioned his great excellence was perfectly understanding Brewing & the care of Beer. If you are already provided or do not chuse to take him – be so good as to write me a line in a post or two, should you think of hiring him direct to Poulton at Bookers No. 56 New Bond Street where he will call for his letters he will not be in London before next Thursday . . .

> I am very truly Dr Mr Turviles faithful & obliged
> Humble Servant
> M. Blount

> (LRO, Turvile Constable-Maxwell, DG39/1634)

The Revd William Alderson to Sir Henry FitzHerbert at Tissington Hall, Derbyshire, 19 August 1817

Aston Rectory, Yorkshire

My dear Sir Henry,

. . . I have this moment had a conference with the Coachman, who is a man of all others that I should like to have in that capacity; he has lived in the Stables (where there are very good apartments) since he came to Aston. His character in the village is very good, his manners are extremely mild, and he has always been regular at church. He lived sometime with Mr. Foljambe before his death and continued with Lady Mary at the same wages, which were 35 guineas a year and the Cloaths you are in the habit of giving. He has taken a small house at Worksop where he would wish his wife and three children to live for the present at least; she is well spoken of and appears a very good sort of body. I told him the wages were much greater than you were accustomed to give, but begged him to state the lowest and I would inform you. He said he could not possibly provide for his Wife and family for less, otherwise he should willingly do it. He prefers a Country life to that of Town, and quickness to that of bustle . . . I think I can say no more on the subject, and you will now judge for yourself, I gave him no reason to expect that you would take him. I forgot to ask his age which appears to be about Forty . . .

Same, 27 August 1817

. . . I have engaged the servant for 30 guineas and the cloaths etc. I am confident you will find him a great treasure . . . He is not afraid of any work or <u>waiting</u> or <u>going</u> or even teaching the Young Masters to ride, [as long as] he is with a quiet place where he may hope to continue; as he is not given to change. He is ready to come whenever you please to commend, and refers you to Colonel Lumley, Cuckney near Ollerton or to Mr Savile or any of the Family who have all offered to give him a Character, but he seems to think the former is the most rational and will be found at home . . .

(DeRO, FitzHerbert, D239M/F/8406–7)

Many of the letters exchanged between Kenelm H. Digby and Major Huddlestone at Sawston Hall, near Cambridge, in the 1830s and 1840s concerned finding servants or placing promising youngsters.

Kenelm H. Digby to Richard Huddlestone, 6 December 1840

. . . But now I must come to a piece of business. There is a little boy here, a native . . . who wants a place as any thing for which he may be taken. Well there are plenty of boys in the same case; yes; but not plenty like him. He is a shy timid delicate but most willing, dutiful & pious child. He has so endeared himself to us all here that though our place is full we keep him till we can place him. He can serve at Mass; he is a rare one for dispatch in going on messages; he has a great love for being in service; he has moreover a certain style & tone of <u>innocence</u> that would make him a treasure to many people. He would have money in his pocket to fit him out in the best new clothes & I have no doubt that at the end of six months he would be found of that sort of rare merit that is often imperceptible on first sight. Now I thought that if <u>along with Harris's brother</u> you should want a boy, here would be the lad for you. But not for the world would I have him to endanger the brother of our Harris to lose his place. Indeed that would be a sine qua non of our sending him. Perhaps Mr Scot would need a boy, or you might know of someone else that did . . .

(CCRO, Huddlestone, 488/C3/DG 70)

Some friends went to great lengths, almost to the point of acting as agents. This was the case with John Trevanion, a sporting companion of the 6th Earl of Stamford. While in London he helped to recruit senior servants for his friend's new household at Dunham Massey, near Manchester, newly inherited from the Earl's late father. Here he has selected a butler, Philip Osgood, who was eventually appointed and remained a kingpin of the Earl's household for many years.

John Trevanion to the 6th Earl of Stamford, 17 July 1819

Mount Street,

My dear Lord Stamford,

. . . After my letter had gone to the post yesterday I saw Philip Osgood, as Butler; form at Newberry in Berkshire, 5ft 10½ inches high, 36 years of age, lived six years with the late Mr. Wyndham M.P. for Glamorganshire, as Valet and afterwards Butler, five years with Sir Saml. Hood as Butler & six years and three months with L' Carhampton, who parted with him upon making an alteration in his Family in consequence of Lady C's health, upon the whole I think him a more likely servant to suit you then Bray, and he may be easily put off as being a Scotchman as I told him I feard that would be an objection . . . Osgood is a married man but his wife (whom I yesterday saw) appears a most respectable woman and is settled in a very good business as Ladies Dress Maker in Davies St. They have two children at school, he had 70gs per annum with L' Carhampton, and of what he has always heard of your Family is most particularly anxious to live in it, as he wishes to get into a place where he is likely to remain . . .

Same, 21 July 1819

. . . I have engaged Philip Osgood at 70 gs per annum for you without any perquisites, if his character answers . . . he has just sent me the enclosed as a specimen of his hand writing which I think very tolerable . . .

Philip Osgood is <u>rather</u> marked with the small pox and a little freckled but is in my opinion certainly a respectable & genteel looking servant.

(EA G2/2/3/12/10)

FINDING THE RIGHT PLACE

Servants, of course, could take the initiative and approach potential employers or an ex-employer.

James Atkins to Sir Henry FitzHerbert, 13 May, nd

Ashborne Grove

Sir,

I understand that you are or will be shortly in want of a Groom, am not feeling myself comfortable in my <u>present situation should be glad to take that place as soon as it may be vacant</u>. I have this morning been to Tissington and Johnson the Keeper (who knows me very well) said that I might in all probability get the situation if you were not already suited – My age, sir, is about thirty.

I have liv'd, sir, with the Earl of Chesterfield's guardian

Mr Williams of Cubley Rectory near Ashborne and my present situation, or rather, master, sir, is J.T. Silvester Esq., Ashborne Grove, to whom a reference for my character may be made.

I have, sir, had the care of five horses under the latter gentleman – Sir, your reply as soon as convenient will very much oblige

Your very ob[t] humb[l] Serv[t]
James Atkins

(DeRO, FitzHerbert, D239M/F/8786)

Requests for work were often made by an intermediary. Here a Quaker tries to find a position for his sister.

Samuel Tennant to a fellow Friend, 4 April 1858

Newcastle upon Tyne

Respected Friend

Thou wilt please excuse the boldness of a stranger, in thus addressing thee, but having a sister who is in want of a situation & having heard that thy wife wanted a servant, I thought thou might probably look over the liberty I am taking.

My sister is about seventeen years of age, was in Manchester with a friend of the name of Henry Nield, about two years, as a nurse maid, but left there in consequence of indisposition: she has now recovered her health & is at present with my Father; whom probably thou may know 'John Tennant' of Counterside in Wensleydale.

Should I have been misinformed relative to thy wife wanting a servant perhaps thou would have the kindness to let me know if thou hears of any other person who may have a situation vacant, as my Sister is very anxious to be doing something for herself.

The address Henry Nield (of whom any particulars relative to conduct & character may be had) is Confectioner, Oxford Street or Road, Manchester. Any further particulars thou may wish to know may be obtained either from my parents or myself. My address is at C. Bragg & Sons, Newcastle.

I think that either a Nurse or Housemaids place would suit

my Sister, in the latter there might be some things she would have to learn. Trusting thou may hear of some likely situation, & with further apology for the trouble I am giving thee,

> I remain thy Friend,
> Very respectfully,
> Samuel Tennant.

(DRO, Hodgkins, D/Ho/C52/315)

Annie McSkimming, housekeeper for the Leveson-Gowers at Lilleshall, Shropshire, sent regular little notes to her employer, away in London.

Annie McSkimming to Millicent, the 4th Duchess of Sutherland, 6 January 1891

> Lilleshall Lodge,
> Newport, Salop

My Lady,

I am very sorry to trouble you at this time but I have put it off for some time. Kitchen Jessie would like to make a change at the end of this month as she would like to get a better place as second kitchen maid as she wants to learn more cooking. I will be pleased if your Ladyship should hear of any place for her. I am pleased to tell your Ladyship that Puggie and Jackie are both quite well and also the birds. I hope your Ladyship is a little better and will soon be able to come down here again.

I am, my Lady, faithfully, Annie McSkimming

Sometimes servants were faced with difficult choices.

Susan Watts to Lady Alexandra Leveson-Gower, daughter of the 3rd Duchess of Sutherland, 11 October c. 1888

> 96, Westbourne Terrace
> Hyde Park, W

My Lady,

I write to thank you very much for kindly offering me your situation as housemaid. You will, I am sure, agree with me when I explain how I am situated. The lady I am living with,

Mrs Argentes, as been very ill, in consequence of which has caused great unsettlement, although she is most kind to me having had a deal of trouble with former servants she looks to me as her responsible servant. She is very elderly and the dr says she must live quietly. Therefore I think they will give up their present house and take smaller for Mrs Argente. Nothing has been arranged with the servants at present. Mrs Argente raised my wages to £26 per year before going to Brighton. So you see, my Lady, I am most awkwardly situated. The lady having been so ill lately I fear would take it unkind if I left her . . . although it comes hard to me to refuse your kindness in offering me your situation. I sincerely hope, my Lady, you will not think me ungrateful after taking such an interest in me, trusting you are quite well, believe me,

Your humble servant, Susan Watts

(SRO, Sutherland, D593/P/29/1/20)

Servants must often have had misgivings about their future employer. When Jane Hatt's mistress Emma Dunn died, Jane returned to her parents in Aberdeen, from where she looked for a new place. Here she writes to Emma's sister, Winifred Salvin of Lartington Hall, Leeds, about a prospective employer in Congleton, Cheshire.

Jane Hatt to Mrs Salvin, 28 July 1864

Ruthrieston Cottage,
Nr. Aberdeen
Dear Mrs Salvin

. . . I have received another letter from Mrs Swetenham she offers me now £20 a year & my Father & Mother think I ought to take the situation in the meantime, till a better turns up, they say it is better than nothing at all, I was some days after returning an answer to her, she has not written again, so it may be she has got another, should she write again, will you kindly allow me to refer her to you should she want a reference. I really think I ought to have one of hers, as I do feel as if she were very odd, still what can I do . . .

> With kindest regards to Mr William and Mr Charles,
> believe me yours,
> very sincerely
> Jane Hatt

Same, 22 August 1864

. . . I received a letter from Mrs Swetenham this morning . . . she wishes me to visit her & we will see each other, she asks for your address so I will send it to her, I shall be very glad to take the situation being so long out of one & so much debt to pay. You remember the letter I got from Liverpool said she was close on derangement, but I will see and judge for myself & if I think I cannot remain I must be on the look out for another . . .

(DRO, Salvin, D/Sa/C/286/2–6)

Correspondence and records kept in 1855 by Charles Palmer, agent to the Harpur Crewes at Calke Abbey, Derbyshire, about the employment of a cook, Mrs Sarah Fogg, reveal something of the complicated personal circumstances of some servants.

Internal memo by Charles Palmer, giving information from recruitment agency

Experienced Cook aged 38, Mrs Sarah Fogg
Has previously lived with Sir Wm. Worsley, Hovingham Hall, Yorkshire, where she married the Butler & having lost her husband she wishes to go into service again. She has been 2 months at Mrs Peels, Burton-on-Trent where she refers to for her character, their situation did not suit her and she left by her own wishes.

Sarah was given a first interview with Palmer, then a second interview with Lady Crewe, which, however, she found she needed to postpone.

Sarah Fogg to Mr Charles Palmer, 18 February 1855

Mrs Wilson's
Nelson Street,
Derby

Sir,

Since our letter of yesterday (Friday) I have accepted an engagement for perhaps two or three weeks which . . . will prevent me waiting upon Lady Crewe on Monday as appointed . . . I still aspire to that honour should it be convenient to wait for me. I must explain to you that the engagement above named will be of great advantage to me as it will furnish me with the means of obtaining suitable apparel for a Gentleman's Establishment without making the sacrifice I otherwise must have done, that is to have disposed of some articles of Household Furniture which I have left and which I have a great desire to retain, for my dear children's advantage.

Sir I should feel greatly obliged to you if you will be kind enough to explain this circumstance to her Ladyship

I am yours obediently
S. Fogg

This seems to have been accepted, but there was a problem with obtaining her character from her previous employer.

Same, 27 February 1855

. . . Mrs Peel informs me that she is very much indisposed which has been the cause of her delay. She also says that she will not give but one character, she never as made a practice of doing so – therefore I think I would rather come to Lady Crewe upon trial as I proposed . . . Should I come it will be with the desire of remaining a very long time both for my own good & that of my young family . . . An early answer will oblige

Eventually, Sarah started work at Calke Abbey, but neglected to pay her fee to the recruitment agency run by a Mr Bull, from whom she had also borrowed money.

Mr J. Bull to Charles Palmer, March 1855

Mr Palmer

This is in confidence to you, when the Cook Mrs Fogg was coming to Calke Abbey she call'd on me being short of cash and borrowed ten shillings also 2/6 for her Place, total 12/6. May I beg the favour of you to see me pay'd as soon as she receives any part of wages, also the upper Footman Shepherd has not paid the office fee of 2/6 which if from Mrs Massey's would have been 5 shillings or 7/6 for such a Place – but I have met with so many shabby jockeys am now determined to expose. If sir you please to see me Righted I shall be much obliged,

am sir, your obed^t serv^t
J Bull

Theoretically Sarah was paid quarterly but she could not afford to wait so long and asked for an advance.

Sarah Fogg to Charles Palmer, 17 May 1855

Sir,

I shall esteem it a very great favour if you will be kind enough to pay the one months wages. I received a letter this morning from the person that as the care of my children requesting me to send them some money and I have no alternative but applying to you . . .

According to a memo kept by Charles Palmer, Mrs Fogg did not stay long at Calke.

Mrs Fogg came to Calke Abbey on 5th of March 1855, & left on the 24th of May 1855,

Credited:
2 months, 2 weeks & 5 days, at £40 a year.   8-15-2

One month extra	3-6-8
Allowed travelling expences	4-4
	12-6-2
Debited:	
May 17 1855 Paid Mrs Fogg 1 month wages	3-6-8
" 18 " " Mr Bull at her request	12-6
" 24 " Paid Mrs Fogg	8-7-2

But Mr Palmer had not heard the last of Mrs Fogg. Four years later she wrote to ask for a character, explaining about her 'lost' husband.

Sarah Fogg to Charles Palmer, 12 December 1859

> Mrs Tunnley
> 19, Railway St
> York

To Mr Palmer,

I hope you will excuse me taking the liberty of writing to ask you if you will be kind enough to give me a recommendation for the time I was with Sir John. I have been living with my husband ever since I left Calke Abbey but I have decided upon going to service again to enable me to go into some kind of business. I have a situation in view and a recommendation from you would I am sure ensure it for me, but cannot apply for it until I know whether you will be kind enough to oblige me. It is at the request of my husband that I apply to you. I wish I had been in the same state of mind when I was at Calke Abbey as I am now, I might have been there yet but the trouble that was on my mind was almost more than I could bear. I am happy to say that my husband and I are quite reconciled to each other and live on the most comfortable of terms. I wish I had the chance of coming to Calke Abbey again, I should appreciate a good situation, & I never served a Lady with more pleasure than Lady Crewe. If you will be kind enough to give me a recommendation, please oblige me by enclosing it to me and you will confer an everlasting obligation upon

> Yours obediently
> S. Fogg

The last we hear of Sarah is a note from her new employer asking for her character.

(DeRO, Harpur Crewe, D2375M 242/16/4)

Many servants tried to lift themselves out of service, but this was risky as it was difficult to get back into it. Two letters from the Sutherland papers illustrate this problem.

John Penson came from a family with a long tradition of service to the Leveson-Gowers at Trentham, Staffordshire and had himself been their coachman before taking a pub tenancy from the estate. Vantini was the Duke of Sutherland's Italian house steward.

John Penson, to Vantini, 3 May 1838

Sutherland Arms Inn, Tittensor

Mr. Vantini, Sir,

I understand that Mr Hitchcock is going to leave the Duke's establishment. And in consequence of the Railroad being open it has tuck traffick off the road. And the trade his so very bad in the Potteries that I am doing nothing as like where I am. It certainly has been a very unfortunate speculation for me coming here. But we cannot foresee these things. And the only alternative I have left his to go to service again and I should very much wish to be placed in my old situation again providing it should meet with His Grace's approbation. Which I hope my conduct in the duke's establishment whas that which will induce them not to forget me,

I conclude with my best wishes to you
and remain yours has ever,
John Penson jun.

Penson's request was not successful as three years later he, his wife and three children were still at the Sutherland Arms.[6]

The second letter is from an ex-governess.

M.A. Ochsenbein to the Duchess of Sutherland, 14 July 1887

18

Highland Road
Upper Norwood

Honoured and dear Madam,

I have no right whatever of writing to you in order to interest you in my behalf. Therefore kindly forgive me in addressing you these lines.

The signature of this letter, I believe, will not inform you of who I am, therefore have to give a little outline of incidents of the past which will help you to do so.

For more than 3 years I have been Institutrice at Argyll Lodge, and my pupils were Lady Edith and Lady Elizabeth Campbell. During that time I was one afternoon at Stafford House with Lady Elizabeth Campbell – it was I believe the anniversary of your son's birthday. The Duchess of Manchester came also, I believe with two daughters and you asked me to make tea. On the table was an artificial small tree with birds which chirped etc. Perhaps these details will bring you to mind who I am. In the meantime I wish to interest you in my behalf which is, should you hear of any one looking out for a Companion to remember me kindly – I feel so lonely – salary no object.

In the meantime,
Believe me dear Madam
Your most obedient and humble servant
M.A. Ochsenbein

(SRO, Sutherland, D593/R/8, D593/P/28/13)

AGENCIES

The way an agency worked was explained in a letter from a Mr Norman, who ran a servant recruitment office, writing to an unnamed enquirer who wished to set up a correspondence agency.

J.H. Norman, 13 November 1804

. . . no employer would treat with an Office keeper for a Servant he never saw . . . A Servant wanting a situation applys personaly at my Office and according to Character, Abilities and

Appearance I select from my Book of Orders such Situations . . . as I conceive will answer their expectations, in like manner a person wanting a Servant applys either personaly or other ways with the Office fee of One Shilling and with the Order is entered the sort of servant wanted, such Servants are then sent as above stated until suited . . . the tempers of both employers and servants are often alike whimsical and not satisfied one without they see a number of Servants and the other without they go after a Number of places to choose as they think the Best . . .

(BRO, Stevens, D/ESV(M)B19)

John Reid seems to have run an agency in London in the 1780s and among his clients was Francis Fortescue Turvile of Bosworth Hall, near Welford, Northamptonshire.

John Reid to F.F. Turvile, 25 June 1789

Old Slaughter, London

Hon^d Sir

I have to thank you for your Indulgent, kind & obliging letter as well as for your goodness in sending me Remittance.

I have took some time to find such a Servant as I thought would Answer your family but am sorry to say have not been able to please Myself the only person I have seen that I think likely is an Irish man who certainly is Well Recommended he has lived more than two years with Lady St John as Butler. He is Recommended to me as a patron of good Moralls and honesty he says his Lady will give him the Best of Characters and I find the Reason of Parting was concerning some Dispute about Cards he wore Livery and had twenty pounds a year, has Refused severall places to be in the Country but would not except of any of them because of his Religion, has no objection to the Country where he can Enjoy his Religion

. . . I am
Hon^d Sir
Your honours
M^o. O^b. Serv
J^{no} Reid

This man not being suitable, Reid found another applicant.

Same, 7 July 1789

I made it my business to go to the Person but not finding him at home was obliged to wait 'till this morning. He has no objection to wear Livery can Dress Hair was Mr Lawson's own man & Dress'd him, lived with Mr L. seven years & in the younger part of his life with the late Earl of Shrewsbury, has had the small pox is thirty two years of age a likely person but not so tall as your Hon. The wages he expects is twenty Guineas & any little matter that may if any belong to the place as Butler.

As your own servant he expects your Old Cloaths but that is a matter for Sir to consider of . . .

NB He can come of a days notice.

(LRO, Turvile Constable-Maxwell, DG39/1315, 1317)

The Harpur Crewes of Calke Abbey, Derbyshire, were perhaps unusual in relying heavily on domestic service agencies. Correspondence between Charles Palmer, the Harpur Crewes' agent, and Mrs Moseley, who ran a recruitment agency in Derby, spans twenty years. Letters relating to an unsuccessful application in 1868 by a footman James Willow show how the system worked.

Mrs Moseley to Charles Palmer, 1 August 1868

36, Cornmarket
Mrs Henry Moseley
Office for Domestic Servants
Open from Ten till Four

Sir, I have this morning had an application for a Footman's place from James Willows, age 26, height 5 11½, he is now living as single handed Butler with the Revd Blandford, Spondon, nr Derby but prefers being in livery, therefore is leaving at the end of his month which expires on the 11th before going there he lived 18 months with Mrs Johnson, Blundstone Lodge, Suffolk, as Footman under a Butler. The wages he asks are 26£. He said he should be glad to take a 2nd Footman's situation in a good family if you think he would be likely for Calke Abbey will you kindly write direct to him and give him all the particulars or if you like and will fix the day and time, I will write for him to meet you in Derby.

Waiting your reply
I remain
Yours respectfully
F.J. Moseley

Charles Palmer to James Willows, 2 August 1868

Calke Abbey, Derby

Mrs Moseley has recommended you as second Footman to Sir John Harper Crewe, Bart, Calke Abbey. I shall be glad to know what experience you have had, what Families you have lived in & how long in each situation & to whom you refer for a character & if you are a member of the Church of england, also the lowest wages you require for the situation as second Footman.

Your reply by return of post will oblige
Your obd^t. Servt.
Chas. Palmer

James Willows to Charles Palmer, 3 August 1868

Spondon, Derby

Sir,

In answer to your letter received this morning I write to say that I lived at Mrs Johnson's, Blunderstone Lodge, Suffolk 18 months under a butler, and with Admiral Robinson of 61 Eaton Place London 3 months as head footman, leaving as London did not agree with me. I have been here a month and am leaving as it is not what I want. I enclose the recommendation from Mrs Johnson and Mr Blandford will forward my character from both places upon application. The wages I shall require 27£ with all found. I am a member of the Church of England. Will you please to return the recommendation if this does not meet your approbation as soon as possible as I leave here on Tuesday Aug 11th

> I remain Sir
> Your obed[t]. Servant
> James Willows

Same, 5 August 1868

Sir, In answer to your letter received this morning I write to say I will meet you on Friday at the place stated at 12 o'clock . . .

Same, 13 August 1868

I was very sorry my character did not meet with your approbation. I hope you will return my recommendation that I gave you. My expences were 5 shillings.

(DeRO, Harpur Crewe, D2375M 242/16/6)

Such transactions were very different from the atmosphere of a large London agency. More akin to an indoor hiring fair, one such agency was described in the 1870s by Hannah Cullwick.

. . . I went to the Registry for servants at the Soho Bazaar, & sat in the office with several more servants, young & old, waiting my turn for my name to be put down. They have prayers there together at a certain hour in the morning, & the man over it all wears a white tie, & speaks to us each about religion & gives us tracts before going up stairs to sit in the room where the ladies come to look at us. So the Soho bazaar is reckon'd a good place to wait for a place . . .

I paid ½ a crown, the price for the lower servants – it's 5/- for cooks or upper ones. I was shown the way upstairs & where to wait – among a good many others of all sorts & sizes & some talk'd & laugh'd together. Then the ladies began to come in, & I felt very nervous till one lady spoke to me & she ask'd me to follow her, & that was to another room where the ladies sat & hir'd you or ask'd you questions after they'd walk'd round &

pick'd you out. This was one Mrs Milne who call'd me out, & I stood before her answering her questions.

(Stanley, *Hannah Cullwick*, pp. 54–5)

Respectable landed families rarely used newspapers to find servants, but they would ask agencies to place discreetly worded adverts on their behalf. Here is a reply to one such advert placed on behalf of the Harpur Crewes.

William Holmes to Mrs Moseley, 14 April 1857

Longnor Hall
Lebotwood
Shrewsbury

Madam,

Having seen an advertisement in the Times of yesterday for an Upper Footman to apply to your offices, I beg to inform you that I shall want a situation of the kind early in May – I am a native of Derbyshire (Holerway near Matlock) and have lived in some very good families amongst other I may mention Hurts of Alder Wasley, the late Lord Denman's of Stoney Middleton and Mr Watts Russell's of Ilam Hall and I know London thoroughly and am well practised in travelling and valeting. I am leaving my present situation entirely of my own accord and with an undeniable character. My age is twenty-six and my height is 5ft 9½ inches of course ½ inch shorter than the advertisement requires. If you think that would not be objectionable I should be glad to have a letter from you stating the name of the Family and all particulars. I may as well add that I should expect good wages as I am perfectly master of my work . . . I should like to have an answer from you as soon as possible and I have the honour to remain

Madam yours very respectfully
Wm Holmes

(DeRO, Harpur Crewe D2375M 242/16/6)

CHARACTERS

In large households, the task of following up a reference, or 'character', as it was called, was left to senior servants.

House steward John James lists the questions to be asked of a lady's maid:

> Is she thoroughly trustworthy, sober and honest ?
> Is she quick and obliging and kind in illness ?
> Is she a handy dressmaker, blouse maker and renovator, a careful
> packer and handy traveller ?
> Has she a good memory and is she tidy and methodical in her work and duties ?
> Has she a good temper or is she easily irritated ?
> Is she thoroughly discreet and not inclined to make friends all over the place, and is she really reliable ?
> Is her health good and has she good eyesight ?
> Do you know if she is engaged to be married ?

(James, *House Steward*, p. 96)

A successful interviewee would be appointed subject to a satisfactory character. A request was then sent by the prospective employer to the previous employer, asking for a reference. Such exchanges were usually formal and brisk.

Lady Godolphin to Mrs Boon, 13 April 1802

> Lady Godolphin presents her Compliments to Mrs Boon, hopes she will excuse giving her this trouble which is to enquire the Character of James Proctor; who has offered himself to her as a Footman, & says he has lived with Mrs Boon a year, would be much obliged to her to inform her if she thinks him honest sober cleanly & a diligent good tempered servant, & must beg to know the reason of her parting with him.

Mrs Boon to Lady Godolphin, 14 April 1802

> Mrs Boon presents her Compts to Ly G. & has the honour to inform her that James Proctor lived with her 8 months, during

which time he has behaved himself very well, remarkably attentive, & good tempered, her reason for parting with him was that he could neither read nor write, which is particularly inconvenient to her.

(NRO, Fitzwilliam, F(M)G 1039)

Characters were kept for future use and survive in their thousands, good and bad.

Lord Hawarden to Samuel Whitbread, 9 September 1814

Taplow Lodge
Near Maidenhead

Sir,

Your note of the 1st instant respecting Edward Penford reached me the day of my departure from Ireland.

I have now the pleasure of stating to you in reply that Edward Penford has lived with me since the 21st April 1810 during which time I have found him perfectly honest, sober and industrious, good tempered, active and cleanly, and <u>thoroughly</u> understanding the care of horse, carriages and harness. He has drove four in hand for the last two years. He last summer drove me in my barouche with four horses from London to Holy Head and from Dublin to my place in the county of Tipperary, and returned with me in the Autumn.

My only reason for parting with him is my disposing of my Horses previous to my going abroad

I have the honor to be Sir
Your ob[t] Humble
Servant
Hawarden

(BLARS, Whitbread, W1/3586)

S. Cottam to the Countess de Grey, Wrest Park, Bedfordshire, nd

Oxford Street

Madam

I have the Honour of your Ladyships Letter of the 21st instant and as to Mrs Lemon I really think she will fully answer your expectations as a Housekeeper, I have known her ever since she came as Housekeeper to Lady Anson and am assured you may depend upon her Integrity & Care as well as her ability in the several matters you mention of making Cakes, Jellyes & Sweetmeats, in so much as not to be exceeded by any, in my opinion; I think she has pretty good health & strength to do her business as a Housekeeper. She hath given great satisfaction in the several places she hath lived in, for any thing I have ever heard to the contrary; Ld Jersey gave her, to Lady Leicester, an excellent Character with whom she lived till her Ladyship's death, being near 2 years, since then she lived about a year & a quarter with Sir Robt Clayton. Mrs Lemon will obey your Ladyship's commands . . . and will be ready when ever you send

I am
Madam your Ladyships
Dutifull & Obed^{t} humble Servant
S Cottam

(BLARS, Lucas, L30/11/79)

P. Gell to Sir Henry FitzHerbert, Tissington Hall, Derbyshire, 29 January 1818

Hopton

My Dear Sir,

I am sorry that you have had the trouble of sending over twice. Yesterday I was unavoidably obliged to go to the Prison at Wirksworth to visit a Boy of 18 who I had sent there for further Examination in suspicion of felony. This circumstance makes me fearful of saying anything in favour of a servant who is leaving me, for the youth in question was in my family 3 years and was recommended by Mrs Gell and myself and Mr Thornhill, and in less than six weeks he has been guilty of robbing his master in various ways. With respect to the character of W.

Woodhouse I may however venture to say the exact truth, that I have found him sober, honest attentive and trustworthy and he leaves me by his own choice after 10 years service, for the sake of Promotion . . .

I am Dear Sir,
Yours truly
P. Gell

(DeRO, FitzHerbert, D239M/F/8414)

Mr Arkwright to Lady Crewe, 5 February 1853

Mr Arkwright presents his compliments to Lady Crewe and will in a few words answer her numerous queries. Mrs Parsons lived at Sutton nearly 6 years and left that place according to her own wishes. Mrs A did not wish to part with her, and can give favourable answers to all her questions excepting as to temper. She has a rather hasty temper and Mr Arkwright is afraid that he is sometimes unreasonable.

Lady Crewe must not expect Perfection

(DeRO, Harpur Crewe, D2375M 242/16/5)

J. Penleaze to George Bowes, MP, 22 January 1754

Sir,

John Ravenor, born in Midx: single, has had the Small Pox, wears a Wig, is about 5:7 inches high and 40 years old, who says he served you 6 months as a coachman, had £12 wages & left your service at Michaelmas last, your former coachman who had been ill, returning to your Service: this Man has offered his Service to a very worthy friend of mine in the like Station, at whose request it is that I give you this Trouble, desiring you will please inform me if what he says is true, if he is a sober, honest, good natures & capable person, & what Character you had with him. Your speedy & impartial answer directed to me at Mr Wm Penleaze's in Seething Lane will very much oblige

Sir Yr most Obed^t Servt
J. Penleaze

Reply from unnamed servant

My Master read yours of the 22nd instant last Post & has ordered me to acquaint you that John Ravenor served him near six months as a coachman & hopes he will answer your Friends expectations in that capacity but I'm to acquaint you that he was not discharg'd for the reason assigned in yours, but for some impertinent expressions to my Master.

(DRO, Strathmore, D/St/C1/3/27)

Elinor Packe to Lady Alice Packe, 18 April 1887

Shangton Rectory
Leicester

Dear Lady Alice

I am afraid I cannot answer all your questions quite satisfactorily about Mary Anne Millington. She was certainly very dirty but perhaps with a strict servant over her she might improve. She was only here six months as kitchenmaid & it was her first place. My Cook is a friend of her Mother's who tells me she is very clean herself. Mary Anne was good tempered & I believe her to be honest & steady but she had been kept at home too long & wanted a thoroughly good training. I daresay she would get that at Prestwold but my Cook is young & did not like to be severe with a Friend

Believe me
Yrs very truly
Elinor Packe

Lady Middleton to Lady Alice Packe, 7 October 1884

Wollaton Hall
Nottingham

Lady Middleton prests. her compts. to Lady Alice Packe & begs to answer her questions abt Margt Gunston from Mrs Hill the housekeeper as Ly M herself has only been here during 2 months of Margts service . . . Mrs Hill found Margt thoroughly sober & respectable & a good worker. She was not the least accustomed to the routine of a large establishment but has learnt something since she has been here.

She is <u>not</u> aimiable with the underservants, but Mrs Hill has found her respectful to herself.

Lady Middleton does not wish to be prejudiced but honestly thinks Margaret has shown no consideration either to <u>her</u> or to Mrs Hill. Her reason for leaving is that Wollaton is <u>dull</u> – this she might have found in the first 3 months here – & all was explained to her before she took the situation. Ly M believes Margaret has simply used this as a stepping stone to a more lively place – & given Mrs Hill all the trouble of teaching her for nothing. She moreover threw up her place the day after Ly M & party had arrived here – driven out of Birdsall with very few servts. owing to an infectious illness breaking out there – & thereby added much to Lady M's anxieties – as it is not an easy matter to get a reliable housemaid at short notice for an important trust like this situation demands.

(LRO, Packe DE/1346/439)

LEAVING HOME

For youngsters, getting their first job meant a poignant leaving of home to start their new life.

William Lanceley left home in 1870, taking little with him:

a carpet bag, containing an extra pair of trousers, a change of underclothing, and five apples. With fivepence in his pocket he walked five miles to begin his career as a foot-boy in the local squire's beautiful home.

(Lanceley, *Hall-Boy to House-Steward*, p. 9)

Aged 12 in 1894, Frederick Gorst's job as a counter-boy in a pub meant he had to get up at 4 a.m. He preferred the idea of going into service:

Like any young boy with a fixed purpose, I would not accept my mother's opinion. I pleaded doggedly with her to let me go. It was the first thing I mentioned in the morning and the last thing at night. Finally, either because I exhausted her or because she saw some wisdom in my logic, she reluctantly consented. . . .

The last week at home was spent in preparation for my leave-taking. Lily mended and wet-brushed my Sunday suit, and my two white shirts and linens were clean and tidy. I took a tin-type of my parents, my hymnal and an album of mottos and pressed flowers which Davey Driscoll, my best friend, gave me when I said good-bye to him. . . . I promised Davey I would write to him once a week and describe everything I saw and learned. But at that time, all I knew was that I was to have a page boy's livery and ten pounds a year. I could hardly wait to begin. . . .

The day finally came for me to leave. August 10th, 1894. Mama took me on the tram to the Birkenhead Ferry Landing. She bent down to kiss me and whispered, 'Be brave and do your best'.

As I watched Mama walk away, I realized that I was alone for the first time in my life. For an instant I wanted to run after her, but instead I carried my battered tin trunk on to the deck and ran to the bow of the ship. In a moment the bells signalled and the landing gates closed. . . .

(Gorst, *Carriages and Kings*, p. 12)

TWO

'I know two sixpences make a shilling' – conditions of employment

Domestic servants were subject to many of the same legal restrictions on labour as other workers. In particular, the Law of Settlement of 1662 governed the right of strangers to work and claim poor relief within a parish, limiting entitlement to such 'settlement' to those who had worked in apprenticeship or service for over a year. Since poor relief was funded by the parishioners, employers tended to avoid claims of settlement by setting on people for twelve months less one week – this in effect became a week's unpaid holiday. At the end of the fifty-one weeks servants could finish or be asked to sign on for another year. The practice of employing servants for fifty-one weeks lasted well into the nineteenth century. Senior servants such as stewards or particularly valued craftsmen might be set on for longer than a year, in which case they would gain settlement. In return they were usually bound by a written agreement or even some sort of financial guarantee.

Whether set on annually or under a longer-term contract, servants were entitled to receive their wages after the year was up, or whatever period was stipulated in the agreement. In other words, a servant worked a year in hand. It was, however, possible to ask, and usually get, an advance on the annual wage. Married men seem to have done this frequently, for they had families to support. Single women could more easily manage without advances on wages; many, after all, were saving their wages to send home and they had few expenses. A surprising number of servants seem to have accepted payment once a year. As the nineteenth century progressed, however, more and more servants were paid quarterly, then monthly. Even this could be a long time to wait for your first money.

Wages fluctuated widely, of course, according to a number of variables.[1] The super-rich households such as the Sutherlands paid more than a country squire. Men received more than women – as a rough guide women doing equivalent work to men were paid half the amount. Rewards increased with experience and skill. Some households paid an increase after a month's satisfactory trial and further increases after several years. For the unfortunates at the bottom of the pile, a totally inexperienced youngster with few skills, work might be rewarded only in kind – food and clothing.

Wages were not the only financial rewards of service and several other forms of payment were expected. Board wages were paid when the family were absent from home – a cash sum in lieu of meals. Later in the Edwardian period, some aristocratic households gave up the tradition of providing meals altogether and servants were put on board wages permanently. Tipping was another important aspect of servant life, an acknowledged source of ready cash. Personal servants such as footmen or valets did better out of tips than a housemaid who rarely saw her employers personally. In addition, perquisites – unofficial extras derived from the nature of each servant's work – could be sold for small sums of cash. Finally, on the death of an employer, the household might be broken up and servants dismissed, but this fate might be ameliorated by the gift of a legacy to each member of the household. Long-serving servants in such circumstances might even receive an annuity.

It is clear that some servants in favourable circumstances could accumulate fair sums of money. Escaping the temptations of extravagance, they could ask their employers to save their money, receiving interest in return. The lack of an assured pension and the threat of a destitute old age were strong motivations to saving.

TERMS OF EMPLOYMENT

In the eighteenth century, workers who were set on for more than a year might be subject to a formal agreement, sometimes sealed by an extra payment 'in earnest', similar in some ways to articles of apprenticeship.

Contract of employment for John Coats, blacksmith at Streatlam Castle, Durham, 1718

Mem^d of Articles of Agreem^t wth Sam^{ll} Burton of Keverston in the County of Durham on the behalf of Wm Blak Bows Esqr in the County afors'd and John Coats of Barton in the County of York Black Smith; touching the s^d John Coats working Black Smith work at Streatlam Castle in the manner & form following (viz) that the s^d Jno Coates doth hereby hier himself & become serv^t to the s^d. Wm Blak Bows to perform and do all smith work about Streatlam Castle to the proper use of the s^d Wm Blak Bows . . . and shall finde & provide for himselfe all the work toolls usefull to his s^d work & Imployment and the s^d Wm Blak Bows doth hereby promise to pay to the s^d Jno Coates the sum^m of Fifteen pounds per ann^m for his s^d work by Quarterly paym^{ts} and to provide him with a work house and a room to Lodge in and that the s^d Jno Coats is hereby Hyerd for the tearme of two years, from the Date hereof, and the s^d Jno Coats shall have the Liberty of Working for any tennants in the Lordshipp to his own Use and Profitt . . . And the s^d Jno Coats shall have Coales found him for the s^d Wm Blak Bow's Work for his Use; for which the s^d Jno Coats confirmed by reciving five shill. in Earnest which is given him over and above the s^d fifteen pounds; to all which particulars the s^d parties Agrees & setts their hands this sixth Day of Decr 1718

(DRO, Strathmore, D/St/E1/5/1)

In cases where the employee was under 21 years of age, the agreement would be made with the father.

Samuel Heathcote to Daniel Houghton, 25 July 1704

London

If your son be at Liberty to come from Mr Hurts, and have his Masters free Consent; I shall be Willing to take him into my Service upon the following terms & Conditions.

That He come up hither with the first opportunity of the Carrier, that He Serve me as a footman, or in any other Business for the term of four years; that I will give him every year a New hatt, Coate, Wastcoate, Breeches, 1 pair of Stockings, & 1 pair of Shoes, that the rest of his Cloths He is to find himselfe, that at the end of the four yeares haveing faithfully & honestly performd his Service, He shall have fifteen pounds, and shall be then free either to leave my Service, or continue longer in it, as We can then Agree. That if his Vails should fall short of Supplying him with such necessarys as he may want over & above the Cloths I am obliged to give him, that I will advance what he may want out of the fifteen pounds above. If you and your son are Contented with these Conditions, do you both subscribe to them here below, and returne this paper to my Cousin Ash. I am

Your Loveing friend
Sam: Heathcote

Acceptance written on the bottom

Chesterfield, July 1704

We have Read & Consider^d this letter and all the Contents of it and do freely Consent & Agree to all the terms & Conditions therein mentioned

Daniel Houghton
ye Father

Daniel Houghton
ye Son

(HRO, Heathcote, 63M84/252)

Where senior posts involving the handling of large sums of cash were concerned, something even more binding might be required. A prospective employee might be expected to sign a money bond as guarantee of his good behaviour. Since a young man would be without such substantial resources, his father would bind himself as joint guarantor.

Joseph Walker binds both himself and his father to the sum of £400, payable to his employer if he fails in his service, 9 February 1788

Know all Men by these Presents that We Joseph Walker the younger, and Joseph Walker the elder, both of Bampton Grange in the Parish of Bampton, in the County of Westmoreland, Yeomen, are held and firmly bound to the Honourable Sir Henry Vane of Long Newton, in the County of Durham, Baronet, in the sum of Four Hundred Pounds . . . to be paid to the said Sir Henry Vane . . . for which Payment . . . We bind ourselves . . .

Whereas the above-named Sir Henry Vane, Baronet, has retained and engaged the first-above bounden Joseph Walker the younger to be his Agent or Steward; Now the Condition of this Obligation is such, that if the above-bounden Joseph Walker the younger . . . shall . . . as often as requested by the said Sir Henry Vane . . . well and truly pay or cause to be paid unto the said Sir Henry Vane . . . all such Sum or Sums of Money as he . . . shall have had or received of, from, for, or on Account of the said Sir Henry Vane . . . and shall render to the said Sir Henry Vane . . . a true, just and perfect Account of all and every Sum and Sums of Money that shall be by him had, received, paid, laid out or disbursed of, from for or on Account of the said Sir Henry Vane . . . and of all other Things whatsoever relating . . . to the said Agency or Stewardship as shall . . . be committed to his Care, Management or Disposal and also well, justly, truly and honestly, in every Respect behave himself in the said Office . . . then this Obligation is to be void . . .

(DRO, Londonderry, D/Lo/F/221(4))

WAGES

The usual domestic servant, however, was set on for fifty-one weeks and was not entitled to any payment until after the fifty-one weeks was served. Working a year in hand did not suit everyone and, with many requests for payments in advance, wage records could get complicated. Wages books record not only wages and advances but also often the reasons servants left.

The wages book from Tabley Hall in Cheshire was kept in the form of a double-entry account book. Extracts here are taken from the right-hand page which recorded the payments to which servants were entitled.

Cr[edit] Housekeeper   Mrs Hannh. Moore

1817 Dec 31	By one years wages due this day	60	0	0
1818 Dec 31	By one years wages due this day	60	0	0
1819 Dec 31	By one years wages due this day	60	0	0
1820 Dec 31	By one years wages due this day	60	0	0
1821 March 25	By ¼ wages due this day when discharged Sir Jno granting her an Annuity for life of £30 (see Int Book)	15	0	0

Cr[edit] Scullery Maid

1816 Dec 31	By bal. due this day	0	11	6
1817 Dec 31	By one years wages due this day	10	10	0
	By ½ years allowance for look of Fowls	1	1	0
Total		12	2	6

Cr[edit] Baker   Dan. Whittaker

1820 Dec 31	By one years Wages due this day	18	18	0
	By 43 weeks and 5 days Board Wages from the 19th Oct 1819 to 21 Aug '20	19	13	5
	By one years allowance for the care of the Lodge	5	0	0
	By a Pig for the Use of the House weighing 11 score at 5½ d lb	5	7	8
	By 3 duks for the Alderney Corn		7	6
	By 30 nights on Watch and Ward, from the 20th Dec 1819 to the 26th Feb 1820 at 2/6	3	15	0

The entry for James Tomlin, underbutler promoted to butler in 1818, is exceptional and shows how some servants could become relatively wealthy. Not only was he receiving interest on a loan of £230 he had previously made to his employer, but for the three years as butler he asked the family to save his wages and allowances for him, thereby earning extra interest at 5 per cent.

Cr[edit] Under Butler James Tomlin

1817 Dec 31	By one years wages due this day	26	5	0
	By one years int. on £230 Note	11	10	0
	By amount of Disbursement as pr. account with the receipts	13	4	1

Cr[edit] Butler   James Tomlin

1818 Dec 31	By one years wages on this day	52	0	0
	By one years allowances for Plate Brushes	1	1	0
	Total	53	11	0
1819 Dec 31	By one years interest on the above sum of £53 11 0 from the 1st of Jan to this day.	2	13	0
	By one years wages 1st of Jan to this day	52	10	0
	By one years allce. for Plate Brushes	1	1	0
	By one years int. on Note for £230	11	10	0
	By amount of Bill for Parcels etc	1	9	6
	Total	122	14	6
1820	By one years int. on £122 14s 6d	6	2	9
	By one years wages	52	10	0
	By one years allce. for Brushes	1	1	0
	By one years int on £230 (Note)	11	10	0
	By Bill for Parcels etc paid	4	9	6
	Total	198	9	3

(CRO, Leicester-Warren of Tabley, DLT 4996/40/7)

The two-volumed wage record kept by the Dyotts of Freeford Manor in Staffordshire covers the years 1813 to the 1840s.

<u>1813 William Mullins, Footman</u>, hired 27 Jan at 24 guineas

March 19 Advanced		1.0.0
May 4	"	5.0.0
Aug 31	"	3.0.0
Nov 20	"	5.0.0
Total advanced 14.0.0		
Wages		25.4
Dedct		14.0.0
Due Wm Mullins		11.4.0

Pd his wages to 27 Jan 1814
Discharged
Afterwards was sent to the Hulks for a felony

<u>1814 Wm Townsend hired as Coachman</u> 1st July at twenty five guineas a year and two compleat suits of clothes, Boots & Breeches – Four shillings a Day Board Wages – 1/6 dinner, 1/3 Breakfast & supper each
January 11th, 1814 advanced   7.0.0
Discharged for insolence

<u>18 Oct 1816 Sarah Cheadle</u> came at fourteen pounds for fifty one weeks
26th May 1817 pd wages & agreed to serve again at fourteen guineas
28th June Gave a months warning [crossed out]
Sept 7 advanced   5.0.0
18 Oct 1818 Pd wages
Married to Butler Welch

<u>23rd May 1820 Mrs Jersey</u> hired at 30 guineas per ann. – we find sugar, she finds tea. If she continues the year to have some allowance in lieu of kitchen perquisites.
To 23 Nov is six months   15.15.0
Went to Mr Dolphin 23 Oct 1820

<u>6 Dec 1823 Henry Welsh</u> from Yoxall came on trial. Agreed to give him ten guineas a year and clothes – if he behaved well promised him two guineas more.
From 6 December to 6 April is 4 months   3.10.0
Discharged – idle and the truth is not in him.

<u>12 Aug 1835 W Lally</u> engaged as Bailiff
Discharg'd 8th Sept 1835 – Out all night fighting on the town
common. Gave him £2.10

<u>February 22, 1836 Usherwood</u> came as gardiner, wages twenty-
four pounds pr ann.
June 22 Pd wages & disch.   8.0.0
Did not know his trade & very idle in executing the little he did
know.

<u>1837 Oct 9 Brindly as Butler</u> from Mr Strutt Derby came, & in
two days gave notice – Discharged him forthwith, gave him £1,
was to have 50 guineas a year.
Stay'd two days

<u>1838 Nov 3 John from Mrs Madan</u> came as coachman, wages
£20 a year. Livery suit, fustian coat, Overalls, Boots, Stable
Waistcoat, & red Driving Jacket & Leather Britches when
wanted, also Great Coat.
From Nov 3 to Sept the year   16.17.6
Sept 1839 Discharged for Drunkeness

<u>1839 August 12 James Bellow</u> from Mrs Boulton Kings, came as
Gamekeeper. Wages 12 s a week as long as he dish in the house.
From 12 Aug to 27 Oct   6.6.0
Discharged for being impertinent to Bailiff and Worthless.

<u>1840 Mary Copestake</u>. The girl from Ashburn came as House
Maid, Wages £6.6.0
24 July 3 months   1.10.0
Discharg'd Giddy

<u>1842 Frances Stephenson</u> from Derby hired as Cook
22 March – wages twenty guineas pr ann.
Paid a months wages 31 Mar 1842. Discharged 1.15.0
No cook, No go.

(SRO, Dyott, D661/12/9)

By the twentieth century, servants were usually paid monthly, but as Jean
Rennie found out, there could be problems even with this.

We should be paid on the first of the month. Some months it was the ninth or tenth, and it has been the sixteenth before we were paid . . . To any tentative enquiries by Mrs Preston, her Ladyship would reply with such infinite boredom that 'Really – Sir James has so much to do – the servants think of nothing but money!'

So that between not knowing when we'd be paid and not knowing when we could get off to go even up to the village to send some home, even if it was only a pound out of my two pound a month, it always seemed as though we were working for nothing.

(Rennie, *Every Other Sunday*, 1955, p. 51)

Even in the late nineteenth century, it was not unheard of for young girls in their first job to work for no wages at all.

Mrs Wrigley

I had been at home a few days when the doctor's wife came to our house and said a lady and gentleman wanted a little nurse for their child, to go back with them to Hazel Grove, near Stockport. My little bundle of clothes was packed up and I went in full glee with them. Instead of being a nurse I had to be a servant-of-all-work, having to get up at six in the morning, turn a room out and have it ready for breakfast. My biggest trouble was I could not light the fire, and my master was very cross and would tell me to stand away, and give me a good box on my ears . . . I fretted very much for my home . . . Not able to read or write, I could not let my parents know, until a kind old lady in the village wrote to my parents to fetch me home from the hardships I endured. I had no wages at this place, only a few clothes.

(Wrigley, 'Plate-Layer's Wife', p. 58)

ASKING FOR MORE MONEY

Servants did ask for rises or loans against their wages.

William Parsons to Samuel Whitbread, 10 December 1813

Sir,

I am very sorry to be under the Necessity of Again asking you for Money, But perhaps you will recolect that it was on Account of the Change of Landlord under whom I Rent a Small House for my family, that I was Obliged to Ask before, the House has only 3 Rooms and a Washouse for £28 a year which is more than I am able to Pay the Present Landlord wants to raise it to £30 which sooner than submit to, I have been looking out, and Have found a House not quite finished which the Owner has Promised to fit up to my Wife's Liking Providing I Deposit £5 to be reducted out of the first Quarters Rent which I am to enter upon on the 25 of March or sooner if I like. The rent is 42 Guineas per Year it has 8 Rooms a Washouse and Good Cellars so we are in Hopes if we keep the Lodging Let to live almost rent free, I shall have Copper [to] hang & to Buy which will come I suppose £5 more, so should be glad if you would Please to Advance me £10 I have received £20 last year and £20 this year on Account of Wages so that at the end of this Month there will be Due to me £10 on that Account. But then the Mangle is not Paid for, and I should be very glad, Sir, if you would Please to say what it is to be. And I also beg if you Please that it may stand over for the Present, and be Settled out of my Book Account whenever that is Paid.

I am to give my Answer on Monday. And it entirely depends upon you Sir to say whether I shall have it or Not. I am doing it for the Best I hope it will Prove so. And Am with the greatest Respect,

> Sir,
> Your Humble Servant To Command
> Wm Parsons

Wages and board wages, paid in lieu of meals, were often the cause of discontent, as both Samuel Whitbread and his housekeeper Mrs Holloway found at Southill, Bedfordshire.

John Shield to Samuel Whitbread, nd
> Sir

I am now two years in your service and it seems I can't give you Satisfaction therefore I think it Best to leave. The wages you allow me is to little providing none own Clothes and allowd Board wages that is not sufficient to maintain me keeps me from doing any good for myself you will Be so good as to provide a man in my place. Ill stop till you get one to answer with pleasure. I would serve if the place answered me But it realy does not . . .

I remain sir
Your humble
Servant
John Shields

Same

> Sir

I have considered your letter and assures you it was not your reproff that Occationd me to wright to you & I have no fault to find except my wages Been as little and I declare it takes all to provide nessaries & I am now in the prime of life and if I do not save something now I cant when Old Age comes on therefore if you advance my wages so as to do me any good I am willing to stop, you allow all the rest nine shillings Board wages and me But six which is not sufficient to maintain me now sir if you allow me the same Board wages you allow the rest and half a guinea a week when the famaly are hear I will be Content to stop . . . if you consent to this I will continue your servant as long as you are pleased to keep me and will do all in my power to regain your good Opinion . . . if you Consent Be so kind as to Destroy this letter that none may see it I ask Pardon for my negligence and will be more particular for the future

> I remain Sir
> Your humble
> Servant
> John Shields

Ann Girdle to Whitbread's housekeeper Mrs Holloway, 15 August 1816

> London

Dear Mrs Holloway I wrote you a line to Ask you a favour if you will be so kind as to Ask My Master to ad something More to ouer Bordwaiges for it is so verey lo I cannot make it do things are so verey Dear William did not like to Ask My Master as he refused him last year but things are more now then they ware then I thought perhaps My Master wold hear wot you had to say . . . I wold be much obliged to you to Ask him I do not like to be dissatesfied or to meake any Complaint if I can help it you must think yourself: 10 shillings is to litle I hope you and all friends are well as it leves me beter than I heave bine I heave bine verey unwell but thank god am beter now Dear Mrs Holloway I heave nothing particular to say I don't know when I shall heave an oporunity to send the beds donne

> I am your Duty full sirvent
> Ann Girdle

(BLARS, Whitbread, W1/3557, W1/3575–6, W1/3552)

OTHER REWARDS

Allowances varied from house to house. They were specified at interview and took the form of agreed quantities of foodstuffs (usually beer, tea and sugar), sometimes candles, soap and clothing. Like board wages, allowances often caused trouble. Here the Duke of Sutherland's agent at Trentham writes to his senior, the chief agent.

William Lewis to James Loch, 12 January 1832

... Beekie has been making unreasonable demands upon Mrs Kirk for candles, soap etc and if I mistake not claiming wages for the woman that cleans out his Room. His Lordship has handed me a copy of his agreement and it really appears to me that he is neither entitled to candles or soap, but before anything more is said to him upon the subject I beg to know what you consider him entitled to so that matters are put straight with him ... Lady Gower has more than once said that his wages were not high but in my opinion a great deal more than he is worth.

(SRO, Sutherland, D593/K/3/2/12)

Tips could be expected from family members and guests who had been valeted, or tradesmen who were prepared to reward custom by paying a commission.

William Tayler in 1837

January 12th ... The old Lady's daughter that's married and her husband called this afternoon. He gave me a sovering for a Christmas box for which I was greatly obliged to him for, but it's no more than he ought to do as they very frequently dine here ...

January 13th. ... Took a walk this afternoon; called on a tradesman. He gave me five shillings for a Christmas box for which I was not sorry.

Oct 16th Went out and paid a bill. The person gave me half a crown. Went and paid another where I only got sixpence, but I did not refuse it as I know two sixpences make a shilling.

December 4th These perquasites jenerally amount to about ten or fifteen pounds pr. year more or less, but it's more frequently very much less as service is getting very bad business.

(Wise, *William Tayler*, pp. 12, 54, 59)

Thomas, a footman in the service of the 2nd Duke of Sutherland at West Hill and Trentham, 1838

23rd July ... We have just had our new liveries and put them on yesterday for the first time the Tailor gave us 20s amongst us so we proposed to have a dance and something to drink and was fixed to be tonight at Stafford House which came off I am told very joyfully though several of us was at West hill they had a very pleasant dance and kept it up till 4 in the morning

Sept 16 . . . just at dinner time Mr. Barry[2] came he was not expected till tomorrow Charles says to me you must valet him I says not I, I have got sufficient to do already. O but you must says he, presently I meet Mr Vantini O you must attend upon Mr Barry very well sir because Charles has got Mr Gilpin says he. I got to bed about 11 . . .

Sept 18 Got up this morning ½ past 6 it was a very fine morning set about my work & got it done by 12 I then cleaned myself and then had orders for to prepare Mr Barry's things as the Post chaise was ordered round to the door directly I went into his room and found his things all ready to come down I brought them down & then the chaise was at the door I carried his bags etc & put them in & when he was got in he put 5/- into my hand

A footman like Thomas, in the service of one of the richest men in the land, could also earn extra money by waiting at the many dinners, parties and balls held during their stays in London, sometimes at prestigious venues.

July 13. 6 o'clock the Duke was dressing in His military dress and his carriage was at the door and he is going to a dinner at Guildhall given to all the foreign Ambassaders The Duke took Lord Francis Egerton and me and his footmen went to wait at dinner we got there a ¼ before 7 . . . after we had set down we servants were a long time before we could get in, at last the servants were called according to their master ranks, the Ambassadors first and so on. I got in in about an hour after we had set down, the Duke had done his fish and was having some beef when I got in the hall looked very rich . . . our Duke sat with the Duke of Wellington on his right and the Marquis of Salisbury on his left . . . we got 4/- for waiting there was a great many servants who could not get in to the hall because their masters name was not on the list but they all got 4/- for their waiting out side When it came 9 o'clock I went to find our coachman and found him at the White Boar in Bassinghall Street expecting to have a little supper as I put some meat in the carriage but to my disapointment he had eat it all, ½ past 10 we got away from the hall.

(Thomas, 'Daily Journal', SRO, D4177/1–2)

Jean Rennie's first post as cook taught her how the commission system worked. She presented her tradesmen's bills in a book to her mistress, who went through them, eventually agreeing them and giving her a cheque to cover both the bills and her wages.

The grocer would change the cheque for me, and I'd go off in the afternoon to pay the tradesmen.

I don't know how to describe my astonishment when the girl in the greengrocer's gave me £2. 10s.

I said, 'What's this for?'

'Commission, dearie. Haven't you had any before?'

'Good gracious, no. This is my first cook's place.'

'It's nothing like it used to be. The head staff of big houses used to be able to give the accounts to the tradesmen who would give them the most commission. This has been lying for about three months. You can have it every month if you like; but it makes a little more if you leave it.

(Rennie, *Every Other Sunday*, p. 161)

Gordon Grimmett learnt about tips while in Lord and Lady Astor's service.

It was then [Ascot week] that the job of valeting assumed enormous proportions. I would be looking after about six gentlemen throughout the period, with often a change of clientele at weekends. . . . Not only for Ascot week but before every weekend a list would be put up in the brushing-room of gentlemen that the footmen would have to look after. I'm a little ashamed to say we studied it with some interest and for the wrong motives . . . an American Episcopalian parson arrived at the front door one weekend with his suitcases. Mr Lee summoned me, and after a quick phone call to the housekeeper, a room was found for him. I made a mental cash assessment of him as I took him to his room, and gave him a zero rating. This was confirmed next morning, because it was the custom for men to empty their pockets onto the dressing-table before hanging their clothes. I glanced there and saw neither small change nor a wallet. 'My reverend travels very light,' I remarked to the other footmen as I gave his clothes only the most casual sort of brushing, and ran a cloth over his shoes. He got scant treatment from me during the next day and night.

On the Monday morning Mr Lee called me and said, 'Your reverend is leaving and wants packing up.' I slung his things in in any old way and was just closing his case when he came into the room. 'Oh, Gordon,' he said, 'will you allow me to do something?'

'What is it, sir,' I queried.

'Will you permit me to give you this?' and he handed me three pounds. Three pounds! I could have wept.

'No, sir, it's too much,' I heard a voice saying which sounded like mine.

'Please, Gordon, you looked after me so very well.'

So very well! If only I'd known what was coming, he'd have had the royal treatment from me.

Gordon also acquired clothing.

It was . . . possible to accumulate a small wardrobe from some of the visitors. It was Mr Dana Gibson, Lady Astor's brother-in-law, who put me wise to this. I'd been valeting him during a long stay he had with us and as he was leaving he gave me his customary generous tip, then slung some ties at me. 'You can throw these away, Gordon, I've no use for them any more.'

I looked through them and could find nothing wrong, many of them seeming brand new to me, so I took them down and showed them to Mr Lee. 'This is the way gentlemen of breeding offer you their old clothes as a present. You may keep them.'

It was a different story some months later. Flushed with the success that Mr Dana Gibson's ties had in my social skirmishes with the ladies and finding my other charges showed no anxiety to throw anything my way I began 'accidentally' to leave the odd things out when I was packing a case at the end of a stay until I had a tidy collection of shirts, vests, underpants and socks. I even 'won' a pair of shoes from Mr Reggie Winn, though this was a genuine mistake.

But he took other liberties.

I was looking after [Mr Billie] in the holidays and finding that he only wore shirts, vests and pants for one day and knowing that he took a bath twice a day I decided that this was an extravagance, so I wore them for another couple of days before putting them into the laundry basket. Although I wasn't found out I was shown the red light by Nanny Gibbons who one day went to the basket, held up some of Mr Billie's things and said, 'Look at these, Gordon, fancy you letting Mr Billie wear his clothes until they get as dirty as this.' I stopped wearing them after that. I was lucky because a week or two later one of the footmen was caught wearing Mr Bobbie Shaw's socks and was sacked on the spot.

(Grimmett, 'Lamp Boy's Story', 1976, pp. 67–70, 73–4)

Eric Horne recalled one footman who took advantage of the tipping system.

It was usual for them to put the tip for the housemaids under the pillow of the bed. We had a very smart footman who knew this. As soon as the visitors left their bedrooms on the last morning of their visit he used to pop round the bedrooms and take the tip from under the pillows, and then disappear downstairs . . . the butler was told, who laid a trap for him, by putting a marked half sovereign under the pillow. Sure enough he fell into the trap. When he came downstairs the butler told him to turn out his pockets. He had the marked coin and the sack as well.

(Horne, *What the Butler Winked at*, pp. 79–80)

For Mary Ann Dodd, one tip had more than monetary value.

> The Prince of Wales stayed at the Castle [St Fagan's] and he was a lovely gentleman. When he left there was a present for us all. The Housekeeper had a brooch and I had ten shillings which was a lot of money. I kept it a long time then it looked as if it might go mouldy so I used it.

(Stevens, 'St Fagans Castle', 1986)

Perquisites (perks) were unofficial extras generally acknowledged to be part of the rewards of service. They were usually in the form of goods which could be sold for cash. Thus butlers sold used corks, cooks sold grease, scullery maids sold rabbit skins, valets and ladies' maids sold clothing.

George Washington explained about corks.

> As hall boy I had my 'perks'. Mine were the empty wine bottles and corks that, whenever guests or the young Lord Ilchester were in residence, came down from the dining-room. These had a second-hand value and every so often a man would call to collect them, giving me twopence or threepence a dozen for the bottles. Corks could bring in much more. All the wines we served were vintage and had the year and origin stamped on the corks. An exceptional year for champagne, clarets and ports could fetch as much as five shillings, and a good year one and six to two shillings. They were resold to villains, who put them into cheap bottles with forged labels, or to wine waiters at expensive hotels and restaurants. Wine waiters were expected to put the corks of the bottles at the side of the table for the host to see; so a tipsy host paid vintage prices for cheap wines. I put the money I got from these sales aside so that when Maisy [the stillroom maid] asked me to go home with her for a week's holiday I was able to say 'yes', and to take a tidy sum with me as spending money.

(Washington, 'Hall Boy's Story', p. 186)

Jean Rennie as kitchen maid

Grouse, rabbits, chickens, ducks, geese, then pheasants and woodcock and snipe and partridges. I did them all.

Only, to my very pleasant surprise, I was told to keep my rabbit skins and hare skins. As I often had about two dozen rabbits in a week, with occasionally a hare, I soon found the reason for this.

An old travelling packman came round every week, and for each rabbit skin he gave me fourpence and for each hare skin a shilling. But they had to be really nicely skinned and not broken.

So I was *really* well-off!

(Rennie, *Every Other Sunday*, p. 100)

Eileen Balderson

The young girl who was scullery maid at Rise . . . ran away. Hilda shared a room with her and awoke one morning to find she had left a note beside Hilda's bed, and gone. She left her luggage behind, but took her rabbit skins. She knew her luggage would be sent on, but not the rabbit skins and these represented money to her . . .

(Balderson, *Backstairs Life*, p. 32)

An occasional windfall and a formal goodbye gift might come in the form of a legacy left by an employer. One year's extra wages seems to have been usual for general servants, with special provision made for long-serving personal attendants.

Extract from the Last Will and Testament of Jemima, Marchioness Grey, proved 20 January 1797

. . . I give to all my menial Servants who shall have lived with me twelve months next before my decease one years wages over and besides what may be due to them at the time of my death. I give to my Servant Jane Boad if I shall not have made some provision for her in my lifetime fifty pounds a year to be paid by equal quarterly payments for the term of her life . . . I desire that three charitable donations I have made to old Servants viz Ann Fairborn who lived at Wrest Sarah Stanley who lived at Richmond and Martha Standforth who lived at Wimple may be continued to them for their respective lives . . .

I give to my Servant S Brasier if I shall not have made some provision for her in my lifetime the sum of twenty pounds a year . . .

(BLARS, Lucas, L32/44–45)

Extract from the Last Will and Testament of Ann, Countess Dowager of Effingham, 20 April 1774

. . . I give to my own Waiting Woman and my Butler Thirty Pounds each and to my other Men Servants and maid Servants twenty pounds each. The said several legacies to my said servants to be paid to such of them only who shall not have given or received Warning to quit my Service and over and above all Wages and other sums which shall be justly due to them respectively at my decease and I give to Robert Archer my late servant the sum of twenty pounds . . .

(SHC, Effingham, 388/1)

THREE

'Cinderella couldn't have had it worse' – the duties of menservants

The numbers of servants employed in a country house varied greatly with wealth, status, the type and size of family, even geographical position. A country rector's house might manage with ten or less, whereas Frederick Gorst recalled that even into the early twentieth century the great aristocratic Welbeck Abbey had over sixty indoor servants and well over a hundred outdoor.[1] Service in such households was highly specialised, structured and departmentalised. Clear job demarcation was one of the attractions of service in the larger establishments, encouraging a pride in skill. Such complex communities needed regulation and many households issued a written set of rules.

Both employers and employees commented that country-house servants needed to start young. Good servants were 'bred up' to it. A boy might start as servants' hall boy, steward's room boy or lamp boy. He could then progress to the post of footman, under-butler, butler and, in the larger households, groom of the chamber and even eventually to house steward. Servants were trained by other servants, usually by serving their seniors in the staff hierarchy. At this lower level, work was hard and unremitting. The duties of hall boy and steward's room boy were defined by waiting on servants and doing the menial tasks such as washing up in the butler's pantry. Here they practised the skills of their calling, became familiar with the social traditions of service and learnt how to survive the bad temper of masters or the spitefulness of fellow servants.

Footmen were one of the kingpins of the country-house world, both in fact and in the modern view of that world. Autobiographical sources serve to emphasise this, for a successful footman became a butler, and successful butlers were exactly those people who wrote memoirs. Nevertheless, footmen were vilified as 'flunkeys' by contemporaries and as 'ornamental parasites' by more recent writers.[2] Yet their hours were long and their duties were multifarious and ill defined. They included the care and use of all the silver, glass, china and lamps, serving meals, polishing the downstairs furniture, cleaning outdoor clothes, valeting male members of the family and their guests, accompanying them out of doors, delivering messages and securing the house at night. The nature of much of their work does not help their image. What was known as 'close waiting' required attendance on family members, simply waiting to be needed – for serving meals, helping an invalid or delivering messages. This was usually worked out on a rota system alongside carriage duty – if a house had three footmen, each one would be in close waiting one day out of three, carriage duty on the second day and the third would be a day off waiting, with only the normal duties of the pantry, meals and valeting.[3] In the largest aristocratic households footmen were supplemented in the rota by grooms of the chamber, a middle-management post with responsibility for the care of the living rooms.

One of the major trends in domestic service throughout the nineteenth and twentieth centuries was the replacement of men by women, who were cheaper to employ and considered more biddable. There was also another financial incentive: from

1777 until 1937 employers had to pay tax on male servants, as well as other symbols of status such as carriages and hunting dogs, but not on women servants. In the Edwardian period, even footmen were beginning to be replaced by parlourmaids and only the great houses retained male cooks.[4]

Extracts from Regulations for Domestic Servants at Wimpole Hall, Cambridgeshire, c. 1790

1. The Strictest Cleanliness, Decency of Demeanor, Respectful Conduct & Obedience to the Upper Servants is ordered.

2. The Time of Rising for the Servants will be between the hours of 5 and 6 in Summer and 6 & 7 in Winter. (Note: Summer from the 1st of April to the 31st of October. Winter from the 1st of November to the 31st of March).

   The Hours for meals will be

	Summer	Winter
Breakfast	8 am	8.30am
Dinner	1 pm	1pm
Supper	9pm	9pm

3. Prayers will be read in the Chapel, at which all the Servants are desired to attend. In Summer at 9 am, in winter at 9 pm

4. Under Servants (except the Footman, who may be required for Drawing Room attendance) are to go to bed at 10 pm. The Upper Servants (except the House Steward & Butler) at 11pm. The Ladies' Maids will retire to their beds as soon as their Mistresses have dispensed with their further attendance . . .

7. The House Steward & Butler is ordered to see weighed, & enter in a book every morning all descriptions of provisions that are brought to the house; and all persons whatsoever, bringing meat, fowls of all sorts, Game, Fish, eggs for Kitchen use . . . are to make the same known to the House Steward & Butler, that he may make his entries.

In like manner, Coals, Oils & Wax candles are to be duly entered into his book, on the day of their arrival.

8. The House Steward & Butler is to be most particularly careful to see the fires & lights completely extinguished after all are retired to rest & to see the doors locked & Windows secured, at 10 o'clock every night.

9. The Housekeeper, in like manner, will enter in a book which she must keep for the purpose all Fruits, Jams, Jellies (made or received), Tallow Candles, Bread, Butter, Sugar, Salt, in short anything of House Provisions that would, according to custom, fall under her immediate charge. These books will be liable to weekly inspection, by either Lady H. or myself.

10. No Servant is to order anything of any trades-person or Shopkeeper whatever without the order in the handwriting of Lady H or myself, or without one of our signatures attached to a given order.

11. No Servant is to keep an Account Book against me or Lady H. with the exception of the House Steward & Butler, and any small sums expended for Turnpikes etc or necessaries for the Stables (being ordered by myself, or in my absence if necessary by the Coachman) is to be immediately repaid by the House Steward & Butler . . .

14. No Servant is to absent him or herself from the House for more than two hours at any time (& that only once a day) without asking leave thro their Butler or Housekeeper or Lady H. or myself; and no servant on any pretence whatsoever is to absent him or herself from meals, or from the house after 10 pm without special permission from either Lady H or myself.

15. Gentlemen's servants coming on business to the House or near Meal Hours are to be invited to partake of the Meal; or coming distances Refreshments may be offered them, a Pint of Ale therewith. Post-boys are not to be entertained in the house, nor their horses fed in the stable . . .

18. The upper Servants will be allowed their Washing while the family are at Wimpole only. Maids will be allowed to wash for themselves. The under Servants (Men) will find their own washing.

20. Times of bringing Stores and Provisions to the House to be regulated by the House Steward.

21. All Servants are expected to attend Divine Service in the Church at least once every Sunday.

NB. No perquisites are to be allowed to Servants

Hardwicke.

(CCRO, Wimpole, 408/F7)

George Washington began his career as hall boy at Little Missenden Abbey.

I was a sort of dog's body, at every-one's beck and call; no sooner would I settle down to do one thing than I would be told to do another – Cinderella couldn't have had it worse. The nick-name that I was given, 'Washy', I think describes my condition and state of mind. One consolation was that I was within cycling distance of home and could see my family occasionally.

Then he went as steward's room boy at Holland House for the Earl and Countess of Ilchester.

Speaking personally I don't think I've ever worked harder in my life; I think that there I learned almost everything I know about private service. My specific job as steward's room boy was to look after the steward's room and to valet the butler. I got up at five-thirty and woke Mr Pettit at six, with a mug of tea and a can of hot water. I would lay out his clothes and clean his boots. Then came the lighting of the fires. This in retrospect was a little ridiculous. I had to light the ones in the stillroom and the breakfast-room, while the stillroom maid lit those in Mr Pettit's bedroom and the housekeeper's sitting-room, and the under housemaid lit the one in the steward's room. There were two fireplaces in the breakfast-room with surrounds of steel. These I had to burnish with a leather pad lined with chain mail. I felt like a valet to a knight in shining armour. . . .

Unfortunately the odd man was an old retainer of some seventy years or more, only capable of pottering about, so that the heavy jobs that normally would have been his responsibility fell on me. Perhaps the hardest of these was carrying the coals, and since all the rooms, including some of the bedrooms, were heated by coal fires this meant climbing to the top of the house with two galvanised buckets of around 56 lb each. At the time I was only just tall enough to get them off the floor; they seemed to wrench my arms out of their sockets and it's my opinion that's the reason why I've got such long ape-like arms today.

Another soul-destroying task was scrubbing the passage which ran the whole length of the house below stairs. I would start at the back door and end up a hundred yards later at the butler's office. My journey was broken by small flights of stairs and here I had to take particular care as Mr Pettit's eyes were most likely to fall there and if he noticed the slightest bit of fluff he'd ring the bell for me, and I was for it. He was a cunning bugger; his office was near the front door and knowing we could hear him as he came from there to the pantry, he'd sometimes take his boots off and walk in his stockinged feet expecting, even I think hoping, to find that we were up to no good. I was able to sort him out for a time. There was a loose tile under the rug outside his room; I ran a wire there and connected it up to a bell in the pantry so that when he left we were given a timely warning. I can still feel the pain on my backside when I recall the day he discovered it.

(Washington, 'Hall Boy's Story', pp. 178, 182–3)

Gordon Grimmett started as lamp boy at Longleat during the First World War.

I was up next morning at six and Bob and I went round the house collecting the shoes. Eventually we had about sixty pairs (family and nurses) down in the cellar waiting to be cleaned. From time to time one of us would break off and go to a landing, fill a number of white enamel jugs with hot water and take them round the bedrooms. Six at a time I could manage, three in each hand, though I clanked about a bit as I carried them.

. . . every day I had to collect, clean, trim and fill four hundred lamps. Actually here I'm not telling the truth because it would have been humanly impossible to have done so many. . . . From time to time the odd men, steward's room boy or hall boy would be sent down to help, and if I got very behind the butler would send a footman down to give me a hand. But officially the lamps were my responsibility. In other words if things went wrong with them I was called to account.

Collecting and replacing them itself meant a few miles walk every day, though again the bulk were delivered to me by the housemaids and the footmen. They came in all shapes and sizes, bracket lamps, standard lamps, table lamps, hanging lamps. Many of them were of great beauty and value, gathered from all parts of the world.

First I would examine the wicks and trim them if necessary with special scissors. . . . Then I would fill the lamps from the large oil tanks, paraffin for the corridor and staff lamps, and colsa oil for the house. It was considered that colsa oil gave a kinder more mellow light, and also that it didn't smell so much. I didn't care for colsa as it was thicker than paraffin and, if by chance I left the tap on in the tank the oil fell silently to the floor. So many times my cellar was flooded before I became aware of what had happened. Then there was the polishing of the funnels or the chimneys as they were called, the glass globes, and finally the cleaning of the stands. Fortunately these couldn't be polished, but they had to be free from any traces of oil.

As each batch of twenty or so were finished there would be the journey round replacing them and collecting others. The sheer monotony of the job took some beating. . . . Candelabra and candlesticks were used in the dining rooms and the drawing rooms, but fortunately these were the responsibility of the footmen. Some of the lamps were counterweighted from the ceiling, and were in groups of three, each hanging on chains in the galleries. These I had to clean and fill on the spot, as they were too heavy to carry.

Grimmett was promoted to footman at Longleat. His day was split up into clearly divided duties. First came the morning chores.

Every morning would see us up at seven, running down to the stillroom, eventually emerging with six small morning tea trays arranged on one large butler's tray, distributing them round the guests' rooms, opening curtains and gently but firmly waking them. We didn't want them slipping back to sleep again and blaming us for their having missed breakfast. Then collecting their clothes from the night before, whipping them into the brushing-room, sponging, brushing, folding and hanging them. Then laying up the breakfast table, and bringing in the various dishes, kidneys, bacon, eggs, fish on one side of the dining-room – hams, brawns and galantines and game pies on the other. And the constant running to and fro with fresh toast and hot rolls.

After breakfast came the cleaning of silver, then hall duties: at St James's Square the duty footman would be stationed all day in the front hall sitting in a large hooded leather chair. There were constant callers of all nationalities to see either Lord or Lady Astor. Unless they had appointments the reply was always the same, 'They are not at home'.

(Grimmett, 'Lamp Boy's Story', pp. 19, 22–3, 61)

Waiting at table and serving food was an important part of a footman's work.

Frederick Gorst explained the system at the Duke of Portland's.

We handed the dishes in order of their importance and our own rank.

Since there were sixteen guests, there were two joints served. Mr. Parley, as the butler, handed one platter, and I, as first footman, handed the other. Trowbridge was the second footman, so it was his right to hand the sauces and gravies and back me up as soon as the entrée was served. Weaver, the third footman, handed the vegetables. . . .

When there were more than twelve at a dinner party, it was customary for Mr. Parley to have an extra footman engaged for the evening to act as an assistant wine butler. He would help Mr. Parley with the uncorking and sometimes help him serve. But no one but Mr. Parley attended to all the finer details, such as choosing the wines and seeing that they were served at the proper temperature.

After dinner, the ladies retired to the drawing room, and the gentlemen remained at the table for their port, brandy, and cigars. I served the ladies the coffee and liqueurs, and Mr. Parley and his assistant attended the gentlemen. I particularly enjoyed bringing the shining silver coffee service into the beautiful drawing room and waiting on the lovely guests individually. Her Ladyship liked to pour the coffee herself, and I handed each lady her demitasse. It was customary for me to pass the liqueurs, and to ask each guest which kind she preferred, cointreau, Benedictine, or crème de menthe. Then I waited in the large white entrance hall for the rest of the evening until the guests went home.

(Gorst, *Carriages and Kings*, pp. 113–14)

In the world of the butler and footman, stories of dropped trays and jolted elbows became part of the folklore, and usually involved scalding food dropped down a lady's décolletage. Eric Horne's is a little different, a vivid word picture of an unnamed castle in the north of England.

I had a large tray loaded with dishes of desert from the stillroom: on one of the dishes was a round green melon. . . . To get to the dining room I had to open a green baize door, which would only open by pulling it towards me. I rested the tray on one knee, opening the door; on doing so the melon rolled off the tray, and being downhill, it went rolling off down the passage. . . . All right, thinks I, I will come back for you directly. On going back there was no melon to be seen. I asked the stillroom maid if she had seen it; she said no. . . . I looked everywhere, then I went out on the drawbridge. There I saw the melon bobbling about in the moat. I rushed to the front door, got the punt, poled round and captured it. The stones in the passage had become so worn through the years of use, that a channel had been made in the centre, just the place for a round melon to go careering in, the farther it went the faster it went. . . .

(Horne, *What the Butler Winked at*, pp. 102–3)

In the evening, footmen were responsible for drawing curtains and shutters and lighting the lamps.

William Lanceley

On this occasion the fire broke out in the lamp room. . . . He blew the taper out, as he thought, and put it down on the shelf. Either it was not quite out when he put it down or a draught caused it to flare up again; however, it had been put near some engine waste that was used to wipe the oil from the lamps and this took fire in its oily condition, and soon the whole room was ablaze. A bracket just above the shelf, on which the lamp filler containing about a quart of oil was placed, was set on fire, and this in turn fell to the floor and carried the engine waste now burning furiously with it. Fortunately this was colza oil, so no explosion took place, but the oily waste floating on top of the running oil made almost choking smoke and smell. The outbreak was discovered by the scullerymaid. We had all been warned that in case of fire in the lamp room we were not to throw water on it, sand only. The girl kept her presence of mind, called out 'Fire,' and ran for the coconut mat at the back door which was only a few paces away. The mat was wet and it filled up the doorway, stopping the running oil; she then rushed to her scullery near by, snatched two dinner plates from the rack and plunged them into a sack of sand which was used to clean pewter and copper utensils and threw the sand into the flames. The other servants followed her example and the fire was soon under control, but the smoke was dense and sickening. The footman, returning for more lamps, was dumbfounded. Then collecting himself and tying a lamp cloth over his mouth and nose plunged into the burning room and brought out a four-gallon can of paraffin oil and a four-gallon can of colza oil. Had the paraffin oil exploded, another of the stately homes of

England would undoubtedly have been burned to the ground, as the nearest fire brigade was five miles away. . . .

The next fire was caused through a footman who in this case acted like a madman. He had been out in the afternoon and had cut his time short for lighting up. He was lighting the gas in the gasoliers and side brackets with a wax taper, then holding the burning taper in his hand proceeded to draw the heavy curtains. In so doing he set alight to the lace curtains . . . these blazed up furiously and he tried to tear them down but could not extinguish the flames. . . . The firebell was rung lustily and the fire brigade, trained under the late Captain Shaw's instructions, turned out smartly. Household and outside servants composed the brigade and were fully equipped with helmets, axes and uniform. They had done yeoman service at fires in the neighbourhood and had given the best account of themselves when called upon. Each kept his uniform in his room or at his home, and when the firebell gave the alarm every man rushed for his clothes. Seeing a man running away from the burning mansion, I called out, 'Come here – the fire is in the house.'

He pulled up, saying, 'Our first rule says, "Get into your uniform as quickly as possible!"'

And so mechanically they all rushed to their room and homes as trained to do and some of the homes were half a mile distant. The house was well supplied with hose and fire pumps and the odd man was told to rush one of these to the small drawing-room and with it succeeded in putting out the flames just as the fire brigade, now fully dressed, appeared on the scene. . . .

(Lanceley, *Hall-Boy to House Steward*, pp. 178–9, 181–2)

Footmen's memoirs often relate details about particular duties – especially cleaning silver.

Ernest King

[Rouge] proved to be a very soft, red powder, mixed in a saucer with ammonia. I then did as he did, dipped my fingers in the paste and began to rub it over the silver.

'Harder,' he said.

'But it hurts,' I said. 'It'll blister.'

'That's right,' he said. 'It's better when they burst.'

Cleaning plate is hell. It's the greatest bugbear behind the green baize door, the hardest job in the house. When I began this work, rubbing the silver, the spoons and forks, occasionally getting a prong in my thumb, my fingers grew fearfully sore and blistered, but in those days if you complained you were just told to get on with it and you did. The blisters burst and you kept on despite the pain and you developed a pair of plate hands that never blistered again. In the old days his duties compelled a footman to use his hands and they became as hard as boards. . . .

And hunting clothes:

From horse and rider perspiring, from a fall in a muddy ditch or field, they can come back in a pretty mess, especially the coat tails. When in this state we would ask the housemaid to save us the contents of the chamber-pots, at least a bucketful. It was truly miraculous in getting the dirt out. That was immediately followed, I hasten to add, by brushing with clean water. I've often wondered if all the smart and fashionable hunting folk ever knew of the means taken to keep their coats so smartly turned out.

(King, *Green Baize Door*, pp. 16–17, 19)

In a hunting house everyone wanted a bath at the same time. Charles Dean recalled Badminton.

One of the difficulties in looking after the hunting set was that they generally came back all at the same time, wanting baths immediately, and if I was looking after two or three gentlemen I had to move fast. They were very free with their language and when they'd had a bad day they vented their spleen on me. It was like water off a duck's back; one thing I learned early in service was never to allow myself to get hassled. The bathing arrangements were, even for that time, a little old-fashioned. The baths were contained in cupboards; when the doors were opened they came down on hinges. They weren't very large and if the gentlemen were careless much of the water would end up on the floor, so I was constantly having to mop up after them. Although they were free with their language they were also free with their cash and I did well with tips; I think they looked on it as conscience money.

And the Badminton staff had a particular problem.

His grace the Duke [of Beaufort] was a great character, both mentally and physically; he weighed twenty-four stone. . . . His hunting days as an equestrian were of course over, but he followed the hunt in an old open Ford. . . . He had a most unfortunate complaint; he was incontinent. Of course opportunity would have been a great thing, because once strapped in the car he couldn't get out, and it wasn't pleasant for us men servants, when after a day's hunting he had to be carried upstairs; two poles were inserted in slots in the Windsor chair and he was lifted by four of us. Invariably I got the rear end, and the odour that went with it. I comforted myself with the thought that his valet had it worse than I did, he had to bath him. To do this he had to use a block and tackle to lift his grace in and out of the bath.

(Dean, 'Boot Boy's Story', 1976, pp. 140–1, 143–4)

Travelling took up a large part of footmen's lives. Carriage duty alternated with 'close waiting', on a rota system. During visits in London, the footman had to be familiar with the etiquette of card calling.

Gordon Grimmett with Mrs Sandford

Many's the afternoon she would summon Dick Williams the coachman to take her 'card calling'. It was the job of the footman on duty to drive with her, riding on the box of the carriage, dressed like the coachman in top boots, long carriage cloak and a silk hat with a cockade 'up' at the side.

. . .

She'd set off about three; in one hand she held a speaking tube through which she'd give a string of instructions to the coachman, and in the other a list of acquaintances she hoped to find at home. We'd be going at a trot, say round Belgrave Square, when she'd yell, 'Stop at number six.' I would dismount. She'd pass me a visiting card for me to present at 6 Belgrave Square. 'Card calling' was quite an operation. I'd ring the doorbell which would be opened by the butler or the head parlour maid, hand them the card saying, 'With the compliments of Mrs Charles Sandford. Is your lady in today?' The door would be closed while inquiries were made as to whether their mistress was at home to Mrs Sandford.

If she was I would, after much effort on her part, get Hett out of the carriage, help her up the steps to the house, and remain standing outside until the visit was over. This could go on at one or two addresses during an afternoon, then we would take a final jog trot round Hyde Park, and return home.

If a person was not at home, and sometimes the alacrity with which the butler or footman returned showed that he had standing instructions if Hett called, the card was left with the corner turned up, which indicated that Mrs Sandford had called personally. Often footmen had the job of going round on their own delivering cards . . . to show that their mistress was in London, and was receiving. In this case the card was not turned up and this indicated that a messenger had presented it.

(Grimmett, 'Lamp Boy's Story', pp. 42–3)

Frederick Gorst travelled with the Portlands by train to Scotland for the shooting season.

It was like moving a small army. It required a special train to transport us to Helmsdale on the North Sea. We referred to it as the 'iron caravan'.

The Duke and Duchess occupied one carriage consisting of several bedrooms, a sitting room, and a dining area; the children and the governess occupied the next; the Upper Ten rode next; then the footmen, the chef and his helpers, and chauffeurs; and the final passenger car was reserved for still room maids and housemaids. The rest of the train was a long string of wagons, each one housing an automobile.

Every time we stopped, Hales went forward to see if Her Grace wished anything, although she had her own personal maid. . . .

The railway served the Duke's and Duchess's meals. All the servants had tea baskets with sandwiches, chicken, hard-boiled eggs, and fruit which had been packed before we left London. It really was a big picnic! Two of us shared a hamper, containing an alcohol stove and a teapot, so that we could make our own tea. We were responsible for the wicker hampers, which were fitted with plates and utensils. Anyone who lost his hamper didn't eat until we got to Scotland fourteen hours later.

(Gorst, *Carriages and Kings*, p. 197)

The highest achievement for an indoor manservant was the post of house steward, usually head of all the family households and responsible for a myriad of mundane duties. Robert Smith was house steward to the 5th Duke of Richmond at Goodwood; Dr Archibald Hair was secretary to the Duke.

Robert Smith to Dr Archibald Hair, 19 May 1858

51, Portland Place

Sir,

The knife cleaner has cost £14-14s-0d it is No 1 size and answers well, the Ice Machine has cost £5-10s-0d being £5-0s-0d less than Lord Derbys and exactly the same, it is working remarkably well the Ice Machine was to have cost £7-0s-0d but for ready Money etc he . . . has taken off £1-10s-0d with which I am very much pleased, I have begun with the same Ice people we get 25 lb for 1/-. The Baker from Park Street is to be kept on as their never was any fault with his bread and he was willing to send at any time . . . I am very much pleased to see 10 rabbits. I think Sir if the Sherry will last this Month out it will be better for you to have the Wine Book to put straight at the End of the Month – I am sorry that there is no Soap come as I have been putting off day after day Expecting it certain today and there is I see exactly 20/- difference per Hundred weight I have not seen Mrs Ewens yet I thought it was as well not until I had made proper Enquiry, her prices are about the same as other Respectable Shops there is a Shop in Great Marylebone Street appearantly a very first Rate Business his name is Clayton he gives me the best Impression of any that I have seen – all his Places are so very clean and his own Slaughter House through the Shop it looks altogether the most wholesome and best . . .

(WSRO, Goodwood, MS 1830 f. 1607)

FOUR

'We have mad four cheses pritey larg' – the duties of women servants

Housemaids were the unsung heroines of the country house. Over the years their duties changed little and they seem to have been among the most hard-working and put-upon members of the staff. Most footmen's memoirs comment on their diligence, for housemaids' and footmen's responsibilities required that they work quite closely together since they were both involved with room cleaning. The housemaid would first clean fireplaces, windows and ledges, then sweep carpets and floors. After a short wait for the dust to settle, in would come the footmen to polish the fine furniture. They were not supposed to be in the room together, however, and certainly this was strictly forbidden if the room were a bedroom.

The successful housemaid might rise to become a housekeeper. Within the country-house world these had a specific role, which was to look after the house in the family's absence and prepare it for their arrival, particularly important given the peripatetic nature of the aristocracy. Their duties revolved around the house itself and its stores, rather than its occupants. They were head of the female household and head of the whole household when the steward or butlers were away with the family, often the main contact between house and master and mistress. A stillroom maid usually acted as a housekeeper's personal servant and the housemaids as her assistants.

Over the years country-house staffs became feminised, women taking over more and more of the jobs previously done by men. In many ways this suited the country-house way of doing things, which had never sat happily with mixed-gender workplaces – women kitchen maids working directly under male chefs, for example. The one bastion of the country-house world which remained unchanged over the years was, however, the nursery – always the domain of women.

Women in country houses either started out at the bottom of the pile in the local squire's house or similar, or as a single- or double-handed servant in an even smaller household. Many of them had the varied sort of work experienced by Annie Norman.

Annie Norman was one servant of two in 1918, working for one of the masters at Repton School.

March 30 We started our spring cleaning. Mrs Singleton had Mrs Surtees in for tea.

March 31 Emily out. Charles' birthday & we prepared for the sweep coming on Wednesday.

April 1 Term ended. The sweep came at 9.00

April 3 I finished my spring cleaning.

Aug 10 I had a rather large wash but it was a glorious day. I dried everything.

Aug 11 It was a very hot day & I was busy ironing. Emily out, but she called in to see me with Dora.

Sept 1 Tuesday. I very busy, not a minute to waste as I have got to boil & cakes to make & beef to boil, ironing to do and it is a very hot day. I have got there lunch ready and they have taken it out for a picnic. Glad to get rid of them. Mrs S gave me 10/- board.

Oct 7 We got up at 8 o'clock, we had breakfast & then we started work. The men put the boiler in. We were working like blacks up to ¼ to 12. We then went to bed after a hard day's work.

Oct 8 We got up at 8 o'clock & had breakfast & started work Lucy came in for tea. We went to bed at 1 o'clock after bathing.

Oct 9 Got up at 8. Had breakfast & we simply had to fly as Mrs S & family were coming at 1 o'clock. We had not got quite straight when they arrived. She said everything looked nice and clean.

(Norman, 'Diary', DeRO, D5161/1)

Harriet Brown to her mother, 1870

My Dearest Mother,

. . . I have been so driven at work since the fires begun I have had ardly any time for anything for myself. I am up at half past five or six every morning and I do not go to bed till nearly twelve at night and I feel so tired sometimes I am obliged to have a good cry. I do think I should have been laid up if it was not for the Cod Liver Oil I am taking it is very nasty but I think it does me good it is very dear half a crown for a pint and it is so nasty. I reach my heart up nearly at the thought of it. Mrs Graves the cook is very kind. She as helped me with my work in the morning. I would never of been done if she had not and the Nurse she as never said so much as are you not well not even offered to do a thing for me but I am much better now so I not trouble her. Dear Mother I should of asked you over next week only we are going to have two dinner parties one on Tuesday the other on Thursday and we shall be so busy so you must come after it is over . . . Dear Mother I can give you plenty of mending when you have time and I should so like to see you but I cannot get away just now so you must come and see me soon. I let you know when to come for I have got lots of things to tell you. . . . With fondest love to all I remain your ever

Affect. Daughter,
Harriet Brown

(Frank Victor Dawes, *Not in Front of the Servants*, 1973, Century, 1989, pp. 22–3)

There was a hierarchy of work within each department.

Margaret Thomas

> I never knew much about the other maids' work, but I
> remember the fourth housemaid worked entirely for the staff,
> the third for the schoolroom, one young lady, maid and
> governess, and helped the second, who had to be downstairs at
> 4 a.m. every morning to get the sitting-room done before
> breakfast. The second housemaid had a medal room to keep
> clean where the medals were set out in steel cases, and had to
> be polished with emery paper every day. I think, because she
> had to get up so early, she was off duty at noon until evening.
> The head housemaid did light jobs. They all did sewing.

(Thomas, 'Green Baize Door', p. 89)

Eileen Balderson at Rise Park

> Wherever we went about the house together, such as to meals
> or to do the lunch and dinnertime tidying, the housemaids –
> Alice, Emma and myself – walked in single file; as we
> approached a door, I had to walk forward, open it, and stand
> aside while they passed through. . . .
>   As in all the houses, we tidied at lunchtime and
> dinnertime. Head housemaid, second, and myself tidied the
> drawing room, library and smoke room. The head folded the
> newspapers and tidied magazines on a table kept for them.
> The second housemaid shook up cushions, and I swept up the
> fireplaces. The fourth housemaid tidied the study and Lady
> Boyne's sitting room, and the fifth housemaid looked after the
> cloakroom. As always, we went everywhere in our correct
> order.

By contrast, as a scullery maid she usually worked on her own.

> Washing up was daunting. Under the scullery window was a
> large sandstone sink. To the right of this fixed to the wall, was a
> long plate rack, 6ft by 4ft, with a draining board underneath.
> For washing up I used two zinc baths about the size of a clothes
> basket, one with hot soapy water and the other with clear water
> for rinsing, then all the plates and dishes were put into the rack

to drain. There were no washing up liquids in those days. Soft soap was used for everything except pans, and soda was used for them. . . .

I had about ¾cwt potatoes to peel for the next day. I used to sing while peeling. One of my favourites was 'Little Grey Home in the West'. I knew how many potatoes I could peel per verse and chorus! But I had many other 'spud peelers', learned from Hilda. They included 'I Dreamt I Dwelt in Marble Halls', 'The Rose of Tralee', 'Songs of Araby', 'Indian Love Lyrics', 'I Passed by Your Window', 'Absent' and 'A Brown Bird Singing'.

If cooking salt was needed in the kitchen, I had a 7lb block to rub through a sieve, which was a painful job if my hands were chapped, as they often were in the winter. After these jobs came all the washing up again. Servants' hall supper was at 9pm, so I was usually finished about 10pm.

(Balderson, *Backstairs Life*, pp. 21, 28–9, 31–2, 54)

Margaret Thomas was first engaged as kitchen maid in a town house in Portman Square.

My duties consisted of waiting on the cook, preparing the food for her to cook, cooking all vegetables, roasts and savouries, making toast and coffee, and all pounding and chopping, all the staff cooking and, of course, all sieving and washing up. As well I had the basement to keep clean. For news of what was to be cooked I was told I must read the slate. This had been 'passed' by the Lady in the morning; it was always written in French, so I spent most of my afternoons, until I got a working knowledge of the language, studying the cookery book, which gave the names of each dish in French as well as English.

. . . That cook and I worked very hard; everything was cooked in copper pans, copper moulds were used for jellies-creams and sponge cakes. There was a large dresser in the kitchen where they were set out, each one had to be cleaned every time it was used with a mixture of sand, salt and vinegar, and flour rubbed on by hand. They certainly looked very nice. Every morning when the Lady passed the slate in the servants' hall she came out to see them, and if one was missing inquired why it was not in its place.

. . . On Friday nights we usually had a dinner party. They consisted of eight or nine courses, and there was usually a luncheon party the next day . . . I used to stay in the kitchen helping the cook all through the dinners; after it was over I had all my washing up to do, then, when she had gone to bed, I started on my housework, cleaning flues, black-leading the range and hearthstoning the kitchen scullery and larder; in the morning I had the long passage from the back door to the kitchen to hearthstone. I always had to be down in the kitchen by 6 a.m. to light the fire to get the water hot for all the cooking was done on a coal range. . . . We never had any help however busy we were, unless the cook paid for a woman to wash up out of her own pocket, which she occasionally did. . . .

Later she moved to a country house in Yorkshire.

. . . The next house in Yorkshire was very primitive after what I had become used to. But in that house I learned to make bread and had to bake it twice a week for the staff as well as baking fancy bread, brown and white, tea cakes and rolls. I was told I made good bread. I knelt beside a huge pan on the floor and kneaded the dough; it took all my strength and I was always trembling all over when I had finished, but it was rewarding to take the loaves from the oven. We had a huge open fire in that house, with ovens at the side, all the meat was roasted in front of the fire on a smoke jack. The fire also heated the water, the tap to it was outside the kitchen door and everyone had to come there for it. There was no water laid on above the first floor, where there was a cold tap in the housemaids' cupboard, and as there were no bathrooms everyone had hip baths in their bedrooms, family and staff. Even the lavatories had no water, a bucket of water was kept in each which the housemaids had to refill as they were used. We had no gas or electricity. . . . The cook told me to fetch some chops on my first day from a meat safe in the kitchen garden. This meat safe was as large as a room, with a whole sheep hanging up split down the middle. I was appalled when I found I had to joint the carcase, but I soon learned how. The beef came in in huge joints, but the green bacon for the staff came in sides, part of which I had to boil and the rest cut in rashers. In that safe there were great crocks of pickled eggs. I dreaded plunging my hands in during the cold weather, but if the gardeners or the gamekeeper were about they did it for me.

We didn't cook many fancy dishes in that house, but there was a lot of sieving, for the Lady was an invalid, and there was plenty of plain cooking as there were two nurses for her, and three grown-up daughters and a young gentleman in the family. Everything was cooked at home. . . .

(Thomas, 'Green Baize Door', pp. 84, 86–7, 91–3)

The post of housekeeper required a wide variety of skills, as can be seen from a routine letter to Lady Mordaunt from her housekeeper.

M. Withrington to Lady Mordaunt, nd, probably early 1700s

I resaved your Ladeyships letter and am hartely sorey to here your Ladeyship canot com the hous and all things is in order all the beds hath ben clene and all the Rooms are verey well I wish your Ladeyship may injoy your helth in town this hot wether I have fated 10 chikins 12 ducks the darey gows on wel but the cows begin to abat of their milk we have mad four cheses pritey larg I have spent 6 of the old chesis I desire your Ladeyship wil let me cnow if you wil have them spent there is non of the other fit to cut I have spent sum of the fatest pork ther is non of the backon meald with onley a litel when Sir John was at hom the bens and carats are come in I have mad the hinds curtains and put them up the three windows at the upper end the diper is shrunk the cors cloth is pritey whit and the sheets shall be mad Cate hath bene verey ill she cept up a day or 2 she canot doe her bisnes she is mitey short brethd I cannot find what her illness is she cannot bere huring about I am allway at the ches macking Ann is slow but gud naterd and willing she hath clend the hous verey wel Mr Clark tould me what Sir John sad conserning the Rasbureys and currends I have provd resepts of my one but perhaps your Ladeyship's may be beter so shall wate to cnow your Ladeyship's plesur which is all from your duteyful

Servant
M Withrington

I have got 12 chikins and 2 ducks with 2 hens the hen that sat of duck eggs ett them all but too.

(WCRO, Mordaunt, Cr 1368, vol. 4/62)

Another housekeeper's letter to her master in London.

Anne Baynes to Geo Purefoy Jervise Esq, 27 June 1822

Herriard House

Honoured Sir,

I beg to inform you that Groves is not to be depended upon to supply good Fish. He has disapointed you when you have had company, the Fishmonger Mr Croft recommended sent very good Fish. The Weather is not so sultry and bad for keeping things as it was a Week ago that you might venture to send a small Turtle for soup, when made strong it will keep good for some time, it is a very useful thing to have in the House . . . Pewsey desired me to Inform you that it will be three Weeks before the Pines are ripe, the Peaches and Nectarines will be fit to gather in a fortnight. Rain is wanted very much in the Garden, the Vegetables are Burnt up, I have preserved all the Strawberries that was fit for Creams etc I am afraid the Ice if there is any in the House will not be fit for use, the Raspberries are not ripe, Currants I shall be obliged to buy for Jelly etc. There is three or four lb of Tea in the House that was had a short time before you left Herriard, there will soon be more Wanted 4lbs Hyson @12, 4lb Souchong @10, 6lb of Souchong @7 pr lb . . . I have sent to Basingstoke to make enquiries for the Hamper of Groceries it was not come to the Waggon Office this morning

I am Hon^d Sir
Your Obed^t Humble
Servant Anne Baynes

(HRO, Jervise, 44M69/F10/56/2)

A housekeeper could expect to be notified of the family's arrival a few days beforehand, together with any special instructions and if necessary a list of guests. Mrs Ingram, the Sutherlands' housekeeper at Trentham in the 1870s, received many such letters.

Henry Wright, the Duke of Sutherland's secretary, to Mrs Ingram, 5 June 1872

> . . . There will be a Ball for 400 for two nights, there will be plenty of Hands required for washing china etc. It would be as well to be prepared with the necessary women for the Dance. I hope to get down quite a week before the time . . . at a rough guess I should say 20 women would be wanted. In your letter in answer to this tell me how many beds provided for the Band. I think you said 25, but there were 40 here the other night . . .
>
> Extra beds required
> 31 visitors servants
> 7 kitchen
> 4 illuminators
> 1 china & glass man
> 25 waiters

Same, nd

> Mr. Metyard will be down tomorrow Wednesday to make the necessary arrangements about the Beds required outside. The Band instead of 25 will be 32. I will see what can be done about livery for the man at the gate. The Prince and Princess of Wales will arrive on the Monday. Shall you want any stores, if so write me a list and I will send them down the Co-operative.
>
> I am sorry Mr Roberts thinks the water <u>hot</u> is all right. I am convinced there is a defect somewhere. I have however done all I can so far in the matter – There will be someone down to look at it. I cannot run risks on such occasions if I am to be held responsible. There will be a quantity of large jugs required from the Potteries. Have you tea and coffee things enough? All glass, china etc will leave London on Monday and 2 men will be down on Friday to unpack the same and take charge of it . . .

Same, 13 July 1872

> The Duchess desires me to say she is very glad to have the list of rooms but she will not settle about who is to occupy them until she comes down which will be on Thursday. She will then devote Friday to it and as only a few visitors will be at Trentham until Monday there will be plenty of time.
>
> I dare say you are as busy as you can be 'and so say all of us'. Take it easy – it will all shake up right . . .

> (SRO, Sutherland, D593/R/10/4 & 5)

A good housekeeper would take upon herself her mistress's interests. In 1860 the Salvin family had rented out their main house, Croxdale Hall near Durham, and had moved to Croxdale Wood House, where Margaret Linsley was housekeeper. Within the main Hall, the Salvins had restricted access to some rooms under the terms of the lease, using them to store furniture. The tenant, however, had other ideas.

Margaret Linsley to Mrs Salvin, 11 May 1860

> Croxdale Wood House
>
> Madam,
>
> I write to inform you that Mr Dycin the person that lives in Croxdale Hall has broken into the room above the kitchen and removed all the things out but whar to I cannot tell . . . brother John was on the Lawn yesterday and saw the Workmen at the Window . . . Madame this I think will show you that Mr Dycin is no Gentleman . . . I am glad to hear that Mr Salvin is so much better. I hope Master Charles and yourself is well. I only wish you was back again,
>
> > From your obedient
> > Servant Margaret Linsley

Same, 13 February 1861

> I write to inform you that we began last Tuesday Feby 5th with the Inventory at Croxdale and we have not gone on as I wished . . . Madame I will give you an account of the rooms we

have been in as well as I can. Rose Wood Cabinet and Billiard Table and a few Pictures and too Book Cases is nearly all that is left in the Billiard Room. . . . The next is the Green Bed Room and Dressing Room, India paper and Pink Room, they are all changed very much. Next is room above the Dining Room we have gone through it and found it corresponds very nearly like our old Inventory taken in 1856, but they had been in and taken a Basket of old keys out and they have it yet but I intend asking for them. We then went to Strange Men Servants room and found too Cupboards with Glasses in wich has been removed from Billiard Room boath locked, we did not see in to them and also too Dining room chars lether all torn; I took and locked them by.

Ash Wednesday We went to the Inner Study but our key would not open the Door so we could not get in thar. We then went to the Attic and we failed in getting in, than the House Maid standing by said Oh Mrs Dyson has a key that opens it, she went and got it, and we got in and to our surprise we found Mattresses, Feather Beds as black and as dirty as the ground and is crammed as full of things as ever it will hold, not a cover over the Beds, one of the good large covers I had for them Dysons was under the Billiard Table. They have taken any thing that they thought fit. I firmly believe thar is not room or closet but what they have been in, when they have failed with false keys they then have forced them open . . . Madame I cannot discribe half the Distruction thar is, they have <u>cut</u> a Carpet of yours and put it round the Library and have one of their own in the <u>Middle</u> of the room . . . I am very much dissatisfied . . . Madame you must not let Mr Dyson have the Billiard Room whatever you do . . . I will write again in a few days and tell you how we come on . . .

(DRO, Salvin, D/Sa/C/299 I, 4)

Another classic country-house figure was the nanny. Sarah Sedgwick was born into a tradition of family service and herself became a nanny. Like many girls she started looking after children at an early age.

I was one of a family of ten. My father was one of the gardeners on a big estate. . . . I was earning by the time I was twelve. . . .

Children were staying at the house, and I was engaged to take them for walks. I earned four shillings a week.

I enjoyed looking after these children, so my parents decided I would do well in a nursery. I had to wait until after my fourteenth birthday of course but then I went to my first place. I was engaged as nursery maid, my wages were to be ten pounds a year.

The house was near Doncaster, a very large place. Downstairs there was a staff of twenty-two. There were two children in that nursery, the baby and a little girl aged two. It seems strange to-day, but to look after them there was the head nurse, the under nurse, the nursery maid, and a maid to wait on the nursery, and in the winter a footman who came up every two hours to make up the fires. But there was plenty to do. I had to get up at five-thirty. The nurseries were a day nursery, a night nursery, a lavatory, the room I shared with the under nurse, and a kitchenette. I had to light the nursery fires at six o'clock, and I had my fire guard to clean. This was made of brass and ran right round the grate, all its bars and its three rails had to be polished each morning. At 7.30 I had to call the head nurse with a cup of tea, and at eight o'clock the children had their breakfast.

. . . Everything had to happen to the minute. At ten sharp we were out with the prams, and pushed them until half-past twelve. Luncheon was one o'clock. Then from two until half-past three another walk with the prams. This was followed by tea at four o'clock. Then there was dressing up the children before they went downstairs, and they were taken into the drawing-room to the minute, and brought up again to the minute. Then there were their baths to get ready, all the water had to be carried. Then bed. I was supposed to be in bed myself at 9.30, but that was something which could not always happen to the minute, for with the washing, ironing, and running in of ribbons I couldn't get done in time.

We in the nursery lived very much on our own, in our separate world governed by the head nurse. Each day after breakfast the housekeeper, in her black dress with a black silk apron, would come up herself for orders for the nursery. In the evening the head nurse changed into something simple, but evening dress when there were visiting ladies' maids and valets, and went to her supper in the housekeeper's room. But the under nurse and myself never mixed with the rest of the staff, we had our supper in the day nursery. We spoke to the downstairs servants if we met them, but we had no contact with them, and at no time went into the servants' hall. . . .

She stayed two years in her first place, then moved to Scarborough.

. . . When I first started in a nursery there was no specially prepared sieved and strained food for babies. . . . All milk had to be sterilised. We had a big steriliser in the nursery, it stood on the fire, it had holes in it for bottles, and a thermometer to show when it reached the right heat. All water had to be boiled; no child was ever allowed water from a tap. Babies had sieved vegetables, but they were sieved in our own kitchen under the supervision of the head nurse. The older children ate a richer breakfast than children do to-day. They would start with porridge . . . served with thick cream and sugar. Then they had bread which had been soaked in whipped-up egg before it was fried. On this they would have a little roll of bacon. To drink they had milk. Before their morning walk the children had fruit from the kitchen gardens . . . if it was apple we always shredded it and the child ate it with a spoon. For lunch there would sometimes be jellied soup, and fish or chicken. This was always followed by a milk pudding. For tea there was thin bread and butter, little jam or banana sandwiches daintily cut, and always a sponge cake. To drink there was milk. Children in my nurseries always had to begin and finish their tea with a slice of bread and butter. For supper there was a glass of milk with perhaps a piece of bread and butter. . . .

. . . A baby wore long clothes from birth until it was six weeks or two months old. Then its clothes were shortened to foot length. It was not until the child was six months old that its legs were allowed to show. Underneath a baby wore a vest, woolly binder, mackintosh knickers over its nappy, woolly knickers, a long flannel which tied at the side with sarsnet ribbon, and an enormous starched petticoat. On top went the robe, and on top of that a woolly coat. Outside the house baby wore a pelisse, which was a loose-fitting coat with big cape collar. When the baby was laid in its pram the pelisse cape was spread out over the pillow. All babies at that time wore bonnets. . . . Looking back, I wonder little babies were not smothered with all the clothes they had to wear. . . . It was the way the children had to be turned out that made so much work. Although there was a laundress for large things, we did all the small washing, and the nappies, and of course all the children's mending. The clothes to be worn the next morning were always pressed over-night, but it was ribbons that took the most time. In those days drawers had ribbons run through them, and little-bows sewn on them. Petticoats had ribbon round the neck, sleeves, and round the bottom, and party petticoats had extra ribbons, and all those ribbons had to be pressed before they were threaded.

(Sedgwick, 'Other People's Children', pp. 14–22)

Nannies were often unpopular with other servants because they were reputed to think themselves 'a cut above' the normal. One reason for this was the opportunities they had to travel.

In the 1880s Harriet Messenger accompanied Mr and Mrs Leveson-Gower of Titsey Place, Limpsfield, Surrey, and their three children on numerous trips around Europe, sometimes lasting six years. She leaves us with a final picture which is far from the usual view of the Victorian nanny.

August 12th 1885, Dresden It is no wonder Continental folks consider England a dull place – it certainly is when compared with places abroad, people live such out-of-door lives here – I think I should consider it dull, if I had to go about in England much now. I am sure I should greatly miss the little round tables, with the laughing groups sitting at them taking their coffees.

September 11th 1887, Berchtesgarden Marie and I went down the salt mine and found it most interesting. Dressed in white trousers, blk jacket, blk and blue cap, and a leather protector on our backs, we first walked a long way in the mine each carrying a lantern, then, mounted a dark staircase, till we came to a little lake, lighted by tiny lamps, a boat was waiting and we got in, and was rowed across it to another part of the mine, here the Guide shewed us the layers of salt in the walls . . . then came to the 'shute' that was to take us lower down, on this sat a man, and we were told to sit on it too – in any but a comfortable position – my hands on the man's shoulders, and my legs round his body – Marie next to me – the Guide behind, in this manner we slipped to the bottom, going so quickly. More walking, and another 'shute' brought us to a pretty grotto of salt lighted up by little lamps, here we got on a tiny traincar and at great speed we were propelled thro' intense darkness into daylight again.

(Messenger, 'Diary', SHC, 498/6/2)

FIVE

'The water in the jug had a thin layer of ice' – servants' accommodation and clothing

Walking around the cold deserted attics of today's country houses it is difficult to see them as comfortable or welcoming. Yet in many instances indoor servants must have thought themselves lucky. After an over-crowded home, having at least a bed to oneself must have been luxury, particularly as many inventories show that it was usual to provide indoor servants with a feather bed on top of a wool mattress. The home-sickness and loneliness might be helped by dormitory living. Accommodation was certainly better than for many town servants, who often had to sleep near or in their place of work. Even the lowly steward's room boy or under-footman, who might have to sleep guarding the basement safe, had the prospect of betterment and promotion ahead. For with promotion came privacy – your own bedroom and eventually even a private sitting room.

Male and female sleeping quarters were of course strictly separated. There were usually separate staircases and entrances, overlooked by butlers' and housekeepers' rooms. Young women servants were carefully guarded, placed in the most inaccessible attics or towers. The room where the sexes came together was the servants' hall, the centre of the servants' social life. Here they ate and passed their leisure time. Here too they learnt the unwritten self-regulating rules and traditions of their trade. Inventories show that servants' halls were often spartan and sparsely furnished, though Edwardian houses tried to offer more comfort as servant expectations rose.

Rules and traditions governed most aspects of servants' lives and none more strictly than appearance. Good-looking but not flashy, wholesome, clean and neat – these were the attributes of a successful servant. Yet menservants' uniforms – livery for footmen and carriage staff – was nothing if not flashy, a deliberate throwback to an earlier fashion, marking the servant out as not a gentleman but belonging to one. A sign of status and conspicuous consumption for the employer, livery was the opposite for the wearer – promotion to the post of butler meant leaving behind livery and powdered hair. The last was an archaic custom which to the modern eye gave footmen a most unfortunate slick and untrustworthy appearance. One of the purposes of livery was uniformity; liveried menservants standing either side a door looked so much better when all of the same height and appearance. For this reason much attention was paid to footmen's looks: anyone with even a mild deformity such as a squint would be liable to dismissal. As Margaret Thomas said, 'No wonder footmen were always so conceited.'[1]

Women's clothing was less uniform as they were not generally on public view. Ordinary patterned 'washing frocks' were the norm, with plain or striped aprons and a white cap. Yet here too rules were strict, governing the type of material, the cut of the dress, the degree of decoration. Above all the wearing of caps and bonnets was regulated. In some households even in the mid-twentieth century, to be caught without a cap by the mistress was a sacking offence, a stricture harking back to the centuries-old tradition that no respectable woman would be seen outside her bedroom without some sort of cover to her crowning glory. Black hood-shaped bonnets were worn to church, a tradition which was especially resented if the church was in the village rather than on the estate.

Clothing was thus a visual marker of respectability, servility and ownership – the belonging to a household.

ACCOMMODATION

The early traditions of servant accommodation were pretty spartan.

Born in 1833, Christian Watt lived as a young girl as laundry maid at Lord Saltoun's house at Philorth, on the Aberdeenshire coast. Most of the twenty-nine servants slept in attics or bothies around the estate.

> Annie Trail, Jock Jye's daughter, Nellie Massey the under housemaid and I slept in another chaumer at Thief's ee. The roof was thatched, with a hanging lum and small 4 pan window, we put on lace screenies and a valance on the box bed . . .[2]
>
> The cook and the housekeeper had nice beds, but the others had only chaff sacks. We brought our own blanket, so as we were four to a bed we were not cold with four blankets. We also had our own pillow slips and towels.

She described another bothy

> . . . two windows about a foot square let in the light, also a glass tile set in the turf roof; the long length of the back wall was bulging and falling outwards. Like all the other chaumers it got a lick of limewash in the spring when the stables and byres were done. In the one bed slept . . . two older men, and in the other bed was . . . two halflin loons[3] always up to some tricks. Bits of harness and all kinds of things hung about the walls. I have seen many a more comfortable hen house.
>
> (Fraser, *Christian Watt Papers*, pp. 36, 38, 39)

In the Victorian and Edwardian tradition of country-house service most of the lower servants slept in attic dormitories. In London, footmen usually slept in the basement.

In 1915, the lamp boy at Longleat slept in a dormitory.

Tea over he took me upstairs to show me my sleeping quarters. These were in a kind of small dormitory with six beds in it; mine was in the corner. There was linoleum on the floor, a dressing-table and about four rickety chairs; that was the sum total of the furniture. I was sharing, I was told, with two under footmen, one of the odd men, the pantry boy and Bob the steward's room boy. I didn't know whether to be pleased or disappointed with the conditions; having nothing to compare them with I just accepted them.

(Grimmett, 'Lamp Boy's Story', p. 15)

It was common for one of the footmen or steward's room boys to sleep near the safe, as a guard.

George Washington at Lord and Lady Tweedmouth's

There were none of the sophisticated burglar alarms that there are today. It wasn't thought necessary when you could get a human alarm also performing household duties for twenty-six pounds a year.

I was that alarm. I didn't have a room, I slept in the pantry on a bed so arranged that it pulled down on hinges from a cupboard and fell across the safe door. This meant that any intending thief would have to slit my throat before he could get to the safe and it was hoped that I would be able to give some sort of warning before I was done to death.

Later in his career he was to sleep in relative luxury, as first footman to the Trees at Dytchley Park, Oxfordshire. Mrs Nancy Tree was a famous professional interior decorator with superb taste.

She didn't confine her interest in the house just to herself and her friends. I remember when I first arrived at Dytchley and was shown my bedroom, I thought I had been put temporarily into one of the guest rooms. It had a fitted Wilton carpet, a comfortable bed with a matching chintz valance, bedspread and curtains, an antique chest, fitted wardrobe and wash basin, and of course central heating, an untold luxury for any servant's room at that time.

(Washington, 'Hall Boy's Story', pp. 179, 196)

Eric Horne

The under butler and the second footman slept in the pantry in let down beds. One night the second footman (a six foot young fellow) did not want to play any longer, but wanted to go to bed, but could not do so, as the card players were in the way, he could not let down his bed. He kept worrying them about it, saying, 'I want to go to bed, you fellows; I got to be up early.' 'Oh, shut up, you silly fool', but he would not shut up, so they bundled him into the plate room; a kind of vault with an iron air-tight door to keep the plate from tarnishing, but they forgot about it being air-tight. When they had finished playing cards they unlocked the iron door to let him out. There he lay on the stone floor, apparently dead. We carried him out, and by putting the ammonia bottle under his nose and rubbing him, he gradually came round. . . .

(Horne, *What the Butler Winked at*, pp. 107–8)

Women servants starting out on their working life might have even worse conditions than men.
Aged thirteen, Mrs Layton's first job was in Hamstead.

I was fairly happy, but had to sleep in a basement kitchen which swarmed with black-beetles, and this made me very wretched at nights.

(Layton, 'Memories of seventy years', p. 24)

Travelling servants had to put up with temporary conditions which might be very much worse than they were used to at home.

In 1837 William Tayler went with his employers on holiday to Brighton.

July 9th This is Sunday. Had a very bad night's rest last night. I slept downstairs in a little room but, when I came to lay down, I found the bed covered with bugs. I began to kill them but they were so numerous that I found it imposible to kill all. Therefore I shook the bedding and layed it on the floor. There a great many found me, so that I could get but little rest. Took a walk this morning along the beach to view the sea. This being Sunday, I shall be under the necessity of passing this night as I did the last.

10th . . . I am going to sleep in one of the upper rooms which is much more airey and more healthy . . .

(Wise, *William Tayler*, p. 44)

Even when houses were provided with plumbed-in family bathrooms, servants usually had no regular use of them.

Dorothy Fudge at Colonel and Mrs Adams's, Marnhull

There was only one bathroom, which we staff were not allowed to use, but when our employers were away we had a special treat of a hot bath every night! Otherwise, we maids had a hip bath in our bedrooms, which meant carrying the hot water up to them when we had a bath. We also had a basin, and a jug with cold water. On frosty mornings, the water in the jug had a thin layer of ice on it, which I used to break before splashing my face and neck with it: it was lovely how warm it made me feel afterwards! But the other maids wouldn't wash until the breakfast was over and they were able to take hot water up to their rooms.

(Fudge, *Sands of Time*, p. 30)

Many houses were great gloomy buildings on isolated sites and young servants were impressionable.

Edwin Lee

I was also a fanciful youth, easy prey for any ghost story, so when we visited Belham Fort and I was told that in the next room to mine a baby had been suffocated in its cot, and that its cries and shrieks could be heard around midnight, the story stayed with me. One stormy night, with the wind whistling in the fir trees and the gulls screaming in their flight against it, I couldn't sleep for thinking about this unfortunate child. I got up and looked out of the window; then I heard a screaming and a crying. I must have got some courage from somewhere because I dashed out of my room and into the one that was supposed to be haunted. There under the window I could see a wooden cot on rockers swaying from side to side – and then I heard a noise coming down the passage.

I went to the door, there was a flickering light approaching. I didn't wait to see any more but dashed back to my room, into bed pulling the bedclothes over my head, and I lay there shivering with fear until I eventually fell asleep. The next morning at breakfast the housekeeper said to me,

'Was that you rushing about on the landing last night, Edwin?'

I was a bit cagey with her.

'Yes, I thought I heard something moving about.'

'It was me,' she said, 'there was a shutter banging so I got up and fixed it.'

She looked at me a bit searchingly as if she knew I'd been frightened out of my wits.

(Lee, 'The Page Boy's Story', pp. 99–100)

The main living area for all the lower servants was the servants' hall. These varied considerably in comfort.

In 1826 at Swynnerton in Staffordshire, the home of Thomas Fitzherbert, furniture was strictly functional.

Large Oak kitchen table, 3 oak forms, cast grate, Iron fender and Poker, 3 Old Benches, Stool, Two Mapping frames, Painted table, 3 large and 3 small Copper Cans, 6 Horns, Pewter Salt, Can Waggon and lanthorn

(SRO, Stafford, 641/5/P(1)4)

By 1905 at Kelmarsh Hall in Northamptonshire, the list of servants' hall furniture included window curtains, a couch and chairs rather than benches.

Three morone figured and plush curtains. 4'0" Wire brass mounted high fender . . . Marone and yellow ground Axminster carpet. Black Rag hearth rug . . . 7'0" Stained deal table on turned legs . . . 3'6" Mahogany bookcase with five shelves enclosed by pair of panel glass doors and cupboard under enclosed by pair of panel doors. Ebonized frame Chesterfield couch covered in cretonne and two pillows. Six mahogany frame chairs, seats covered in crimson linsey. Beech frame Windsor arm chair . . . 'Singer' hand sewing machine in walnut case . . . Five photos and coloured prints framed and glazed. White and blue figured festooned tea service of 40 pieces.

(Lancaster, Inventory taken for fire insurance, December 1905)

APPEARANCE

Those servants who were seen in the front of the house needed to be reasonably attractive or at least normal-looking. Anything other might be cause for dismissal or refusal of employment.

From Lord Fitzwilliam to Francis Guybon, 9 September 1697

. . . I recd: a letter this weeke fro: Mrs Ullit of Thorpe, about her sonne James; lett me know by yr next how he is, if he be not much deformed, if his Eye is not a great Blemish to him, for I would not have unsightly servants: & if he be not very much grown, for if he be to Tall he will not be fitt for a footman: his Father was a very propper man . . .

(NRO, Fitzwilliam, F(M)C 1012)

Eric Horne

Did anyone see a crosseyed servant? No they are as scarce as dead donkeys. A servant must be absolutely perfect in form, disposition and action. . . .

(Horne, *What the Butler Winked at*, p. 279)

Footmen especially were chosen for their looks. In the 1750s John Macdonald, who had gained a reputation for womanising, found his good looks more important than a good character.

At last a hairdresser sent me after a place, to be butler and dress hair, with a gentleman in Kent, and to wear a livery. The gentleman went after my character. I went for my answer. He said: 'I went to inquire about you, and your master did not giver you a very good character; but I will take you by your looks.'

Later in life, when looking for a new place in London, he had trouble with his appearance.

I met one of Mr Maine's clerks, the banker in Jermyn Street . . . John, go to Mr Hill's, who lodges in Pall Mall. . . . Accordingly I went next morning; and being very well dressed, with a gold-laced vest and other things in form, I went upstairs. . . . As I was coming out, I met a German going up. I went into the next public-house, and soon after this man came in. I asked him if he had success. He said he had, and was to go to France with him. 'He spoke to me about you, and said you were more like a gentleman than a servant; now, I am plain dressed and I have got the place.' Three days after I went after Sir Francis Hobburn's place. I was dressed plain, without lace. . . . When he saw me he said he had got one. When I came downstairs he rang the bell, and said to his footman: 'How came you send that fellow to me? Is he dressed like a person for my place or like an interpreter?' When he came down, he said: 'I am sorry I did not tell you to dress yourself finer, for Sir Francis is very nice.' After this, I was sent to Sir William Abdy's place. I went at night, and well dressed. Sir William not being at home, Lady Abdy told me she did not want a servant. Three days after I saw the servant that sent me after the place, who said: 'I am sorry you went dressed in a gold-laced waiscoat. Against the candle light it made a more rich appearance. She said you were too grand for a family servant.' I said to myself: 'A man does not know what to do for the best in this world.'

He described his appearance in greater detail in 1778, when he was again looking for work in London, having recently taken up a new fashion.

Having good clothes, with rich vests, I wore my hanger, a silk bag at my hair, and laced ruffles: but, when I went after a place, I dressed in the common way. If it rained, I wore my fine silk umbrella; then the people would call after me: 'What, Frenchman, why do you not get a coach?' In particular, the hackney coachmen and hackney chairmen would call after me; but I, knowing the men wee, went straight on, and took no notice.

(Macdonald, *Memoirs of an Eighteenth-Century Footman*, pp. 80, 180, 236)

Footmen needed to be tall – preferably six foot or slightly over. This was a self-perpetuating preference since livery uniforms were passed on to replacement or temporary footmen.

Frederick Gorst on interviewing agency footmen for special occasions

It was my duty to see that thirty outside footmen who were engaged for the evening would be provided with the Howard livery and placed for their duties. Four of them were stationed at the door, four men took care of the guests' wraps and the cloak room, and the others helped with the service. In great London houses it was customary to have a large supply of extra liveries for receptions and balls, but it was quite a task to outfit all the extra men with coats and breeches that fitted properly.

I always asked the agency to send footmen who were at least five foot ten because the uniforms were tailored for tall men. When a little fat fellow arrived, it was almost impossible to dress him without turning out something which resembled a comic valentine.

(Gorst, *Carriages and Kings*, p. 119)

Prejudices about a servant's height were not limited to menservants, as one of the Sutherlands' agents revealed when writing to the housekeeper at Trentham.

J. Whittaker to Mrs Ingram, 26 April 1876

> Stafford House
> St. James's
> London

Dear Madam,

I cannot understand what you mean about the new Laundry maid. All I can say about her is, that she had a most excellent character as a good strong hardworking and willing young person. If she had not been so I would not have engaged her.

In the meantime I shall be glad if you will not listen to what Janet McDonald or anyone else says against her for the short people often work better than the taller ones. After I had engaged this young person one of Janet's friends applied for the situation: but if I had not been settled I should not have engaged her as she talked too much.

So Janet must make herself comfortable as I shall not think of discharging the girl without just cause.

> Trusting you are quite well,
> I am Yours Truly
> pro. J. Whittaker

> (SRO, Sutherland, D593/R/10/5)

LIVERY

Livery was a deliberately antiquated uniform which marked menservants out as in service to a particular family. Complete with expensive trimmings, it was supplied and paid for by the employer. Here the 5th Duke of Richmond's house steward writes to the Duke's secretary.

Robert Smith to Dr Archibald Hair, 23 January 1858

. . . You must if you please allow me to make them wear the same Stockings to the Drawing Room it seems to me down right waste to give new Silk Stockings for every State occasion I supose the Stables will <u>rebell</u> but if you will give me your authority they may <u>rebell</u> . . .

Same, 6 July 1858

Edward Pascoe has been this Morning & Measured the Servants for their White Liveries . . . [he] says that it takes 5½ yards of Lace for each Suite it seems a great deal . . . I have ordered 5 lace hats . . .

Same, 13 July 1859

> John Wise will have new Hats this season for the Postillions
> I told him that they had only been worn Eight times
> [he considered] it is necessary that they Should have new ones
> So I have wrote to that little Cheap Hatter to come & measure
> them . . .

(WSRO, Goodwood, MS 1830 f. 1539, 1830 f. 1635–6, 1841 f. 1754)

Frederick Gorst had ample experience of livery from an early age when he was first employed as a page boy in St Aiden's Theological College in Merseyside.

> I saw my page boy livery: a dark red jacket, with a brighter
> red collar and white taping, carefully buttoned over the long, dark
> blue trousers. There were eight shiny brass buttons on the coat. I
> could not resist putting it on immediately . . . and looked at myself
> in the small glass over the dresser which, unfortunately, only
> reproduced my reflection from the neck up. So I took it off the wall
> and started at my collar, moving it slowly down to the tops of my
> shoes. Although I was only able to see myself in fractions,
> I felt the composite picture must be a very satisfactory one. . . .

And later at Court Hey, as a footman to Walter and Richard Gladstone, nephews of George Ewart Gladstone

> During the week I wore a full-dress suit of dark grey wool which
> had six silver buttons on the coat, three on each side. With it I
> wore a batwing collar, stiff shirt, and white bow tie.
>   The Sunday livery was cut exactly like the regular suit but it
> was made of plum-coloured wool and trimmed with gold
> buttons.

At his next job with Lord and Lady Howard his livery was more elaborate.

> My dress livery for the London house was also a novelty. I had
> never before put on blue plush knee breeches, white stockings,
> and pumps with silver buckle. I also was expected to wear a
> claret-coloured, swallow-tailed coat with silver buttons, a claret

waistcoat, and a stiff, white shirt. All the staff bought their white bow ties ready-made, which they wore with a round collar. This saved time in dressing.

When I was turned out, I looked at myself in the full-length glass in the hall – I could not believe my eyes. Somehow I had never thought of myself as a 'picturesque figure', but height plus the Howard livery had achieved an amazing transformation. I felt as though I were going to a masquerade but I hoped in time I would feel more comfortable in my costume.

Eventually Gorst rose to become a Royal Footman, normally employed in the household of the Duke of Portland at Welbeck Abbey but sent on royal duty when needed. His livery at Buckingham Palace was accordingly very elaborate.

There were four 'indoor' liveries: the 'off duty' livery; the 'on duty' livery for luncheon and dinner, which was the small, scarlet coat; the formal luncheon and dinner livery which was also a scarlet coat but trimmed with gold epaulets and the full-state livery for important functions. This was the royal-blue Quaker coat worn with purple knee breeches, pink silk stockings, black pumps with gold buckles, and powdered hair.

When we were on the carriages, there were also four liveries which might be ordered: postillion livery, which might require an 'epaulet' or 'small scarlet' coat with buckskin breeches, depending on the importance of the event; a semi-state carriage livery worn with a three-caped scarlet coat and a Napoleon hat decorated with a crest. The full-state carriage livery was the same as the semi-state livery except that we wore a pink feather on the crest of the Napoleon hat, a gilt sword and carried a long, gold-headed stick from which hung a gold tassel. . . .

By the time I had gathered up my liveries, I had two steel cases about five feet long, three feet broad, and two feet high, which contained my full-state and semi-state uniforms, two leather portmanteaux for my smaller liveries and personal effects, and six hat boxes.

(Gorst, *Carriages and Kings*, pp. 15–16, 81, 88, 126)

Ernest King on the old practice of wearing livery to church

At Youlston Park – Major Hamlyn Chichester's house – footmen had to wear their livery to church, the coachman his top boots and cape, even the chauffeur, who came from the Siddeley-Deesey works, a mechanic who knew nothing of domestic service, had to put on his driving coat, his breeches, peaked cap and big leather gauntlet gloves. The women servants wore dark costumes and black bonnets. Those of them off for the afternoon and evening would carry hatboxes and leave them with the lodge-keeper's wife; her little hall would be piled high with them. Then after morning service off would come the girls' bonnets, on went their ordinary hats and they would set out to walk or cycle four miles into town or to their homes. At ten that night they would have to be back in their black dresses, aprons and caps, the footmen in their livery for Evening Prayers.

(King, *Green Baize Door*, pp. 21, 44)

Not surprisingly, footmen who were used to carefully tailored livery tried to keep up to standard in their own clothes and much of their wages went on clothes.

Thomas the footman in the service of the 2nd Duke of Sutherland

18th Aug I went out intending to buy my self a pair of shoes I went to Barrats in Marylebone lane and bought a pair of pumps 5/6 and I bought myself a stock in the Regent circus Picadilly 5/6 and then went home . . .

Oct 15 I then went to Yates the tailors & got myself measured for a morning jacket & a pair of trowsers . . . [and] to Fishers the haberdasher in St James St & bought 2 pair of winter gloves for which I payed 2/6.

Nov 19 I came back to Stafford House first going to Barbers and trying on my cloths, the coat not fitting very well he is going to make a little alteration on it and I am to call again on Friday.

Nov 22 I called at Barbers and got my coat and waiscoat and paid Mr Barber £1 10s as the difference him and me for my cloths

He had to arrange for his own mending.

Feb 18 I took the four shirts that Mrs Rowe made me to Mrs Wright to be new fronted.

He also sold some of his old clothes to another servant.

31ˢᵗ July . . . I sold George Hawkins my old hats two round ones and one cocked hat with all the silver lace upon them for 1£ . . .

Jan 29th . . . I sold Thomas five pairs of old trowsers today and my baraige coat for 18/6

(Thomas, 'Journal', SRO D4177/1–2)

In the eighteenth century, many senior servants, male and female, would have worn a grey wig. From this developed the tradition of powdering liveried footmen's own hair, a tradition that lasted well into the twentieth century. On the whole it was extremely unpopular with those who had to endure it.

John James

Powder money used to be allowed in some houses, while in others the powder itself was provided and was always of the best. Footmen of the younger generation should be thankful that this daily powdering of the hair has gone out of fashion, for it was indeed a very unpleasant business. After the hair had been moistened, soap was put on and rubbed into a stiff lather, and the combing was done so that the teeth marks would show evenly all over. Powder was then applied with a puff and the wet mass allowed to dry on the head until it became quite firm. In the evening the hair had always to be washed and oiled to prevent its becoming almost fox colour, and I remember I was hardly ever free from colds in houses where this hair-powdering was the regulation.

(James, *House Steward*, p. 97)

WOMEN SERVANTS

Women servants' dress became formalised during the nineteenth century and some houses even adopted a system of colour-coding their female servants. Nursery maids, for example, were usually dressed in white and grey.

Nursemaid Sarah Sedgwick

> I was promoted to a bonnet in that house. The strings were white, made of fine linen or lawn. I used to edge my strings with lace. They were put on first, the strings pinned on the top of my head and tied in a bow on the side. The bonnet was then put on top. In the house we always wore white, even white shoes and stockings, outside we wore grey costumes with white blouses, and black shoes and stockings. Sometimes I wore a black tie, but this was not really allowed.
>
> (Sedgwick, 'Other People's Children', p. 21)

Dress restrictions were usually made very clear at interview. Employers did not like their female servants to be fashionable, though ladies' maids were an exception.

Mrs Layton

> She had imposed three conditions on me. . . . First I was to take the pads out of my hair (large chignons being then in fashion); second, I was to cut the tail off my dress (long dresses were then worn); third, I was to wear aprons with bibs on them (which were never worn in those days).
>
> (Layton, 'Memories', p. 28)

In 1928, Rosina Harrison became maid to Lady Cranborne.

> Now that I was a proper ladies' maid, I no longer wore print frocks. I was expected to dress simply, plainly, unassumingly, yet in fashion. I wore jerseys and skirts with a cardigan in the mornings and afternoons; after tea, or if I was going out earlier, I changed into a blue or brown dress. A string of pearls or beads

were permissible, so was a wrist watch, but other jewellery was frowned on. Makeup was not encouraged; indeed later I was rebuked for using lipstick. When ladies and their maids were out together, there could never be any mistaking which was which.

(Harrison, *Rose*, pp. 33–4)

At least male liveried servants had clothing provided for them. Female servants had to provide themselves with suitable dresses. They might be given a dress length as a Christmas present but they still had to pay for it to be made up or make it up themselves.

Harriet Brown to her mother, 1870

Edgware

My Dearest Mother,

I do not know how to thank you for your kindness in doing the aprons for me. I should never have got them made myself for I have not made the print dresses yet that I told you about when I was home last. I must try and finish them this week for I am sick and tired of seeing them about. I have been so driven at work since the fires begun I have had 'ardly any time for anything for myself. . . .

With fondest love to all I remain your ever
Affect. Daughter,
Harriet Brown

(Dawes, *Not in Front of the Servants*, pp. 22–3)

The cost of providing the uniforms required to start in a job was a severe burden to young servants, who might have to take a preliminary job to pay for them.

Margaret Thomas

When I was fourteen Mother decided it was time I started earning money for my clothes for service, so she got me a day place to look after a baby and do light jobs. I went at 9 a.m. and my wages varied; the woman I worked for let her rooms during the summer, and when she had one family in she gave me two shillings a week, and two-and-six when she had two families. Other times it was one-and-six. She used to keep me baby-sitting until nearly 11 p.m. . . . I couldn't save much out of my wages, so when they dropped I got another job as well. I was paid one-and-six a week to clean knives and boots from 7.30 a.m. to 9.30 a.m., before I went on to my other place. Eventually I saved enough and got my uniform: print dresses, morning aprons, black dress, afternoon aprons, stiff collars, and cuffs, all packed into a tin trunk, and set off to my first real job. I was just fifteen.

What did I look like? An old-fashioned touch I should think. A year previously Mother had had a long grey dress given her, with boned bodice, long sleeves and a high collar, trimmed with white braid. When Mother told me I must wear it because I hadn't anything else, I said: 'I can't unless I put my hair up.' 'Why not put your hair up?' she replied. I didn't want to grow up at fifteen, I liked my hair as it was tied back with black ribbon, and didn't know how to do it up; however, what had to be had to be, so I brushed it all up on top, made it into a 'bun' and there I was – A WOMAN. It was as easy as that.

Once she got into her first place, as a single-handed housemaid to a family of seven, in the country, she still had problems.

The cook and parlourmaid were sisters a lot older than I, I think they thought I looked too young and frivolous for they advised me to draw my hair back, braid it and pin it neatly, and to wear a hat which had belonged to the lady of the house, who was middle-aged. I must have given my family a bit of a shock when I went home on my first visit, I must have looked about forty!

In a later place in Yorkshire

All we maidservants in that place had to wear black, navy or dark grey whenever we went out, with small black hats or toques; we had our own places in our pew in church, and I was agreeably surprised to find I ranked next to the head housemaid. The manservants wore livery with top hats. Nobody seemed to mind not wearing colours, nor being told what to wear. Our indoor clothes cost a lot. There wasn't much left for outdoor wear after we had bought them. I had to wear well-fitted hollands all day, changing to clean in the afternoon; my wages in that house were twenty-eight pounds paid quarterly.

(Thomas, 'Green Baize Door', pp. 80–82, 88–9)

Finding the money for a decent set of clothing with which to start in a new place could also be a problem for men.

William Lanceley

I once had a footman under me who had a hasty temper and was discharged through showing it to his master, who likewise possessed a similar temper.

The master's way to punish him was a rather unkind one. He would not give him a character until a month had elapsed; by this time the poor chap was on his beam ends, and when he came to me he only possessed one decent suit of clothes, half-worn-out boots, one shirt and two collars. He was a very proud fellow, hated to borrow and would not ask a favour of anybody. I had to complain to him at the end of a week on account of his shirt front – it was getting very grubby. He did not reply, but promptly turned his shirt. He had a good appearance, but this sort of thing could not go on. The other men noticed it and asked him why he did not open his mouth and handed him over shirts, collars, ties and underclothing.

When I heard of this I advanced him sufficient to buy the necessary linen, and he was soon as smart as the others. The help and kindness he received at that time made a lifelong impression on him, and in after years when he was at the head of a large establishment he never forgot his low-water days and was always considerate to beginners, and was held in the highest esteem by his fellow-servants who, when speaking of him, would say, 'He's all right – he has been through the mill and can feel for others.'

(Lanceley, Hall-Boy to House-Steward, pp. 168–9)

It is perhaps ironic that the only time women servants were provided with extra clothing was when the family went into mourning – just that time when many households would be broken up and the servants laid off. On the 5th Duke of Richmond's death, his housekeeper wrote to his secretary.

Mrs Sanders to Dr Archibald Hair, 23 October 1860

> I have made a list of what I think the maids ought to have it would be much the most satisfactory if you please to Give them the £4 each and let them get there own to appear as they ought they cannot do with less please to excuse this as I can scarcely hold my pen – There is Mrs Griffiths do you give her any

2 dresses Lining and making up	£2 10s
Bonnet	10s
Shaul	10s
Gloves Ribbons Caps Cotton	10s
	£4 00

(WSRO, Goodwood, MS 1851 f. 1465)

At Dunham Massey in 1799 the unexpected death of the house steward, John Arnatt, was occasion enough for all the servants to go into mourning, as described by the agent Isaac Worthington.

Isaac Worthington to the 5th Earl of Stamford, February 1799

> I . . . took Mr Holland in my chaise to attend the Funeral. We had Hatbands and Gloves . . . Mrs Princep and Mrs Staples had Gloves and so had all your Lordship's servants. Six of the Labourers were bearers with Mourning Cloaks and had Gloves. All your Lordship's menservants attended the Funeral . . .

(JRL, Stamford, EGR 4/1/8/3/4–8)

SIX

'Rice on Sundays' – servants' food and drink

It was customary in the country house for servants to be provided with all food and drink whenever members of the family were at home. This was called being 'at housekeeping'. The larger households issued cooks with written guidelines for amounts of food allowed each week or day. These could be in the form of either quantities or value. Generalising wildly, the quality of country-house servant food was probably not too bad. It seems to have been simple – stews using poorer cuts of meat or offal, or roast meat served up cold again and again – and was probably very boring. But it was adequate and helped considerably by fresh home-grown vegetables. Some of the wealthy households probably did very well.

Meal times were standardised and changed little over time, in contrast to those of the fashionable world. Breakfast was usually at eight, after servants had finished their early morning chores. What servants called 'lunch' was a short break at eleven and the main meal, dinner, was between midday and one. There might be a short break at four, followed by a supper usually of cold meat or cheese at nine, after the family dinner had been served. In the nineteenth and twentieth centuries, most houses issued extra allowances of tea and sugar for servants to make their own drinks in the evening or early morning.

Servant dinner in particular was ritualised. Traditionally it was eaten largely in silence and supervised by the senior servants until the end of the main course, when they would remove themselves into the steward's or housekeeper's room to have a better pudding and a drink, thus allowing the juniors to relax. This ritual seems to have been seared into the servant soul, so ubiquitous is it in their memoirs. It speaks volumes, not about the food itself, but about the part played by food in defining the nature of a community and its hierarchies.

When the family was absent servants went on board wages – a cash sum calculated daily or weekly, out of which servants bought their own food. Housekeepers, housemaids and kitchen maids were often on board wages, for it was part of their job to spring-clean the house when everyone else was away. Footmen, butlers, cooks and valets were more rarely on board wages, for they tended to follow the family in their travels from house to house. It would seem sensible for servants on board wages to pool their cash and pay one of the kitchen maids to cook for them. No doubt this happened, but not invariably. Beer-issuing records in some households imply that groups of servants divided themselves by gender and ate separately, probably cooking separately. Certainly the autobiographical record shows that this was the case when households came to be permanently on board wages, a not very satisfactory situation where menservants seem to have had difficulty in getting good hot meals.[1]

The traditional drink of the country-house servant was beer, until the mid-nineteenth century usually provided by the house brewer.[2] Beer was considered as much a food as a drink and was an important part of the work contract – servants were entitled to their allowance and if it was not available they were entitled to be paid beer money in lieu. Country-house beer-drinking was surrounded by rules and traditions. Weaker small beer was freely available throughout the day, ale being restricted to a set allowance at the dinner table. Men were usually allowed twice the amount given to women, and some workers were allowed only beer and not ale, except on special occasions such as family birthdays. Like the ritualised dinner, the beer allowance system helped define the hierarchical systems so beloved of the country-house world.

By the late eighteenth century some households were offering tea or tea money as an alternative to beer, but it was not until after the mid-nineteenth century that country houses began to give up the tradition of brewing. At first the house brew might be replaced with bought-in drink, but finally the system was abandoned altogether.

Abuse of alcohol figures largely in many country-house memoirs. Coachmen, butlers, footmen and cooks seem to have been most vulnerable. Some households had a very strict regime of cellar control; others were much more lax. The nature of coachmen's and footmen's work involved hours of hanging around waiting for their passengers, and pubs were warm and tempting. In households where drinking was not strictly controlled by the family or senior staff, the social pressure of the servants' hall must have been difficult to withstand.

FOOD

List of food allowances for servants and horses in the Newdigate family, 1832

Meat	–	1lb per head per day
Bread	–	1 quartern loaf per head per week
Cheese	–	½lb per head per week
Table ale	–	1 qt per head per day
Tea	–	2 oz per head per week
Sugar	–	¾lb per head per week
Butter	–	¾lb per head per week
Coals	–	2 bushels weekly for the kitchen fire
		3 chaldron per fire per annum
Corn	–	2 bushels per horse per week
Hay	–	12lbs per horse per day.

(WCRO, Newdigate, CR 136/B[3698A])

Guidelines for the value of meals per head per day in the household of
the Duke of Sutherland, 1830s

Family when they dine at home – each per day		22/-
Family when they dine out	"	10/-
Friends to dinner	"	12/-
Friends to luncheon	"	4/-
Grand dinners in London	"	15/-
Children, tutors, governesses, secretaries	"	7/6
Steward's Room	"	4/-
Servants' Hall	"	2/-
People at balls	"	8/6
People at soirées	"	5/-
Musicians	"	4/-
Sandwiches – plates of meat	"	2/-

(SRO, Sutherland, D593/R/11/11)

The quality of servants' food varied.

Footman William Tayler described the food served in the Prinsep
household in 1837.

January 22nd . . . I think I will give an account of our living
during the next week. They breakfast at eight in the kitchen on
bread and butter and toast – or anything of the kind if they like
to be at the trouble of making it – and tea. All most all servants
are obliged to find their own tea and sugar.

For my own part I care but very little about breakfast at all,
therefore I jenerally wait until the breakfast comes down from the
parlour at ten o'clock when my apatite has come and I can then git
a cup of coco, which I am very fond of, and a rowl or something of
the kind. Anyone that like to have lunch, there it is for them but, as
I have breakfast so late, I want no lunch. This day we had for
dinner a piece of surloin of beef, roasted brocoli and potatos and
preserved damson pie. We all have tea together at four o'clock with
bread and butter and sometimes a cake. At nine o'clock we have
supper; this evening it's cold beef and damson pie. We keep plenty
of very good table ale in the house and every one can have as
much as they like. This has been a miserable wet day and I have
spent most of it in reading the news paper.

23rd . . . Had cold beef for dinner with potatos and pickled cabbage, and for supper some fish and cold mutton.

25th . . . Had for dinner today a rost leg of mutton, potatos and suety pudding; supper, cold meat and rested potatos and rabbit.

26th . . . Had Irish stew and rice pudding for dinner. I went out to supper where I had some mince pie that came from Grafton.

27th . . . For dinner had a roast shoulder of mutton and savois and potatos.

28th . . . Had hash and vegitables for dinner, cold mutton and rice pudding for supper. We have more change in our living in sommer and we can get veal sometimes beside what I have mentioned. We get many little nice things that come down from the parlour . . . I have just had a good blow out of egg.[3]

29th . . . This day for dinner had a part of a round of beef with potatos, cabbage and carrots, scimmerlads[4] and bread pudding. For supper roast beef, pickle cabbage &c. &c.

May 14th Breakfast as usual, cold beef and potatos for lunch. For dinner, fish and minced mutton with poarched eggs, curry, which is a kind of hot Indian dish, potatos, rice, greens, cheese and butter, beer, sherry and port.

(Wise, *William Tayler*, pp. 13–15, 35)

Much later, Gordon Grimmett remembered the sophistication of food at Longleat during the First World War.

We fed very well at Longleat; indeed as visiting servants reminded us, 'You wouldn't know there was a war on.'

Each week three sheep of different breeds were butchered for the household, a Southdown, Westmoreland and a Brittany. We also had pheasant, partridge, goose, venison, hare and rabbit. Rarely was beef served. The meat course was followed by a variety of puddings and cheese. Since there was no gas or electricity all food was cooked on charcoal. Again Longleat was the only place I served in where there was a fish still. In it swimming about were pike or trout in their season. They were caught in the lakes on the estate and put in the still to cleanse them of the taste of mud.

(Grimmett, 'Lamp Boy's Story', p. 24)

Margaret Thomas, living in a large country house in Yorkshire

We had plenty of fruit coming in daily, as, besides the large kitchen garden attached to the house, there was another large one about three miles away; the house there was in ruins, but the gardens and hothouses were kept going by about half a dozen gardeners; beautiful melons, peaches and grapes came in, and plenty of fruit for jam-making and bottling. Once when the upper servants had all gone to the races a huge basket of strawberries arrived. 'Surely you don't want to make jam on such a hot day,' the others said to me and I agreed. With a bowl of cream we soon finished those strawberries and no one the wiser. Everyone had good food in that house, but we always found the staff hardest to please. There were always titbits in the cupboard for the servants' hall elevenses, a tin full of cakes, chicken legs, etc. Footmen always boasted they went through the meals with the family, helping themselves to each dish hiding behind a screen to eat out of sight of the butler; afterwards they had the cheek to come down and criticise the food.

(Thomas, 'Green Baize Door', p. 90)

Rose Gibbs at Box Hill, Dorking

But what amazed me was the good food we had in the servants' hall. A bell used to be rung from a belfry, and we all had to get ready for the meal, changed into clean caps and aprons. When I saw the lovely food on the table, I just stood and cried, wondering if my mother and father had any food. The butter was made in the estate dairy, the vegetables were home-grown, and the fruit in the summer included strawberries, raspberries and loganberries, peaches and apricots – everything you could want. Lady Constance used to bring us baskets of it.

(Gibbs, *In Service*, p. 14)

Sometimes servants sent food home.

Harriet Brown to her mother, 1870

> . . . I have saved a small piece of plum pudding for you and will
> save some mince pies and I thought you would like a little
> dripping so I have sent all. Mrs Graves has to spare and I dare
> say next week she will have some more. You must let me know
> if you would like it and I will send it. . . .

> (Dawes, *Not in Front of the Servants*, pp. 22–3)

But some households were well known for their poor food.

Edwin Lee on servants' food at Glynliven, Caernarvonshire

> Strangely the food for the staff at Glynliven was not good,
> consisting for the most part of a plain unappetising succession
> of stew-like meals. When I was first there we were only served
> with one pudding a week, rice on Sundays, tacky stuff. Whether
> our old gentleman suddenly thought that we'd moved into more
> enlightened times I don't know but after I'd been there a year
> we were allowed stewed fruit every Wednesday.

> (Lee, 'Page Boy's Story', p. 99)

In 1892 a butler called John Robinson wrote vehemently about the
unsuitable food given to servants.

> The condition of the servant . . . may often be described as a
> condition of starvation in the midst of plenty. . . . It is a
> principle with most cooks that they are not engaged to cook
> for servants; consequently the servants' hall is left to the
> tender mercies of the kitchen-maid. . . . The result of this is
> that a huge badly cooked joint is sent to the servants' table.
> This appears again and again at a succession of suppers and
> dinners, till someone, nauseated at its continual reappearance,
> chops it up and assigns the greater part to the swill-tub. This
> is followed by another joint, which goes the same round and

shares the same fate. Any variety beyond that of a very occasional sweet is out of the question.

(Robinson, 'A Butler's View of Man-Service', pp. 205–6.)

When the family was absent, servants were given cash in lieu of meals. They usually clubbed together to buy food, often in gender groups. Menservants found this particularly difficult, a situation which has given rise to a genre of horror stories about board wages.

At Charles Cooper's first place

We were on board wages for a time. The first footman doing the catering for us men, and trying to do things as cheaply as possible, ordered a piece of belly of pork; this salted meat he thought would save a lot of extra cooking; it must have been a yard long, and as each meal time came round, upon investigation we found it was still, belly of pork. I think it was used at last to replace a broken paving stone in the yard.

(Cooper, *Town and Country or Forty Years in Private Service with the Aristocracy*, p. 26)

MEALTIMES

It was perhaps inevitable that servants developed their own systems of rank and hierarchy every bit as rigorous as those of the families they served. Markers of rank were obvious at mealtimes.

Frederick Gorst described the hierarchy at Welbeck Abbey.

Position and rank also took precedence in the hierarchy of the servants. They were divided into the 'upper servants' – also called the 'Upper Ten', and the 'lower servants' – referred to as the 'Lower Five'. We Royal footmen occupied a kind of no-man's-land in between the two categories because we were part of the Palace staff, but technically, in the Portland household, we belonged to the Lower Five.

The two groups did not mix socially, the lines were drawn

more strictly perhaps than among those whom we served. Moreover, we ate separately. The Upper Ten took their meals in the steward's dining room and they were waited on by two steward's room footmen.

The Upper Ten had white wine, claret, and beer for luncheon and dinner. The china, silver, and glass which was used to serve them, and which was taken care of exclusively by the steward's room footmen, was much finer than the gentry had in some of the smaller houses in England. Their napkins were rolled up and put into silver napkin rings every day at breakfast, to be used again at luncheon, but at dinner the linens and napkins were always freshly changed.

Mr. Spedding, the wine butler, the underbutler, the groom of the chambers, the Duke's valet, the housekeeper, head housemaid, and ladies' maids – and any visiting ladies' maids and valets – were designated the Upper Ten.

At Welbeck, visiting ladies' maids were expected to wear a dress blouse for dinner, and the visiting valets were required to wear smoking jackets for late supper. The Upper Ten came to the table similarly dressed and full of their own importance. Their evening meal was in the nature of an intimate dinner party except when there were visiting maids and valets, often as many as forty at one time.

We, the Lower Five, ate our meals in the Servants' Hall, the old refectory of the Abbey. We Royal footmen ate at the same table with the housemaids and stillroom maids. The two footmen on duty always carved and the hall porter and the hall boys served the meals.

We had two or three fresh vegetables served with the meat and potatoes – all good, solid food which came to the table piping hot and nicely served. We had delicious bread that came directly from the bakery and freshly churned, country butter.

After the main course, the maidservants left the table. The sweet was served to the menservants and maidservants separately. The maids had theirs in their own departments, in the stillroom or the housemaids' sitting room, where they had a table laid in readiness. Traditionally the men and women servants were always separated before the end of the meal. . . .

(Gorst, *Carriages and Kings*, pp. 132–3)

'Rice on Sundays'

Welbeck's meal arrangements were not usual. In most country houses all the servants, senior as well as junior, ate the main course of dinner together in the servants' hall. Thereafter followed a strangely divided meal.

At the Chichesters' house at Youlston Park, North Devon

> I would sound the bell for the household staff to come to breakfast, dinner (midday) and supper. They were given five minutes to assemble and after that the door was shut and none could enter till the senior servants had left. When all were seated the butler would rise and say grace: 'For what we are about to receive . . .'.
>
> We ate in silence. Immediately the head servants had finished the main course, all the rest would drop their knives and forks and the butler would rise again and say: 'For what we have received . . .'. Then I would open the door and the head-servants – the butler, the housekeeper, the lady's maid – would retire to the housekeeper's room, where I had previously laid the table, for their sweet (in the dining-room, I believe, always referred to as 'pudding', but by us lowlier folk as sweet). Then, of course, the babble would break out, for before the senior servants left we, the lesser fry, the junior footmen, the oddman, me and the housemaids and laundry maids would utter not a word.
>
> There was, I think, a reason for this. It instilled discipline. Had conversation been allowed from the start the meal would have been prolonged. The idea was to get it over and get back to the job. We weren't there to enjoy it. We lower servants had to walk the chalk-line.

(King, *Green Baize Door*, p. 10)

At Rise Park

> . . . butler [was] at the head of the table, my sister, cook-housekeeper at the foot. On her left, lady's maid, kitchen-maid and myself; on the butler's left, footman, chauffeur, Emma, Alice, the old head housemaid, and so back to my sister, Hilda. The meal was also served in the order of one's position in the household. . . .

113

. . . As in other establishments, most mealtimes were passed in purgatorial silence. We longed to talk or laugh, but had to remain silent. I used to exchange sign language at Rise Park with Emma to make up for the monasterial quiet. If I raised an eyebrow it meant, 'Will you please pass me the marmalade?' A twitch meant I fancied the cake nearest to her. At suppertime we were allowed to talk, and we had a fine time gossiping with visiting maids and chauffeurs.

(Balderson, *Backstairs Life*, pp. 22, 52)

Eric Horne

One bank holiday, Good Friday, I think it was, my father came to see me unexpectedly. The butler made him welcome. He sat down to dinner with us in the hall, and would keep on talking on general topics, much to the amusement of all the rest of us, and could not understand why no one answered him. I explained to him afterwards.

Horne also remembered an old tradition.

. . . no conversation was allowed until after the cloth had been removed, and the health drank. The under butler stands up at the bottom of the table, holds a horn of old ale up in his hands, taps the table twice, and says, 'My Lord and Lady', the other reply, 'With all my heart.' This old custom was observed every day.

(Horne, *What the Butler Winked at*, pp. 57, 96–7)

At Glynliven

In the servants' hall we ate at a long slate-topped table. The food was served on enamel plates which I found would skid and bounce on the slate; this was a matter of acute embarrassment for me, for as I slid and rattled my way through a meal the maids would giggle and snigger and since at that time I'd blush when I so much as spoke to a girl, my red face protruding from a hot collar couldn't have been a very pretty sight.

(Lee, 'Page Boy's Story', p. 99)

Where senior servants ate separately, the steward's room boys had a problem.

At Holland House

The trouble with being in the steward's room was that for some time I was half starved, for while I was there the other servants were having their meal in the servants' hall, and by the time I went to get mine there was precious little left. In order to survive I would steal bread from the stillroom and lock myself in the lavatory while I ate it. One day while I was clearing a beautiful York ham from the steward's room I found myself drooling over it. I gave way to temptation, carved two slices and was putting them under the wooden cover of the sink outside when Mr Pettit came from the room and caught me in the act. He exploded, 'What the hell do you think you're doing, boy!' I then knew how Oliver Twist must have felt, but Mr Pettit was more merciful than Mr Bumble. He let me tell my story, said he would investigate the matter and then admonished me for stealing, whatever the circumstances might be. It worked the trick, for from then on my food was portioned out with the others and put into an oven to keep warm. Sometimes when I'd finished serving he'd tell me to cut myself a slice or two to augment mine. In that way I got the best of both worlds.

(Washington, 'Hall Boy's Story', p. 184)

Some households harked back to earlier, less formal traditions. In the 1840s Christian Watt worked at Philorth, Lord Saltoun's house in Aberdeenshire.

We started in the laundry at 5.30, at 4.30 the farm bell would toll and all the staff would be about. All dined in the large kitchen at Philorth, with staggered diet hours, for it was a lot of folk to make brose for.[5] This was ever staple diet, apart from broth. Some of the lovely things Jean Anderson made made my mouth water but none ever came our way. It was the same in every similar establishment. What a washing up old Polly and the Cairnbulg quinie had![6] We had ½ an hour to meals, but what a laughing and joking went on in the kitchen when different crews were seated.

(Fraser, *Christian Watt*, p. 38)

ALCOHOLIC DRINK

Addiction to alcohol was a real problem in the country house, especially for menservants who had plenty of opportunity to escape to the pub. The following letters are concerned with two cases where menservants took to drink.

From Lord Fitzwilliam to Francis Guybon, 12 March 1700/01

. . . This being the time of yeare that I make my new Liveries, James Ullitt told my Wife there should be made none for him, for he would not stay: and because this last Twelvemonth or more he has much neglected my service, being often out, and taking ill courses he has been admonished for it many times, that I the more freely part with him: however, because his Mother desired me at first to have him, pray lett her know so much, that she may consider what to advise him, for he has become a very idle druncken fellow, & extravagant: He was advised by us to write his Mother word he was to leave our service, but he said what should he trouble himself for that, he was old enough now to take care of himselfe without her. His Mother may do well to advise him soone, for though he is at present in my House, as soon as ever he is out, forty to one, but he may be Press't to go to Sea, for they take up all Loose fellows that are out of service, & many servts also . . .

Same, 3 April 1701

. . . I recd: fro: James Elliotts Mother about her sonne, for she never hears fro: him. Pray lett her know, her sonne is well in my House till he getts him a place, which I hope he will do soone:& we part very fairly. I believe now he is sorry he goes fr: Mi:, but I have another in his Roome.

Same, 17 January 1705–6

... I heard last weeke but forgot to write it, that James Ullit died at the Bath this summer, but of what I know not. One of my footmen learnt it accidentally at an Alehouse where he used to frequent when in Towne. You may lett Goody Ullitt his Mother know of it if you think fitt, for she is often sending to inquire of him ...

(NRO, Fitzwilliam, F(M)C 1164, 1165, 1448)

Kenelm H. Digby to Major Huddlestone, Sawston Hall, 27 August 1841

Springfield Manor, Southampton

My dear Sir

I was delighted to hear of your being so much better. I have a sad piece of news to communicate about Harris. Will you have the goodness to inform his Parents that he leaves us in a month from today. We have borne with much & forgiven much; but he is inclined <u>to drink</u> & this odious vice in so young a person might lead to every other vice. Having warned & warned him over & over I think now his only chance is to leave our house & get a stricter master. We shall do all we can for him; but at the end of a month his own interest requires that he should leave. . . . I must now break off; for the Harris affair has given me a headache ...

I remain
My dear Sir
Your Most faithfully
Kenelm H. Digby

Same, 29 September 1841

As Mes Harris leaves us today I was anxious to let you know how his case stands. We part with him more for his own sake than for ours. Had he continued with us he would not have had strength to stand against the temptations of our service: for he had too much liberty; and thereupon he would have settled into a sot. As it is I hope and believe he will quite recover himself &

we have promised to give him an excellent character & that for four years and a ¼ will enable him to do well. If he tires of the new life he has chosen he can easily retrace his steps as the packet will go back in two months. A little more experience and suffering will do him no harm. So I trust he will not have offended you. A golden bridge should be left for every one who seeks to return to himself; and in every other respect he conducted himself always well. We offered to keep him if he would promise to drink only in the houses where he was not stinted, & not go to a public house: but I think he refused this from having the mania of seeing a little of the world in the new way of life. He will be in bad company; but it will be his own fault if they lead him wrong. Have the kindness to show this to Mr Scott & to tell him that we have got a servant.

Same, 7 October 1841

. . . I have heard nothing since of Harris; & I know not whether he is at home or on the seas. Colonel Dalry at Portsmouth told me it was an excellent place in the Y[ach]t Liverpool if he could refrain from drink; but that the temptations that way would be awful as he would have wine, brandy etc ad infinitum at his disposal. We did our best to keep him from it.

. . .

Same, 13 October 1841

. . . It appears that Harris had no place after all in the Yt Liverpool. He call'd one night & left a parcel with one of the servants; but told no one where he was going . . .

(CCRO, Huddlestone, 488/C3/DG73, 75–7)

The nature of service encouraged drinking. Coachmen and footmen on carriage duty had to wait around for their masters and mistresses. When they were asked into other servants' halls, drink was always on offer.

William Tayler in London, at the Prinseps' house

April 25, 1837 . . . took Miss P. to her sister's in Belgrave Square where she staid to dinner and spent the evening there with many others. Went at half past twelve this night to fetch her home. It poured with rain. When I got there, I was asked into the inner apartments as I live with some of the famley. There was a large party of gents and ladies at supper. I went and looked in the room where they were forty sitting at supper; everything was butiful and splendid. These people very often gives such parties and they spare no expence; the best pastrey-cooks and confectioners are imploid in London. After I had looked at them and heard them sing some good songs, I went downstairs – first into the pantry where the footman gave me a tumbler of sherry which I drank. I then went into the housekeeper's room, and she gave me a tumbler of mulled port wine and a lot of sweetmeats which I very soon devoured. After sitting and talking to the ladiesmaids awhile, I went into the pantry again where the butler would insist on my haveing a glass of champane, and after a little, he gave me a glass of sherrey. I then began to get very talkative and after helping wipe some of their glasses he gave me another glass of muld port and by the way of a finish he gave me a glass of sherey. By this time I am sertain I had drunk a bottle of wine and to get off from drinking more, I went up to the entrance hall to be out of the way, where there were many servants sitting that had not tasted a bit or drop as they were not in any way connected with the famly. We got home a little before three o'clock.

(Wise, *William Tayler*, pp. 29–30)

While waiting for Lord and Lady Howard, Frederick Gorst often went into pubs.

The evening that 'Rupert of Hentzau' had its premiere at the Lyric Theatre I was on the carriage with the coachman, Derwin, when he took Her Ladyship [Lady Howard] to the theatre. After leaving her at the door and finding out when the play was expected to be over, Derwin and I went to a public-house for a drink. This was, strictly speaking, against the rules. However, we felt that a beer or two would not be too far out of line.

We went into the 'private bar', because we were both in the Howard livery. The bars were really one huge room, separated by an ugly, stained-glass screen built onto a wooden partition. Because of my height, I was still visible from my chest to the top of my black silk, high hat to anyone standing on the other side of the screen in the public bar.

The place was practically deserted except for two fishwives who still had some fish left in their baskets after the day's work. . . .

One of them caught sight of us and burst out, 'Blimey! Will ye get a look at them flunkies!'

This outburst struck us both as humorous, and we began to laugh. Unfortunately, this angered one of the fishwives, and before I knew what was happening, she picked up a fish and threw it over the screen. It hit me on the chest, leaving a large unsightly stain on my fawn-coloured coat. . . .

I did everything possible to remove both the stain and the odour so that I would be presentable when we went back to the theatre to fetch Lady Howard.

We arrived there in good time and I met Her Ladyship as she came out. As I escorted her to the carriage I noticed that she was eyeing me somewhat oddly. And when I helped her to get in, she said, 'Gorst, you have a large spot on your coat. Did you have an accident? . . . And there is an odour of fish somewhere about, Gorst. Do you notice it?'

'I'm sorry, Your Ladyship,' I said, 'there *has* been a slight mishap and I will do what can about it as quickly as possible.'

Lady Howard looked completely mystified but she seemed to sense a secret joke, and she began to laugh.

(Gorst, *Carriages and Kings*, pp. 112–13)

At home, too, many employers encouraged the drinking of alcohol. Ernest King recalled his master Mr Chichester of Youlston Park, North Devon.

Whenever Mr and Mrs Chichester went out for the day, the moment their carriage was out of hearing, down to the cellar the butler would go and ring the bell to summon all the stablehands, gardeners and workmen. 'Come on, boys,' he would cry, 'another b . . . anniversary.' And the beer would flow . . . I know that both the butler and a footman died of drink. Many an insurance company then would refuse to insure a butler because of his ready access to drink. Indeed, when I first took out a policy the agent advised me not to put down my occupation as butler, but as valet to ensure acceptance by the company.

The wine-cellar at Hall was never locked. Once suspecting a loss Mr Chichester pinned at eye-level the following notice: *The same man who took a bottle of my very best port has now taken a bottle of my very best brandy, C.C.* Twice, three times a week he would invite the butler and the two footmen after dinner to fill their glasses with whatever they wanted. 'My men servants are my friends,' he would declare. They were. No one ever left. . . .

The Chichesters were also liberal in their distribution of beer.

. . . the men servants all had beer for breakfast. It would be drawn from a barrel in the cellar into a huge two-gallon copper jug and the jug placed on the sink in the pantry and they took a glass whenever they wanted it. The postman, the butcher, the oil-man, the grocer, all who called were offered a glass. The men from the stables came in for a drink. No beggar – and there were many then – was turned away with an empty stomach. It was the normal hospitality of a gentleman's house. . . .

We had 'elevenses'. For the maids there was cocoa or tea and a piece of cake or a scone. The footmen had beer and bread and cheese. I was considered a bit of a sissy because I had cocoa. I was rather horrified by all the drinking.

(King, *Green Baize Door*, pp. 10, 12)

An addiction to alcohol however, could put a job at risk.

Thomas the footman was concerned about his friend James the porter at Stafford House.

Nov 7 Went to Stafford House when I got there I found that James had been drunk & the housekeeper had sent him out of the house so as soon as I got there I dress'd myself & saw the housekeeper & she said that I must stay there till James came back, so I was porter all day. His wife came & said James was at home very poorly . . . I slept in James' bed.

Nov 8 I got up about 7, cleaned the door & about etc . . . about 11 o'clock James Porter came back he was quite well. He asked for Mrs Galleazzie[7] I said she was showing some of her friends round the house so about 12 o'clock they went. She did not come to speak to him neither did he go to her, presently little Sarah brings a note from her to James which I believe was to tell him to send his account to her & she would pay him & he might go about his business. She said she would not see him . . . little Sarah then went back to her & beg'd her to see him . . . James was quite frightened when he came back from her . . . he said it was all right again he had promised her that the like should not happen again.

(Thomas, 'Journal', SRO D4177/1–2)

There could be even worse consequences.

William Lanceley

I had noticed two of the men a little stupid occasionally, so kept an eye on them. Their stupidity was always late at night, though neither neglected his work nor were they ever absent from their duty. One day one of them caused a great sensation in the servants' hall. While helping the dinner he fell to the floor in a kind of fit and I called in the doctor, who at once said that it was through alcohol. I could not at first believe it, but he was sure on that point and the man was sent to a Home for inebriates. This steadied the other for a time. Then the climax came. The first man was discharged from the Home as cured and joined up during the war. On leaving for England he either fell overboard or jumped into the St. Lawrence River and was drowned. His body was recovered three months afterwards in a block of ice and was buried in Ottawa. Some months afterwards the other man died a miserable death. It was then discovered that both these men had been shown how to make whisky from wood alcohol or methylated spirit, of which a large quantity was used in the house for tea urns, kettles, breakfast dish-warmers and many other things. They concocted this in their bedrooms with darkened windows and a curtain over the door, so that even the night watchman was deceived, and here they would imbibe the vile poison until after midnight. . . . One of them had been with me twenty years, the other twelve.

(Lanceley, *Hall-Boy to House-Steward*, p. 164)

It was not only men who took to drink.

Ethel Stanbridge

The staff at Burwood were ruled by the butler who was always drunk by lunchtime, everybody knew he was drunk, but in Lady Ellesmere's eyes he could do no wrong and he was there for forty years. The lady's maid was also drunk, part of her allowance was beer at dinner, beer at night and beer when she went to bed and she never missed any!

(Stanbridge, 'Below Stairs', p. 335)

Margaret Thomas at a large country house in Yorkshire

The cook was uncertain-tempered so I wasn't surprised when I was told she had once been discovered the worse for drink. The staff were told to report at once if they saw any signs of her drinking, so she was surrounded by spies, poor thing, for nobody liked her, but I think she made out all right for she used to visit the grocer's in the afternoon; and come back very good-tempered after spending a social hour in their parlour. As well she went to the butler's cottage every evening to take dainties for his invalid daughter. I expect she got a little drop there too, for she was in high spirits on her return, though they had evaporated by bed-time.

(Thomas, 'Green Baize Door', p. 93)

Alcoholism among servants was usually associated with the illicit drinking of wine or spirits. Beer-drinking was less of a problem since the households brewed their own and could therefore regulate the strength. It was also an accepted part of country-house life, formalised, even ritualised.

Extract from the Regulations for Wimpole, *c.* 1790

13. The Allowance of ale is to be: for Men 1 Pint at Dinner, 1 Pint at Supper; for Women, ½ Pint at Dinner, ½ at Supper. Small Beer may be drunk (under regulation as to time) as necessary, but not wasted.

14. No ale or Beer to be given away in, or carried away from the House; & it is most particularly ordered that no ale or Beer be drawn before 1 pm or after 9 pm . . .

16. The Butler will draw Beer & Ale at Certain times in the day, so as to not be going continually to the Cellars and the Servants are to conform to any regulations he may make.

(CCRO, Wimpole, 408/F7)

The beer allowance was a management tool, a means of keeping discipline, as seen by the list of rules still displayed in the servants' hall at Chirk Castle.

Rules to be observed here
That every Servant must

Take off his Hat at entering here
Sit in his proper Place at Table
Keep himself clean becoming his Station
Drink in his Turn[8]
Be diligent in his Business
Shut the Door after Him

That no Servant be guilty of

Cunning or Swearing
Telling Tales
Speaking disrespectfully of any one
Breeding any Quarrel
Wasting Meat or Drink
Intermeddling with any others Business unless requested to
Assist

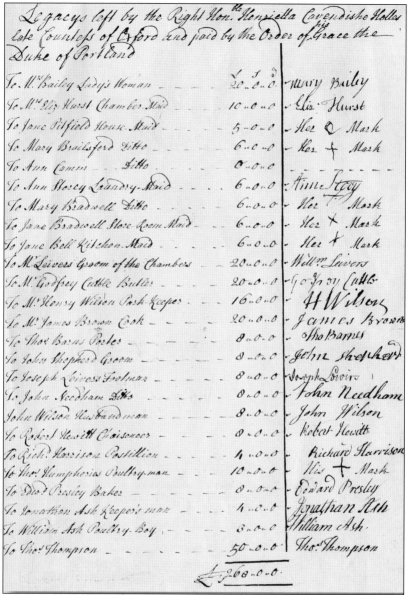

Legacys left by the Right Hon.ble Henrietta Cavendishe Holles late Countess of Oxford and paid by the Order of Grace the Duke of Portland

	£ s d	
To M.rs Bailey Lady's Woman	20 – 0 – 0	Mary Bailey
To M.rs Eliz: Hurst Chamber Maid	10 – 0 – 0	Eliz: Hurst
To Jane Pilfield House-Maid	5 – 0 – 0	Her ⊙ Mark
To Mary Brailsford Ditto	6 – 0 – 0	Her † Mark
To Ann Camm Ditto	0 – 0 – 0	
To Ann Hosey Laundry-Maid	6 – 0 – 0	Anne Hosey
To Mary Bradwell Ditto	6 – 0 – 0	Her † Mark
To Jane Bradwell Store-Room Maid	6 – 0 – 0	Her × Mark
To Jane Bell Kitchen-Maid	6 – 0 – 0	Her × Mark
To M.r Leivers Groom of the Chambers	20 – 0 – 0	Will.m Leivers
To M.r Godfrey Cuttle Butler	20 – 0 – 0	Godfrey Cuttle
To M.r Henry Wilson Sash-Keeper	16 – 0 – 0	H Wilson
To M.r James Brown Cook	20 – 0 – 0	James Brown
To Thos Barns Porter	8 – 0 – 0	Tho Barnes
To John Shepherd Groom	8 – 0 – 0	John Shepherd
To Joseph Leivers Footman	8 – 0 – 0	Joseph Livir
To John Needham Ditto	8 – 0 – 0	John Needham
John Wilson Husbandman	8 – 0 – 0	John Wilson
To Robert Hewitt Chaisoneer	8 – 0 – 0	Robert Hewitt
To Rich.d Harrison Postillion	4 – 0 – 0	Richard Harrison
To Thos Humpheries Poultry-man	10 – 0 – 0	His † Mark
To Edw.d Presley Baker	8 – 0 – 0	Edward Presley
To Jonathan Ash Keeper's man	4 – 0 – 0	Jonathan Ash
To William Ash Poultry-Boy	3 – 0 – 0	William Ash
To Thos Thompson	50 – 0 – 0	Tho: Thompson

£ 268 – 0 – 0.

According to this list of legacies left to her servants at Welbeck by the Countess of Oxford in 1755, only three of the eight female servants could write their own name, whereas all but one of the sixteen men servants could sign for themselves. Part of the explanation for this must be that the men's jobs were more senior than the women's.
(*Nottinghamshire Archives, DD4P 37/85*)

Dr.   George Cooke to the

George Cooke Debt: to the last Account Settled 29th September 1788 .... 25 : 55 : 9

13 Oct: 1788 Received of Mr. Isaac Worthington on Account for the Earl of Stamford ...... 500 : 04 : 0

27.   Received of Mr. Isaac Worthington on Account for the Earl of Stamford .... 500 : 0 : 0

31st.   Received of Mr. Isaac Worthington on Account for the Earl of Stamford ...... 500 : 0 : 0

3. Novr: Received of Mr. Isaac Worthington on Account for the Earl of Stamford .... 100 : 0 : 0

6. Dec: Received of Mr. Isaac Worthington on Account for the Earl of Stamford .... 200 : 0 : 0

13th Dec: Received of Mr. Isaac Worthington on Account for the Earl of Stamford .... 500 : 0 : 0

20 Dec: Received of Mr. Isaac Worthington on Account for the Earl of Stamford .... 500 : 0 : 0

20th Dec: Received of William Ashton for 600. Bricks .... 0 : 7 : 6

                            Total Debt: .... 826 : 3 : 3
                            Total Cred: .... 713 : 52 : 9½

George Cooke Debt: to this Account the 31st. December 1788 .... 112 : 50 : 5½

This Account was Settled between us, the Balance due to
the Earl of Stamford being: 112 : 50 : 5½ Witness our Hands

                            Stamford.

                            George Cooke.

Above: Typical of the painstakingly neat writing of the senior servant in the late eighteenth century, this extract is from the account books of George Cooke, the house steward at Dunham Massey, dated 1788. It also shows Cooke's numeracy and the degree of trust placed in the hands of stewards. These are the amounts of cash handed to Cooke by the land agent for the purpose of settling household bills – anything from buying salt to framing pictures. (*John Rylands Library, University of Manchester and National Trust, EGR7/14/1/66*)

Hon^d Madam   F(M)G 864   London Jan^{ry} 18: 1779

I am sorry to trouble your Ladyship
with these few lines, as I am Opposite your
Ladyships house I cannot help taking notice
of your Ladyships house maid, whom I see
lazing shirts on the Grass two & three times
a week whome I find by inquiry is a sweet heat
heast of hers & she boards him likewise
& if your Ladyship will give her self the trouble
to Inquire the Gardener can Inform your
Ladyship of the Same,

          I am Hon^d Madam
          a neare Neighbour

Servants were not even safe from surveillance when their employers were away from home. Here the generosity of one of the Fitzwilliam's housemaids in cooking and washing for a male friend has been noticed by an anonymous correspondent. (*Northamptonshire Record Office, F(M)G 864*)

Opposite, below: A servant to her sweetheart. Ruth Barrow, a servant in Leicestershire, writes to John Spendlove, who worked in Gretton and whom she later married. They were both non-conformists and much of their correspondence is religious and exhortational in tone, as well as being written in crossed writing to save paper. (*Northamptonshire Record Office, SpG 355*)

Extracts from a trade catalogue of Joshua Taylor & Co. Ltd, of Cambridge and Ely, makers of livery and uniforms. The first Joshua Taylor store appeared in Ely in 1810 and the Cambridge branch opened in 1860. As a family business it survived until 1988 when it was sold to the Asda Group. (*Cambridgeshire Record Office, R85/126*)

Servants waiting for registration at Mrs Hunt's domestic employment agency in London. The picture was published in 1903 in a magazine called *Living London*. (*Mary Evans Picture Library*)

The female servants at Elford Rectory, 1860. This picture is taken from an album that shows the whole household turned out into the garden to have their photographs taken. This must have been a new experience, hence the rather apprehensive expressions. (*Staffordshire Arts and Museum Service*)

Below: Servants at the Grange, Erdington, Birmingham, 1890s. On the edge of the growing industrial conurbation, this household was a fair size and belonged to Sir Benjamin Stone, a successful businessman, MP and photographer who took this image of his own servants. (*Sir Benjamin Stone Collection, Birmingham Library Services*)

Servants at Erddig, 1887. In the centre at the front is the housekeeper Harriet Rogers, to her left is the butler George Dickinson and to her right is the head gardener Alexander Stirton. (*National Trust*)

Servants at Speke Hall, Liverpool, 1890s. Notice the maids are wearing waist aprons not pinafores. This was usually a sign of status, but these women are probably housemaids wearing their best uniforms. Maids tucked the corner of the apron into the waistband to keep the apron clean. (*Sir Benjamin Stone Collection, Birmingham Library Services*)

A cabinet portrait of an unknown footman, taken by 'Monsieur George' of Greengate Street, Stafford, who was at that address between 1892 and 1896. The shoulder knot was the trade mark of the footman's dress livery, and is derived from the cord that supported a powder flask as part of an eighteenth-century military uniform. The whole photograph is an exercise in establishing status – not only was the footman in his best livery but 'Monsieur George', though a prize-winning photographer, was in reality plain Joseph George. (*Gillian Jones*)

Above, right: The butler at Rudge Hall, Staffordshire, one of the many servants who went off to fight in the First World War, never to return. (*Staffordshire Arts and Museum Service*)

John Jeffries, coachman to the Lane family at King's Bromley in Staffordshire, *c.* 1910. (*Staffordshire Arts and Museum Service*)

Three servants at Blakeshall in Worcestershire, photographed during the First World War. (*Staffordshire Arts and Museum Service*)

By the early twentieth century, domestic servants had become more expensive to employ and more difficult to recruit. Some of the smaller country houses came to rely on agency staff, especially for cooks filling in during staff holidays or an emergency. Helen Boardman (centre) kept a diary between 1906 and 1932, recording her travels as a relief cook and housemaid in Lancashire, Aldershot and the Lake District, registered at Roscoes in Manchester. This was taken at Dr MacGill's house in Manchester in 1911. (*Manchester Central Library, Misc. 505*)

The indoor male staff at Petworth, 1870s. Back row, left to right: assistant underbutler, footman, underbutler, footman, house steward; middle row: lodgekeeper, chef, lodge keeper; front row: footman, steward's room man, second chef, footman. This is an interesting study of the social gradations of the household. Not only do the senior servants (chefs and steward) not wear livery, but the footmen wear a differently cut jacket and a different tie from the under butlers. (*Lord Egremont*)

Joseph Applegate, usher of the hall at Petworth, 1883. A Hampshire man, he was aged about forty-four when this picture was taken by Walter Kevis, a professional photographer who had been a footman at Petworth for a short time and who worked between the 1870s and 1908. (*Kevis Collection, West Sussex Record Office*)

The Misses Curling and Smith, housemaids at Petworth, July 1899. Petworth seems to have supplied their housemaids with a standard best dress. (*Kevis Collection, West Sussex Record Office*)

Mary Bridges, the Petworth House laundry maid, March 1894. She worked at Petworth from about 1891 to 1896. (*Kevis Collection, West Sussex Record Office*)

The head nursemaid at Petworth, Rachel Sumpter, bathing one of her charges, Everard Humphrey Wyndham, born in 1888. (*Lord Egremont*)

Mlle Clare Bouliott, governess at Petworth, c. 1886. She was born in France in about 1856. (*Kevis Collection, West Sussex Record Office*)

The kitchen at Lyme Park, early twentieth century. Chef Perez is on the right, with his kitchen maids, scullery maid and the odd job man. One of the maids' jobs was to lay the tables out every morning in strict work stations. The chef and the head kitchenmaid would work on scrubbed wooden blocks on top of the immaculately starched tablecloths. Between the blocks would be put out dishes of butter and lard, sugar and eggs and down the table chef's favourite knives, a sharpening steel, spoons, a palette knife, wooden spoons and whisks. (*National Trust, Lyme Park*)

The servants' hall at Lyme Park, early twentieth century. Compared with earlier more spartan halls, this has some degree of modern comfort, but retained the use of old horn cups for beer. (*National Trust, Lyme Park*)

A cheery group of brewers from the Lyme brewhouse pose for the photographer. The brewhouse continued in use well into the 1900s. The brewer is sitting at the front wearing the apron. Footmen and gardeners were obviously called in to help. (*National Trust, Lyme Park*)

Evelyn Christiansen, the head laundry maid at Lyme Park, 1936. (*National Trust, Lyme Park*)

An early photograph of a head gardener, William McMurtrie of Shugborough. He was born in 1781, and died in 1857, so this photograph must have been taken after his retirement. He was head gardener from 1815 to 1836. (*Staffordshire Arts and Museum Service*)

The maids and yard staff at Shugborough, 1870s. The tall man on the left was the estate blacksmith, and he is seen here helping to restrain the guard dog, a huge mastiff whose white paw, chest and studded collar can just be seen.
(*Staffordshire Arts and Museum Service*)

The housekeeper at Shugborough (on the right) with her maids, 1926. (*Staffordshire Arts and Museum Service*)

Monsieur René Pavillard, chef at Shugborough, c. 1927. (*Staffordshire Arts and Museum Service*)

Two of the Shugborough maids with their bicycles outside the brewhouse, 1926. Bicycles were a godsend to country house servants and Shugborough encouraged their maids to visit friends or go local dances. (*Staffordshire Arts and Museum Service*)

Many of the traditions of domestic service were alive and well in houses like Shugborough in the 1930s. Nevertheless there was a more relaxed atmosphere, allowing even servants' children to play with the family. Here Lady Lichfield's lady's maid Gertie Hulme picnics in the park with her charges – on her right Lady Celia Anson, on her left the chauffeur's daughter, Pam Kinson.
(*Staffordshire Arts and Museum Service*)

NB The person offending to be deprived of his Allowance of Beer – for the first Offence 3 Days. Second Offence, one whole Week – and third Offence – his Behaviour to be laid before Mr Myddelton

(NT, Chirk Castle Servants' Hall)

At Holland House

When we speak of elevenses today it's in terms of tea or coffee; this wasn't the case in service – then we were given beer and that included both male and female staff, and if it wasn't provided we had beer money in lieu. At Holland House the drawing and carrying of the ale was my province. Every day I would take the jacks to the cellar, fill them, carry one to the butler's room for Mr Pettit, the footman, the head gardener and the chauffeur; another I would take to the housekeeper's room, another to the kitchen, another to the housemaid's sitting-room, and a small one to the stillroom. Jacks came in various sizes; they were copper jugs wide at the base coming to a small opening at the lip, and their shape and metal helped to keep the beer cool. Those we had measured from a quart to a gallon and a half. The largest one was for the butler and his cronies. They weren't great drinkers and would often leave at least half of it, which had to be poured down the sink. There were always eight barrels in the cellar, four on tap and four set up. The beer was excellently kept by the odd man, it was the one job he did really well. He was up and down the cellar all day like a yo-yo tasting it to make sure it was in good condition – to the detriment I thought of his own.

(Washington, 'Hall Boy's Story', p. 183)

Up until the mid-nineteenth century it was usual for a country house to brew its own beer.

Will Clerke to Lord Mordaunt, 16 March 1705/6

Walton

Honble Sir

I have received yours of the 14th and observed your directions about Brewing but find upon search there is not vessels enough for three Brewings as you have ordered we do intend on Tuesday next to brew 14 strike of coke dryed mault for strong Drink, to be placed in the old Ale Cellar, and a Hogshead[9] and half of Small Beer to keep against your comeing . . . There is three Hogsheads of Strong Drink in the old Ale Cellar, brewed in October, Novemr and Decemr last and two Hogsheads of Small to keep in the Small Beere Cellar, and two Half Hogsheads of Ale in the new Ale Cellar which is all in the House excepting the Small Beere lately Brewed for the Family . . .

Honbl Sir

Your faithful &

Obedient servant

Will Clerke

(WCRO, Mordaunt, CR1368, vol. 4/44)

Many of the smaller country houses still believed brewing was women's work, as shown by a letter from the steward at Bramham Park to Lord Bingley.

Thomas Fleming to Lord Bingley, 14 February 1727

. . . I am afraid of Venturing Sarah to Brew, for a week after you were gone, she had all her Brewing things to wash up. Margaret says you promised her She could Brew, but I fear she is as bad as Sarah. If you think ft I will send for Marjery again for she understands Brewing the best of them all . . .

(LCL, Lane Fox, LF 134)

It was not until the latter half of the nineteenth century that great households became aware that they might be fostering bad habits and so many houses closed their brewhouses and offered cash instead of beer. This marked a fundamental change in the ethos of a system which had been operating for centuries.

William Lanceley could see the advantages of both systems.

Drink is the chief ruin of men-servants, but there is not so much kept within their reach as formerly, and the old ale has nearly disappeared from the servants' hall. The brewing days of old are past, and in many houses beer money is given instead. Where beer is supplied there is not the excuse of going out for a glass of beer. On the other hand, a temperate man finds his beer money a help. I knew one footman who made it a rule to provide himself with under-clothing and boots from this source.

(Lanceley, *Hall-Boy to House-Steward*, p. 163)

SEVEN

'His sheets taken for a lark'
– servants' recreations

The amount of spare time available to servants varied according to both seniority and gender. Junior menservants and maids had no formally recognised time off at all in the early nineteenth century but later were given perhaps a day off every fortnight. What time was available was often negated by the fact that the workplace was so isolated. Servants developed quiet, sedentary pastimes. Even men took up needlework and at least one, Ernest King, bred mice.[1] The more ambitious tried to better themselves – learning to read and write, perhaps, or to speak a foreign language or play a musical instrument.

By long tradition, footmen were the athletes of the country-house world. By the nineteenth century 'running footmen' were no longer seen (in effect security guards who ran alongside the carriage), but even so footmen often walked several miles each day. Some country households had a tradition of 'racing off' – foot races, often with bizarre handicaps, and many employers allowed men to keep fit by rowing on a park lake. Menservants attended other outdoor sports such as 'sparring', badger baiting and cock fighting.

Later, Edwardian servants were allowed, even encouraged, to be sociable with people outside the house, at least within reason. Annie Norman, for example, spent most of her spare time taking tea and walking through the lanes with other servant girls from nearby houses or farms. In this respect many servants have recorded the importance of having a bicycle and some households in the 1920s even provided their servants with a household bike.

Holidays were limited. In a twelve-month period in 1838–9 Thomas, the Sutherlands' footman, was given special permission to visit his family for three days. By the late nineteenth century most servants had a week or a fortnight when they usually went home. They were allowed to take this at a time when the employer was away – perhaps in early summer during the London season. Then servants would take their turn on holiday to suit the spring cleaning, which was also done at that time. Often holidays were not very restful, especially for women servants who were roped into work at home.

In the great titled households where servants might number fifty or more, the servants' hall formed a distinct community. Evenings were passed sewing or playing cards, singing or dancing. Servants were often highly musical – there was usually someone who could play the fiddle, the banjo or even the clarinet. Servant dances figure largely in memoirs – whether the grand annual balls to mark special occasions or the more informal dances which were allowed in some houses every month or so. The formal dances opened by the master and mistress were a mixed blessing – they could be something of a trial, with servants feeling they were on show.[2]

Christmas was always celebrated in the country house, usually by a grand dinner to which many of the outdoor servants were invited. But many recollections of Christmas in service are tinged with disappointment, largely because of the nature of the presents given to servants by the family. Households graded them strictly, according to the status of the servant, and they were usually connected somehow with work. As Gordon Grimmett said, many opportunities were missed for cementing loyalty and affection.[3]

PASTIMES

William Torry was a footman and butler in the household of the 6th Earl of Stamford. For family reasons the household was split between two houses: the first six months of each year were spent at Enville in Staffordshire, the second at Dunham Massey near Altrincham in Cheshire. Torry kept a 'memorandum book' which was arranged alphabetically, so his record of events moves seamlessly from one house to the other. The extracts presented here give a glimpse of a long-lost world of the country-house male servant – tragedies, minor disasters, sport and household pets. They have been rearranged to read chronologically.

Lady Am. Keys footman, William, and Lady Sophia Greys footman Joseph ran a race one hundred yards for a pound each, the former won by 2 yards in the Bollington Meadow, Nov. 11th 1826

William Taylor's son Joseph clothes caught fire at the Workmen's fireplace at Enville Jan 27th 1827
Enville Treat in Commemoration of the Birth and Christening of George Harry Grey took place on Monday 26th of March and lasted till the 31st. Born 7th of Jan. 1827
Lion bit with a mad dog and shot, May 1827, Dunham[4]
Mr Osgood's well cleaned July 27, 1827[5]
Tarter the Coach dog shot Aug, 21st 1827
David Seamman had his shoulder put out at the ford by his horse falling Oct 1st, 1827[6]
The Miller fell into the Mill dam Nov. 1827 at Dunham
Sampson & Oliver sparing at Wol'hampton Jan 23 1828
Enville footraces that should have been run on the Ice, 5th Febr 1828

Badger bate at Enville March 8th 1828 from Mr. Whitmore's.
William Hardwick's horse came home before him from W'hampton, March 12th 1828

Brown & Spring came to Enville for Brown's Training to fight
Sampson, March 17th 1828

Wm Steadman went to the farm yard blind folded in 7 ½ min.
29th July 1828

William Steadman beat William Hardwick one mile on the Race Course for one pound 13th Dec. 1828

Mr Cousens waggner hung himself 22 March 1829

The Dutch oven put hot on Richd Smith's head at Enville, 2 Dec, 1829

Henry Lees race off, with the Keeper's boy W.M. Henry L carry 2 ×14 pounds, one in each hand, 4th Jan. 1830

Joseph Hardwick fell his leg through the ice on the Horse pond, 4th Febr. 1830, Enville

Mr Osgood's bed furniture Raffld for at Enville, 10th Febr 1830

T Kenyon and J Davenport Race on Mosse with Greyhounds 11 March 1830[7]

Old Lion shot at Enville 31st April, 1830

William Hardwick his sheets taken for a lark 18th May, 1830

Dunham Massey: a thief taken in the Stables March, and tried at Chester 4th April, 1831

Fox, William, ate Cyan pepper and mustard in the Hall, 6th April, 1831

Boy taken from a Gipsey and riged out at Enville, 14th April 1831

Lion came from Mr Griffin's 6th Oct. 1831

Lees, Henry, ran one hundred yards agst Jos Toy running the dog cart 70, HL won easy 24th Feb 1832

Collins, Mr., of the Legh, black pony stolen in the night 7th Jan. 1833

Cookly morris dancers attempt to steal one of the Hall horns 15th Jan. 1833

Hardwick Jos & Benjm Lewis run a race 100 yards. B. Lewis won 11th Febr 1833: The same day Thos Steadman run Mr Mosely, footman, 100 yards giving the footman 5 yards, the footman won.

Steadman Thos, ran one hundred yards with Tailor of Stourbridge near Dunsley 19th Febr, 1833, Shrove Tuesday

Bache, Thos., run Henry Beddard 50 yards (with W. Beddard

on his back) against Henry Bedd. running one hundred yards
18th Feb. 1833

Egg broke in J. Topham's small clothes, 22nd June, 1833

Carriage run over Mr. Beddard's Pig, 26th June, killed on the
28th, 1833

Duck & Brandy in the Bakehouse at Enville 6th July, 1833 –
Ratstails[8]

Leathers, Mr, dog went mad and bit the Butcher's dog in the
Park, 24th Oct, 1833

Timporley Sam. head badly cut by a fall early in the morning of
the 1st of Nov 1833 after keeping Lord's birthday, his donkey
raffld for at the Dog 5th Nov. 1833

Lewes, Benjm attempted to run round the new park 5 times in
3 quarters of an hour, defeated the 3rd time round, 13th Febr.
1834

Daller Thos, large pig raffld for, won by Mr Green 27th Febr,
1834

Davenport Wm, sadle, bridle & Thos Fosters Great coat stolen
from the farm Dunham the night of 27th Febr. 1834

Coach Horse shot near Norris Farm after Running away with
the Roller, 29th March, 1834

Alford and Bissell Fight at Mr Gough's near Enville, 20 May,
1834. Alford won.

Supper in the Hall without the table cloth on the table, Enville,
27th May 1834 – a larke because J. was out of the way.

Lion died 2nd Nov 1836, ditto came the 7th of ditto – 6 months
old, he went away, and another came from the Dairy house
Farm, 28th August 1837, 6 weeks old

Cock Fight at Enville between them & Womborn, the Latter won
April 2nd 1838

Coach Dog Nelson, shot at Dunham 24th Sept 1839

Jones, Mrs, grand daughter burnt to death caught fire on the 5th
July & died on the 8th, 1841[9]

(Torry 'Memorandum Book', NT, Altrincham)

Thomas the footman's diary covered the years 1838–9. He was employed
in the highly prestigious household of the Duke of Sutherland. In the
autumn of 1838 he was at West Hill, south London, helping to look after

the younger Sutherland children while the Duke and Duchess were abroad. Thomas did a lot of walking and on one of his walks he had an idea.

19ᵗʰ Oct . . . started to go to London. I took the road to go over Westminster bridge not because it was the nearest way but because I had never been that way and I went more to look about me than anything else I went at a very slow pace and got to the Horse Guards a bout a quarter before one as I was coming along I bethought myself that I would learn the French language this winter and likwise calling to mind that there was a house in Regent St where it was taught by the Hamiltonian system . . . I knocked at the door I enquired if the teacher was at home I was shown up stairs into a front room and there sat a curious man with all the appearance of being a Frenchman I told him my business and asked him what the cost would be he said . . . 'for 3 months it will be 3 guineas and in that time you will be able to write the language very well' I thinking that the price was rather large I said that I was a servant etc etc well says he we will say 2½ guineas which will be very low, so that was agreed upon and Monday was the day fixed for me to begin and to attend twice a week.

24ᵗʰ Nov At home all day learning my lessons

30ᵗʰ Nov I had a new French Grammar of my Master today for which I paid 5/-. I commenced in the 3ʳᵈ part of my reading book today.

12ᵗʰ Dec At home all day doing nothing but learning my lessons which employment takes up nearly all my spare time

Continuing with his lessons he practised his accent on a French nursery maid.

6ᵗʰ Jan after supper I went into the Nursery to say my lesson to the little French Girl . . .

17ᵗʰ Jan Got up about 6 and got my work done and got to my lessons I am now learning the pronouns and am getting on very well

19ᵗʰ Jan I go up to the Nursery every evening to say a lesson to Caroline.

25ᵗʰ Jan I paid for the ensuing quarter at School to day this being the 2ⁿᵈ time £2 12 6 Said my lesson today to another Master the other one being engaged . . . Mrs Bucknall told me tonight that I must not come to read in the Nursery in case if some one should tell the Duchess

30ᵗʰ Jan . . . in the afternoon by appointment I went upstairs to Mme Rouseau[10] to have a French lesson and am to go every day . . .

1ˢᵗ Feb In the afternoon I went upstairs to Madame R and said my lesson think I shall get on very well with her she takes such pains in making me repeat every word so correct.

2ⁿᵈ Feb . . . I went upstairs today to say my lesson and besides me saying a lesson to her she said a lesson to me she reads pretty well much better than I thought she would have done I was upstairs nearly 1½ hours . . .

4ᵗʰ Feb . . . I brought Madame Rouseau a French grammar to day the same sort as mine and a box of ointment . . .

(Thomas, 'Journal', SRO D4177/1–2)

In the 1750s, a young John Macdonald taught himself to read.

When the family returned to Bargeny, I had a great desire to learn to read, and the servants gave me a lesson when time permitted. Wherever I went, I always took the spelling book with me. I thought that if I once could read the Bible, I should not go to hell. . . . When Mr. Hamilton and Lady Anne were informed that I was desirous to learn to read, they put me to school. . . . In the course of time I got reading, writing, and arithmetic; but the coachman became jealous and gave me a flogging. . . .

(Macdonald, *Memoirs*, pp. 27, 30)

Charles Cooper recalled some of the hobbies of servants.

In the old days one used to meet footmen who collected crested livery buttons, putting them in cases, or crests from stationery and pasted them in albums, did fretwork, making brackets, pipe racks, picture frames, etc., and French polished them, did silk and wool work, studied languages hoping this would help them to secure a good place as a valet to travel abroad with some gentleman; others would take up music, the banjo being a popular instrument. . . .

We men being musical, formed a little band of our own, the first footman with a guitar, the boy a violin, myself the mandolin; the hall boy was an excellent performer. In the evenings we managed to find time for dancing and then our musical instruments were appreciated. . . .

(Cooper, *Town and Country*, pp. 181, 198)

Eric Horne

At that place I learned to do crotchet work, and could beat any girl at making lace and wool. During my years in service I have made dozens of jackets for babies: in fact, I think the women used to have the babies in order to get the little wool jackets; also, no end of woollen crossovers for old women.

(Horne, *What the Butler Winked at*, pp. 54–5)

And even steward's room boys had pets, as William Lanceley recalled.

. . . My place was taken by another boy whom I had to coach. He was full of mischief and got into trouble repeatedly. During the lambing season a ewe died at the Home Farm and this boy begged the bailiff to let him have the motherless lamb to rear, so with a broken teapot, a cork fitted into the spout and a quill running through it covered with the finger of a kid glove the rearing began. The lamb was kept in the wood shed . . . but he thrived and was soon as happy as a sandboy. He was christened Billie with due ceremony, old ale being sprinkled over him and his health drunk in the same beverage; and Billie, taking a sip along with the others, was now initiated one of the family. He soon developed bunting, and the boy would walk backwards towards Billie and get a charge from him in double-quick time. Billie was fond of the Servants' Hall and got very friendly with the servants who fed him with scraps and who delighted to see him charge the boy. As time went on Billie grew big and fat, and one day when the servants were at dinner, the hall door not being closed properly, he came stealthily in and seeing the maidservants sitting on a bench with their backs towards him could not resist so glorious an opportunity for a bunt. . . . This was followed by a tremendous shriek and before he could be secured he had charged a second maid in the same manner. The butler was furious and called the boy to take him out and never to let Billie into the house again. Poor Billie's career was soon ended after this, the climax coming through his charging the dairywoman who brought the milk, butter and eggs to the house daily from the Home Farm. She had a milk-yoke with two pails of milk and carried a basket of eggs and butter on her head. She stooped down to unhook the cans from the yoke, not seeing Billie behind her. He charged with dire calamity to the woman, milk, eggs and butter. The squire was very cross, though more or less amused, and ordered poor Billie to be killed, much to the boy's grief.

(Lanceley, *Hall-Boy to House-Steward*, pp. 16–18)

In the old days footmen walked or ran with their messages. Later, the car-bound footman could have problems with keeping fit.

Frederick Gorst

One morning when we came down to our own bailiwick in the footmen's pantry, we found an announcement which we did not like very much stating that Her Grace, the Duchess of Portland, intended to institute a regimen of exercise for the four Royal footmen. First she presented each of us with a bicycle and then with a set of golf clubs. We were to spend most of our spare time exercising, and Her Grace arranged for us to use the golf course when the family and guests were not playing.

Jim and I made good use of the bicycles and the golf course but Osborn and Hales were not so athletically inclined. Hales continued to use his 'foot bath' [afternoon sessions of 'spooning' with one of the housemaids] and Osborn continued to read his 'penny dreadfuls' as lurid fiction was then called.

But the Duchess of Portland was adamant. She decided that all four of us must report for callisthenics in the gymnasium at specified hours and she engaged a Japanese jiu-jitsu expert to train us. Her Grace had made up her mind that we were not to grow fat from drinking beer, and rather than have the beer rations cut, we decided we would do anything – even callisthenics! . . .

All of us stripped and put on exercise trunks in the dressing rooms. When we entered the gymnasium the Japanese instructor was waiting for us, I will never forget the look of amazement that came over five faces when we regarded each other. Jim was a mere six foot, Osborn and I were six foot, two, and Hales boasted one more inch. The Japanese gentleman was five foot, four.

He began with the horizontal bars and showed us how to hold on, and then, with a slight running start, to make a somersault at the end of the dash; I found myself face down each time I tried this manoeuvre.

Breathing exercises came next – followed by a vain attempt to touch the floor with our finger tips without bending our knees. Too much fresh bread and beer – we just couldn't make it!

Finally, we were given a little elementary instruction in jiu-jitsu and I was thankful that the mats were thick and well-padded. The little Japanese tossed Hales over his shoulder like a rag doll. . . .

It was later arranged that we would attend this class twice a week, and the Duchess gave orders that rice was to be substituted on our menu for bread. I was willing to co-operate to any extent, even if Japanese raw fish was to be added to the regimen, as long as there was no cut in the beer allowance.

(Gorst, *Carriages and Kings*, pp. 137–8)

HOLIDAYS

In 1914, Annie Norman was living as a general maid, one of two, with the Singletons at Repton School. Except for her holidays, life was bounded by the local rural community and occasional trips to the nearby town of Burton. She was probably only 15 or 16 years old when this was written, and her friends were girls of her own age and older women met through service or the church. Her activities were limited to taking tea, walking, biking and, for a short time, dancing.

Feb 1 Sunday. I was in the morning and I went out in the afternoon with Dora on the Willington Rd. I met Nellie Williams and Rene B. We then went to Mrs Perry's[11] for tea and then went to Church with Esther Wright then we went another walk till 9.15. I then came in.

Feb 5 I went to the Parish tea at 6 o'clock and Emily & Dora & Lucy & Emily Perry. We all went together and I had three dances and came back to the Pastures at 10 o'clock. Mr Singleton gave us tickets.

Feb 15 We had morning tea at 5.15am in bed. Emily went to Church in the morning & I went to Mrs Perry's for tea with Dora and we had some games & then we went for a walk with Esther Wright & we met Rene Blunt and Jane Cox and we all went to Willington for a walk & we didn't half have some fun all 5 of us.

Feb 18 I went to Esther's for tea and went to visit Mr Wright and Mrs Perry. Ellen was with me & we both went to the rink dancing and came in at 10.15.

Feb 19 Mrs Singleton said I was not to have another evening at the dancing classes as she did not like to be alone 'poor thing'.

Feb 20 Mrs Singleton said I could go to one more class, so as to tell my friends that she could not spare me again. I also went to Burton on my bike & started at 3.30 arrived at 4.30, started back at 6 and arrived at 7.10. A dinner to cook now.

She started confirmation classes instead of dancing.

March 19 I got too late for confirmation class so Lill & I had some fun against the school shop. I then went to Mrs Perry's for tea. Lill & I saw a motorcar run over a fowl at the bottom of the Pastures.

March 29 My Sunday afternoon out. Dora Perry called in & I went to there house for tea, & afterwards Dora, Esther & Jane & I went to Willington for a walk & Jane went into the Green Man & bought a packet of cigarettes. Of course <u>we</u> didn't smoke them!

April 10 Good Friday. I went to Church in the evening with Dora and E.P. & E.E. at 7.00 and we came out at 8 & got in at ¼ to 9. We also got into hot water. But she soon cooled down.

April 12 Easter Sat. Emily at Church in the morning. Bill[12] came over in the afternoon for tea & supper. We went to Mrs Perry's & then went a walk on the Newton Rd & then Bill went back on my bike.

April 13 Easter Mon. I went home on the 10.30 train from Repton. Bill met me at Burton & George Williams came home with me. Bill & I went to the pictures in the afternoon & I saw Vic to speak to and Jim.

April 14 I was weighed & Bill was as well. I was 9st 4lbs & Bill was 9st 5lbs.

April 30 I was confirmed by the Bishop of Derby. Dora came in for tea. I was dressed in cream & there were 24 done at the same time.

May 24 Sunday Emily went to Church. I out in the afternoon. I went to Mrs Wright's for tea, we had the gramophone on. Esther and I went across to Mrs Perry's. Dora was ill in bed, then we went for a walk, it simply poured with rain. Emily Perry, Esther and I and Jane. We sheltered in the fives court. We had some fun because there were some boys there as well.

June 2 It was a very wet day, fine in between showers. I and Esther went to Burton. I asked for 9.30 and Mrs S said it was the last time till 9.30 I could have, so I was not to ask again. We enjoyed ourselves very much.

July 3 . . . I sent Bill a cake to the barracks . . .

Aug 4. The British declare war with Germany.

Aug 9 Sunday. I went to Church in the morning & the service was all about the war. We all sang 'God save the King' just before we came out.

Aug 19 I went to the Red Cross working party at the rink, & I went to Sarah's for tea, after we went for a walk on the Willington Rd. I started to knitt some socks for our poor soldiers.

(Norman, 'Diary', DeRO, D5161/1)

By definition, many country houses were situated far from towns or even villages. Even in the 1930s Eileen Balderson found Burwarton House, the Shropshire home of Lord and Lady Boyne, isolated.

The house was silent. You could hear a pin drop. The deadly atmosphere was enlivened only by birdsong.

At the time I was there, there was neither a bus nor a train service. We used to be taken into Bridgnorth. . . . Half the staff went each Saturday afternoon; also any estate workers who wanted to go. We went in the shooting brake, driven by the under chauffeur. We left the house at 2pm and returned at 4pm, so we went to town for two hours per fortnight!

The under-servants had to be in by 9pm, which was no hardship since there was nowhere to go. Under these conditions it was very difficult to keep staff. I did not stay long. . . .

(Balderson, *Backstairs Life*, p. 52)

While at Trentham, Thomas the footman was allowed to take a short trip home to his family in Cheshire.

Sept 4 A very fine morning. I got up about ¼ before 7 & went out & got the boat out & went out on the water by myself & was out about an hour, got home for breakfast. After that I cleaned up all my cloths & shoes & got myself ready . . . & started for Whitmore just as the clock was striking 12. I had to run & walk nearly all the way it was very hot just as I was past the Inn at Whitmore I overtook a man with a gig & asked him to let me inside he said I was quite welcome he said that he was brother-in-law to Wright the baker at Trentham he took me to the station & I bid him good day.

It was 10 past 1 I got my ticket & paid my fare 4/6 & waited ½ an hour before the train came it was a first class train I got into the carriage & in a few minutes we were at Crew station then stayed there a few minutes and we were at Hartford in about 11 minutes under the hour where I got out . . . I then started for home along the Chester road . . .

Mary D saw me coming and came and met me then sister then Mother and afterwards all. Father was carting his Oats but he came to his tea directly . . . Samuel Woodward came to see me in the evening . . . went to bed about 11, slept with my Father. They were all very glad to see me.

5th Sept Got up this morning about 7 had breakfast and afterwards went with my Father to School Bank to see all my Uncles and Aunts . . . they wanted me to stay for dinner but I promised my Mother to be home for dinner . . . Mother had got a very nice dinner I was at home till teatime, I had tea then went to see old Pritchard Woodwards and then to my Uncle Joseph's . . . and saw little Mary and then got to Delamere House . . . and saw Thomas, John, Mr Garner & the Keeper . . . I had supper and then went into the Kitchen and saw Fanny and the rest of the Maids . . . I also spoke to Mrs Garner Mrs Tomlinson and Mr Bayson . . . they were all very surprised to see me . . .

. . . I went to Norley Bank to see Wm . . . and most of the servants . . . I saw the housekeeper at Norley Bank she used to live at Oulton in the Kitchen . . . she sent her respect to Martha

7th Sept . . . I went to bid sister Mary good bye I could not help crying so that I could not bid the rest farewell, I gave John, Henry and Charles 6d each then mother and me started Wm came with us along the lane to the bottom of the hollow we then called to see Mrs Rayson . . . and then we came on to Davises and met her, stayed there and I run down to see Mrs Lewis . . . and Mother and me came . . . to the Railway Station at Acton when I got there I just went in to see Charles Moulton . . . I met Mr Plumb on the Bridge he said he hoped I was very steady and took care of my money . . . my Mother cried and seemed very sorry at my parting she gave me good advice etc I saw the train coming I then put Mother a sovereign in her hand she thanked me & said I was very good to them by then the train was up I bid her goodbye and we parted and in 1 hour and 10 m I was at Whitmore a distance of about 25 miles I then took my bag and again walked back to Trentham

(Thomas, 'Journal', SRO D4177/1–2)

SERVANT DANCES AND CHRISTMAS PARTIES

Dances figure large in servant memories.

Frederick Gorst described the annual servants' ball at Welbeck Abbey.

The great event, a ball for the staff, always took place on Twelfth-night. It was held in the underground ballroom and the three great reception rooms. The rooms were beautifully decorated, just as though the Duke and Duchess were giving a ball for themselves. The flowering plants were brought down and there were arbors of potted palms and ferns. . . .

All the staff, the tenants on the estate and their families, and the tradesmen in Worksop and their wives had been invited. There were about twelve hundred guests for the ball. . . . An orchestra from London had been engaged, and a swarm of fifty waiters arrived because none of us was required to perform any duties that evening – this was the social event of *our* season!

One reception room had been set up as a cloak room for the ball, and the other huge rooms were arranged with tables for the midnight supper. There were pine festoons on the great chandeliers, and hundreds of small gilt chairs with red velvet seats lined the ballroom walls.

When the Duke and Duchess arrived, Osborne, Hales, Askew, and I followed in their wake as proud as peacocks to attend them for their entrance. We wore our epaulet liveries because we were, in a sense, still on duty, but it had been previously arranged that as soon as the Duke and Duchess left, we would be permitted to go to our rooms and put on our own full dress clothes.

It was quite a revelation to see all of the members of the staff in ball dress. Even the prim head housemaid looked quite chic in a velvet gown, and the head housekeeper, who wore a low-cut blue satin gown, was almost unrecognizable without her stiff, black silk dress and her belt of jingling keys.

Many members of the staff looked so well in their ball clothes that it sparked off the party; and, as I looked around, I found that we had acquired a new kind of individuality and gaiety for the evening, and, stranger still, that we were seeing each other from a new aspect – as people, not as servants.

The Duchess opened the ball by dancing with Mr. Spedding, and as hundreds of couples followed them onto the ballroom floor . . . Naturally the Duchess was the most majestic figure in the ballroom. She had on a magnificent ecru satin gown, embroidered with white passementerie and pearls almost as large as those in the fabulous 'dog collar' about her neck. She wore a spectacular ruby and diamond crescent on her hair and matching pendant ruby earrings. She was the epitome of feminine elegance . . . they left the ball room soon after midnight.

Everything was served from a buffet and the entire silver service was used. Champagne was consumed in unlimited quantities, and the dancing and merrymaking continued until the small hours. With the coming of dawn all the Cinderellas were reminded that this was another day of work, and that the most exciting party of the year was rapidly drawing to a close.

(Gorst, *Carriages and Kings*, pp. 159–60)

Eric Horne thought servant dances were important for servants' morale.

I think what kept them together . . . was we were allowed a dance on the first Tuesday in every month. The mason who worked on the estate played the 'cello, his son played second fiddle, the tailor played the first violin. I played sometimes as well . . . the under gardeners, the grooms, the two whips from the kennels, and perhaps a friend or two would come in, so there was no lack of partners for the maids. . . . The tables were put to one side, which formed a band stand. Our programme

consisted of lancers, quadrilles, waltzes, schottisches, polkas . . .
and country dances. . . . Everything was conducted in a decent
style, no rowdyism. Sometimes some one would sing a song
between the dances . . . I think this sort of thing keeps servants
together, makes them just one great big happy family.

(Horne, *What the Butler Winked at*, pp. 98–9)

At a castle on the shores of Loch Fyne, Jean Rennie found the staff made
regular but secret visits to the gardeners' bothy.

We all trooped out of the back door, we three housemaids, the
cook, kitchenmaid and scullerymaid, and James the young red-
headed footman. . . . The butler saw us out and locked the door.

It seemed that the procedure was that he kept the door locked
until his 'Lordship', the Colonel, had been on his rounds, and
then unlocked it for us. . . .

We crossed the lovely lawns at the back of the house and into
a wooded thicket; through that and out into a clearing, where
there was a long low building lit by oil lamps and seemingly
divided into rooms. It was not unlike the pictures we had seen
of a western shack in American cowboy films. We went into one
of these rooms. . . . There were wooden benches and wooden
chairs and there were tin mugs of tea. Donald played his pipes
and David his fiddle and we danced.

Oh the lovely lilt of the Highland dancing! Oh, the 'Hoochs!'
and the 'Heys!' and the laughter.

It went on till about two in the morning. And I was no longer
tired.

The boys saw us back to the house, and there was much
giggling and kissing, and it was all very sweet and young and
lovely. It made the long day's work seem worth while.

(Rennie, *Every Other Sunday*, p. 28)

Arriving back at Trentham from his holiday in Cheshire, Thomas the footman
found numerous visiting servants in the house – the housekeeper and
stillroom maid from Lilleshall as well as Lord Harrowby's under-butler and
another servant.

. . . having brought my clarinett with me I set about cleaning it . . . some one proposed a dance Charlotte having come home from seeing her friends and has brought Lord Harrowby's under butler with her who is come to see Thomas Grey we got the porter to come and play the Violin for us & we went up into our bedroom[13] & had a very comfortable dance there was about 10 or 12 of us all couples. We kept it up till after one . . .

Later at West Hill

30th July William Knott came here tonight to fetch his Violin . . . he played a tune in the servants hall and they had just begun to dance when Mr Vantini heard them and ordered them to be quiet . . .

1st Aug . . . there was a qeerish party in the servants hall after supper some wanted a song some a dance and there was such a confusion I went to bed at 11 . . .

5th Nov Mrs Adams[14] having gone to town today Omer & me invited the 2 Kitchen maids and the still room and the Dairy Maids to tea with us in the pantry. After supper we had a dance in the servants' hall . . . I did not get to bed till nearly 12 o'clock for after we had done dancing we began playing cards

17th Dec All the talk in the house is about the Ball that is to come off on Wednesday and there is great preparing for it [Lord Stafford's birthday] . . .

18th Dec Got up in good time this morning and the carpenter began to prepare the room for the dance. I was cleaning shoes in the shoe place when Richard came to me and said that we should want some lights in the Ballroom . . . I said that we must have some lamps from Stafford House he said that we must have the room ornamented and he went after the gardeners to do it, as soon as he was gone Mr Wright[15] said that he wanted me I went to him and he gave me 2 bottles of brandy and 2 of rum. I asked him wether there was no wine allowed, he said there was none given out. I directly went to Richard and told him, he said we must make a collection, he said he would be 5/- I said I would be the same. We then went to the Laundry and to all the rest of the servants & collected 1/- of every one. We got about £1-16-0 so there was 16s to go to the Violin players & the other to buy drink . . .

19th Dec Having slept over the stables I got up in good time and got my work done and was very busy doing one thing and another. Thomas brought the lamps from Stafford House . . . and we put them up in the room . . . at 5 the gardeners came in and some of the labourers and had tea . . . there was 2 or 3 dances before 8 o'clock when supper was announced. And as many as could sit down at once came and had supper and the next remained upstairs till these had finished . . . and after supper Mrs Adams and Mr Wright came in and Lord Stafford's health was drunk and then dancing commenced again we had in general punch to drink and plenty of ale and some little wine nagus . . . some of the maids went away about 3 but there was most of them that stayed till the finish which was about 7 or ½ past, we had the cushin dance to finish off with and we had tea in the servants hall about 8 as a sort of finish. I did not go to bed. . . . I got my work done and got on as well as I could, but I was very sleepy. Wm Thomson was here all day and he assisted me to wash up the glasses etc . . . The day passed over very heavy and by 9 o'clock at night there was not a body about the place there was no supper in the servants hall I went to bed about ten . . .

21st Dec I got my work done as well as I could but I was in very bad cue I started for London about 12 said my lessons and found my way home again as well as I could but almost half dead not having got over my dancing yet . . .

On Christmas day, Thomas's diary records things beginning to go wrong among the servants.

25th Dec Today being Christmas Day we had roast and ale in the servants hall and some of the maids came in and had some and some of the farm men . . . all the servants and labourers about the place dined in the servants hall except those in the stewards room & them in the kitchen. We had a very good dinner of roast beef and plumb pudding and all had a mince pie apiece and as much ale as they could drink . . . The housemaids made tea, the laundrymaids not having pleased Mrs Adams on Lord Stafford's birthday . . . after tea there was not much doing but playing at cards till supper time . . . at ½ past 8 we had supper and after supper I got a pewter plate and went upstairs over the hall . . . and we had a turn at what is called turning the trencher and there we kept it up till a little before 12 and then went down into the hall and began to play at cards again, some played at speculation and some at whist, I was in a speculative party, we were playing there till one o'clock when Mrs Adams suddenly made her appearance at the door and said that we must leave off playing and go to bed and accordingly all was obeyed and all the maids made their exit, some of the men went and some . . . began to play tossing, me for one and very soon lost all the pence that I had got, then Tom Gimbert and Omer's friend . . . created a quarrel, I then cut off to bed, after I was gone Tom put him out of the hall and made a great noise which brought Mrs Adams out again but they all went away without further disturbance

27th Dec I then walked to Stafford House I went into the Housemaids room and found them just beginning to have tea there was several strangers in the room but not above twelve in all, after tea a friend of Margrets gave us a tune on the violin and we had a country dance and so continued dancing till 3 o'clock in the morning and the gentleman played on his violin and I did not play at all we had plenty to drink and it was a very comfortable party and everything went on very comfortable we had some songs and different sorts of amusement I did not get to bed till 4 o'clock

The gardeners began preparations for their party on New Year's Eve. They collected fourteen bottles of liquor.

31st Dec I went to Waterloo house and bought myself a black silk cravat for 5/9d. As soon as I got home I shut up the house and lighted up and had some tea in the Kitchen with the maids . . . we have now 18 bottles. But . . . someone had told

Mrs Adams every thing about our goings on – how much drink we had bought and who bought it and how much it cost and every particular and a thousand other falsities, we concluded that Sarah Dairy had been doing it all or at least a greater part of it but however in spite of all about 7 the Gardeners came . . . we had supper at a ¼ past 8 and about 9 . . . they began to move up stairs the Nursery maids came down and the Kitchen maids came in, Richard led off the Triumph for the first dance Croucher and Smith were the violin players, I made some grog gin & water, brandy & water and rum, Sherry & Port . . . We bought some sugar and biscuits from Wandsworth, Anne Stillroom Maid gave me three plates full of biscuits, we kept on dancing and singing and we were dancing when the clock struck 12 . . . and then drunk a happy new year to all they continued dancing till 4 o'clock . . .

Tonight or at least last night after supper I went to Mrs Adams and asked her for some more ale for I said that . . . all the farm men were come up and we had nothing to give them, she said she was very sorry that we were not more united together. I told her I did not think there was any disunion amongst us and there was a great deal said between us but I found out it was Sarah who had been making herself so busy and saying all she could to prevent us having the dance, and I think Betsy had been doing all she could . . . it is all done out of spite & against the Nursery maids because the Gardeners took more notice of them than the rest . . . and so I ended the year 1838.

(Thomas, 'Journal', SRO D4177/1–2)

Frederick Gorst recalled Christmas dinner at Carden Park.

All the staff on the estate had been invited to the Christmas dinner, which was given in the servants' dining room in the Manor House. The gardeners had decorated the room and the fireplace with boughs of evergreen and holly. There was an enormous kettle hanging from a huge hook in the fireplace. It was about four feet in diameter and filled with hot beer, to which nutmeg, Jamaica ginger, cloves, and cinnamon sticks were being constantly added. This brew was kept simmering, but not allowed to come to a boil. All day long we kept replenishing the beer grog, and everyone filled his horn.

Four long tables and wooden benches had been set up for the dinner, which was served at one o'clock. First, a great hog's head, stuffed with sausage meat and pate de foie gras from the Squire's own geese, was carried in by four men and set upon a separate table. It had a shiny red apple in its mouth and the ferns and greens which decorated the huge board lent a pagan touch. Then came the cold meats and roasts. The main dish consisted of the finest joints of beef and Yorkshire pudding and many kinds of vegetables. And finally the plum pudding was brought in, burning and flaming with brandy.

The feast lasted for most of the afternoon, and by the time everyone had left the servants' hall of the Manor House Mr. Ling and I were almost too tired to serve Christmas dinner for the family and their guests.

And at Welbeck Abbey

Christmas Eve was a gala affair for the family and their close friends, and when they had exchanged their own gifts, the Duke and Duchess presented each of the Royal footmen with an envelope which was sealed in wax with the Portland crest. When I opened mine I discovered that I was richer by a five-pound note.

(Gorst, *Carriages and Kings*, pp. 46, 159)

Housekeepers were usually responsible for keeping a record of Christmas presents given.

Christmas Present Book from Alton Towers, home of the 20th Earl of Shrewsbury. Extracts from the list for servants, 1891

Not exceeding 3 guineas

House steward	Sleeve links and collar stud
Groom of the Chambers	Mackintosh
Housekeeper	Black silk dress
Valet	Gladstone bag

Chef de Cuisine	"
Head nurse	Travelling cloak
Governess (Miss Wright)	Timepiece
Stud groom (Malcolm)	Gladstone bag
" (Fred)	2 easy chairs
Head estate clerk (Robinson)	Pedestal lamp
Woodman (Ducie)	2 suits of clothes
Head gamekeeper	Portmanteau
Clerk of the Works	Sofa
Head gardener	Easy chair
Lady's maid	Umberella and
	crocodile bag

Not exceeding 2 guineas	
Second estate clerk (Clarke)	Chair
Foreman gardener (Alton)	Stationary cabinet
Coachman (Wilkinson)	Portmanteau
Under butler	Scarf pin
Not exceeding 30 shillings	
Barber	Trousers
1st cook boy	Kitchen knives
Electric engineer	Woollen shirts
Not exceeding 1 guinea	
Alton hall porter	Woollen shirts
Stable boy (Bob)	Gladstone bag
" (Jack)	Mackintosh
Steward's room boy	Mackintosh
1st footman (new man)	Gladstone bag
Scullery man	Trousers
Watchman	Breeches
Not exceeding 10 shillings	
Grate-cleaning boy	Guernsey and
	shirting
Alton gardeners	11 guerneys
Helen Gordon	Heliotrope dress
2nd Alton housemaid	Petticoat
3rd "	"
5th "	"
6th "	Boots

1st laundry-maid	Black dress
2nd "	Petticoat
3rd "	Print dress
4th "	"
1st still-room maid	Navy blue dress
2nd "	Black dress
Nursery-maid	Grey dress
Under lady's maid	Black dress

(SRO, Shrewsbury, D240/J/10/4)

By the early twentieth century, many of the old traditions seemed tawdry and humiliating, at least to Jean Rennie.

So, after an early dinner on Christmas Eve, we all trooped into the front hall – Mrs Preston in white, Molly and I in our print dresses and cap and apron, black stockings and shoes. The housemaids in black and white, and lace caps; Miss Bentley in a nice dark dress; the butler in his evening suit; and George in his wasp waistcoat and his tail-coat with brightly polished buttons.

We stood awkwardly together in one corner. . . . We all thawed a little at Sir James' patronising joviality. . . . The youngest son, Master Edward, shyly handed each one of us a parcel with a murmured 'Merry Christmas'.

Sir James made a little speech, which we all acknowledged with sheepish giggles, in which he thanked us for our service during the past year, and spoke of the nobility of service in a gentleman's house . . . Mrs Preston and Mr Carter left the hall and in a moment came back, Mr Carter carrying a big oval silver dish. . . . It was piled high with almonds and raisins. . . . The fruit and nuts seemed wet and were glistening under the lights.

Sir James put a match to the dish and all the lights were turned out. The little blue flames leapt amongst the fruit as the brandy burned.

Somewhere among that pile was a sixpence, and we had to put our hands in and grab a handful of the fruit and nuts.

George got the sixpence . . . we went back to our kitchen to open our presents.

I hugged my parcel tightly, dying to open it.

What would it be?

Black velvet? I did so long to be sophisticated in black velvet!

I opened the parcel.

There, in its hideous glory, was a length of that god-awful pink cotton – a length sufficient to make a morning dress – for work.

Not a piece of material for a dress for the very rare times I was off and could dress up. Not a dress to dance in – just the one thing that mattered to her Ladyship – work . . . I never made it up and I never wore it. . . . Next morning Sir James asked George for the sixpence! George just looked at him in amazement, then fished in his trousers pocket and threw a sixpence on the floor of the dining-room and walked out!

He nearly got the sack, but good footmen who would live in the country were scarce.

(Rennie, *Every Other Sunday*, pp. 84–5)

EIGHT

'We have gone through a good deal together' – servants and employers

Servants were wise if they never forgot the gulf existing between themselves and their employers. At times this must have been a difficult lesson, for relationships between the two could be very close, especially with long-serving career servants. The personalities of masters varied of course; some were very strict and distant, while others treated servants as equals; the ageing 5th Duke of Portland treated his like naughty children.

The closest relationships were with nannies and yet here too things could be fraught with danger. Some nannies invested a good deal of affection in their charges and although it might be returned and remembered with gratitude, there would always be constraint. Housekeepers too could become very much part of the family, a sheet anchor in a highly mobile world. Many must have identified themselves closely with family interests. But however close, the servant would need to be aware that they were still employees, with their own way to make in the world – the classic dilemma of the servant.

Servants were required to show deference in their behaviour to their masters, but this did not necessarily extend to their speech outside their presence. Diaries especially show occasional lapses of respect and exploitations of weaknesses.

Some relationships were extremely stormy or eccentric but lasted for decades. Of course personal servants were in a position of trust and confidence and when things went wrong within the family, they might well see things going on which later proved to be of consequence. So they were sometimes called as witnesses to testify about family behaviour, though cases where servants were called to give evidence about abuse towards themselves were very rare.[1]

Oral history does record recalcitrant servants. On one occasion the servants' hall at Dunham Massey rebelled *en masse* and went on strike when pieces of newspaper were found in their stew.[2] Correspondence, too, records a maids' strike at Welbeck and occasional disgruntled letters from individual servants. But if servants became disaffected, the much more likely route to release or redress was dishonesty.

There is plenty of evidence of dishonest, fraudulent and thieving servants. Quarter-session records are full of servants stealing clothes, food and money, mostly from a lower level of society than the country house. Family correspondence shows that servants had ample temptation and opportunity to steal. It was perhaps only in particular circumstances that people were found out. Smuggling food to take home to family was a widespread practice and, indeed, in some houses accepted as an inevitable part of the unchanging traditions of the country house, a hangover from the old days of bonded labour when food was issued in 'messes' which had to be shared out between three or four people.

SERVANT AND MASTER

Long-standing servants came to think of themselves as members of the family. After the death of the 3rd Duchess of Sutherland in 1888, her old housekeeper, Miss Anne Low, wrote to the Duchess's daughter, Lady Alexandra Leveson-Gower.

Miss Anne Low to Lady Alexandra, 10 December 1888

St. Raphaels, Torquay

Dearest Alix,

I have been very unwell for sometime, having heard of your being worse than your last dear lines led me to think. I have been quite unhappy till yesterday, when Lady Symonds sent me the good news that you were much better, for which I am most thankful. When you are really well, dearest, let me hear from you, giving me news of your brothers and their families. It seems so sad, that after more than 50 years of <u>such</u> close connexion with the family I should be so ignorant of all concerning it. I did not even know till the other day that Miss Blake was still with you. All will be well, however, if you be careful of your dear self and get well and strong . . . I wish you were with the young people of your family . . . There is a freshness and charm in the companionship of the young. I know this better than most people. I am busy at my 'bedsock' making again and shall send you a pair or two. May I beg of you not to pay visits in the depths of winter or early spring, as you did last year, particularly in the North of Scotland and the North of Europe. Even strong people do this at <u>great</u> risk. Don't write more than a line, till you are <u>quite</u> well, to assure me you are <u>really</u> getting on well. Remember me to Miss Blake,

God bless you, Dearest,

A. Low.

Mrs Emery was another old Sutherlands' housekeeper at Trentham. Over a period of less than two years there have survived eighty letters from 'old Emery' to her beloved Lady Alexandra.

Mrs Emery to Lady Alexandra, Tuesday, nd

Lilleshall
Newport
Shropshire

Dearest Darling,

Thank you so much for your dear letter this morning. I know, darling, if you do not write often you do not forget me, so do not worry your dear little self too much. I did not know you were in London and sent you a little root of musk to Torquay also a letter.[3] Ask Susan to say when she writes to me if you got them or if they were dead. I will send you some more. The poor little kitten that I told you about is dead. The cat and Jack are quite well. I have rather better accounts of my mother. I am so glad, darling, you are keeping so well. How very very sad about the Prince Imperial's death, tis very sad for his poor mother but I hope she will be able to bear it. I hope Harry is quite well and that you have some nice rides. Give my love to dear Harry with a kiss. I hope you found all your things, dear, accept a great deal of love and a number of kisses –

from your loving old Emery

(SRO, Sutherland D593/P/29/1/18 and 19)

Lady Alexandra seems to have had very good relationships with her servants. Housemaids confided in her about their boyfriends.

Mary Ford to Lady Alexandra, October 1890

209 Lancaster Rd
Notting Hill

My Dear Lady Alexandra,

You will be surprised to hear that it is all broken off with Tom and I. I have [found] out for myself that he is not going on as he ought to do and I find what your Ladyship said was quite true. Of course I feel it very much as it is not to say I have been with him a few weeks, but it is seven or eight years. I think he has got into bad company but I am very pleased to think I have found it out before we were married, it would have been much worse then. I have got another situation at 3 Park Street, Park Lane and I am going in on Monday. I am very sorry for Tom's Father and Mother, I am sure they will be very much upset. I will address this letter to your own house as I am not quite sure where you may be, so will close hoping to hear from your Ladyship soon.

Yours very obedient
Mary Ford

Same, nd

Thank you so much for your kind letter and it was very kind of you to answer so soon. But I think as you say Malady that I have done right by doing what I have done, although it is very hard after being so many years corresponding with each other. His mother is very much upset about it. My Mother has been up here for three days to see about it and expecting to take my things and myself back with her. But as I have just come into a situation and it is very comfortable so far, though it was not just what I wanted I shall try and stay until I can see something better. I am with Mr. Brunton as single handed housemaid. I am told he is a batchelor, he is a large stockbroker.

I shall be so pleased to see your Ladyship when you come to London. Hoping this will find you quite well

(SRO, Sutherland D593/P/29/1/20)

Lady Alexandra's closest relationship was with Miss Blake, the governess who became her companion. The following letters cover a period when the relationship between the two women was becoming difficult. The 25-year-old Lady Alexandra spent more time in London, working as a volunteer at St Bartholomew's Hospital and 'Blakie' was something of a supernumerary in the family's various country houses. In 1890 she left, thinking that she was no longer needed and took up a temporary post as governess with Lady Ilchester.

Miss Blake to Lady Alexandra, 14 June 1890

Easton Lodge, Dunmow, Essex

My dear Alix,

I go on Monday, to Daisy's, Tilney Street, Park Lane, London W. for 2 nights, and on Wednesday to Lady Ilchester's . . . for a month. It will seem strange but I will try and make the best of it. I have always heard they are nice people . . . I have several commissions, I must go to Mrs Chettles as my only garment does not fit and I am shabby enough already . . .

Believe me, yrs sincerely,
Blakie

Same, 15 July 1890

Holland House, Kensington, W.

My dear Alix,

. . . My task here will be no <u>easy</u> one for many reasons. The girl is not studious, backward, and a difficult temper to manage, but I shall have support from Ld and Ly Il. and with God's help and guidance I may, perhaps, accomplish more than I expect. You will feel relieved I am sure, and I am glad to spare you saying what, perhaps, in kindness you would rather shrink from. Y ou remarked to me when I suggested all this, that you could not be expected to live alone. But dear Alix, if your time is to be taken up by periodical visits to the Hospital and friends, I am useless . . .

<u>Please</u> write <u>by return</u> as the time is <u>short</u> and Lady Il. is in treaty with several who might take my place . . . . I should have liked to have come and talk matters over with you, but you might have had an engagement. Please do not leave my letter about. I have not written to Lord Stafford but you will of course tell him what I propose. I <u>hope</u> if we may part, it will be to remain friends. I shall ever look back with a feeling of gratitude to the years spent and made happy to me at Dunrobin and elsewhere . . .

Same, 17 July 1890

Many thanks for your letter. I should be sorry <u>indeed</u>, to put you to any inconvenience, but there is no use in returning to <u>what is past</u> and I <u>really</u> thought that, when a chance offered, it would meet your views, both as regards the expenses of my salary, travelling expenses and also living, that as we had been for the last months I had become thoroughly distasteful to you. Of course I felt it <u>deeply</u>, and you know what else I disapproved of, but all was in your own interest, not in <u>mine</u>. I think too many interfere and give advice. Whenever I venture with mine, I am told not to do this or that. You see, dear Alix, at my time of life it is rather hard to bear . . . Now if next year, please God, you go out in London, you will be with Lord Stafford, well naturally, there would be no room for me in a London house. There is so much to consider. (I am talking to the child and writing this, in between) but it is for you to say candidly if you think I am necessary to you. I have been 6 years with you, we have gone through a good deal together, so you have of course the first claim. At the same time, dear Alix, I must not lightly refuse Lady Ilchester's offer. I could never again go through the same anxiety as to finding a post. Just when I felt too disappointed, this turned up. Can you really say the same would not occur again? . . .

But if you really mean that you care to keep me I can tell Lady I that I feel it my duty to remain with you. I hope, please God, by the end of the year to have saved a sufficient sum which I shall sink (that means never see it again) but purchase with it a small annuity, on which, however, I could not live, but in case of being for months again without a shelter, I should have something to go upon. It does seem hard after a long life of really hard work, one is no better off, but my having remained so long in Germany, although passing pleasant and an interesting life, it has left me a few hundred pounds poorer. If I had them, I should be independent of all my fine rich friends and not owe one of them a shilling, as I do now.

. . . But what will be arranged now, between us, must be certain and remain. You see I have no home to go to, in an emergency, nor the means to be out of occupation for, perhaps, 6 months, as I was before when Mrs Wemyss so generously took me in, and no one else helped. Consult Lord Stafford and be guided by him, he is sure to say and advise the right thing.

Of course the life here would be much more arduous, but there is only one and I might, after all, fare much worse. Wherever I find happiness, I care not whether it be Little Hales or Holland House, or wherever. I think I am liked, really useful, appreciated and subjected to no annoyances. So now no more. I have written fully. Only think what will be for your own convenience, reflect well. I am ready to return and thank you much for the offer of a home. I know you mean it, but are you sure it can be done? In any case . . . at my time of life I cannot knock about any more. This has been offered, shall I refuse? I might get a companionship with some old lady afflicted with a temper, or with young ones where there would be much to contend with. Here Ld and Ly I promised to support me in every way . . .

(SRO, Sutherland D593/P/29/1/17)

Perhaps the fact that Lady Alexandra was obviously not strong was one of the reasons for the close relationships with her staff. Yet she does seem to have been an exceptional woman. Among her correspondence are letters from St Bartholomew's Hospital about her becoming not just a volunteer but a 'special probationer' nurse. She did in fact begin nursing in 1890, but died on 16 April 1891 aged 25, at Argyll Lodge, Kensington. Her death certificate records 'ulcerative endocarditis 5 months, cerebral embolism 1 week'. We do not know whether Blakie went back to live with Alexandra or whether she stayed with the Ilchesters, but she was one of the chief mourners at the funeral.

Nannies, of course, had especially close relationships with their charges. One of the Sutherlands' housekeepers, Mrs Ingram, had been nanny in various previous households and received letters from several 'old children', including the Earl of Drogheda and the Earl of Wharncliffe. Here the latter, Edward Montagu Stuart Granville Montagu-Stuart-Wortley Mackenzie, born 1827, writes to acknowledge his old nanny's congratulations on being advanced to the earldom.

The Earl of Wharncliffe to Mrs Ingram, 31 December 1875

Wharncliffe House, Curzon St., W

My dear old Nanny,

I am going to stick to the old name and be Earl of Wharncliffe – also Viscount Carlton. It is ages since I have seen your dear old face, and I could fall on your neck and kiss you now with as much tenderness as when I was a nasty, dirty little boy. God bless you, my affectionate old Nanny, your letter was a real pleasure to

Your loving old child
Wharncliffe

(SRO, Sutherland, D593/R/10/7)

In the 1830s, the FitzHerberts kept in touch with their old nanny and made great use of her. In semi-retirement, she lived with her husband on the estate at Tissington in Derbyshire, relaying instructions and messages to the house whenever the FitzHerberts were absent. In fact she acted as a sort of land steward – a role acknowledged by Lady Agnes FitzHerbert.

Selina FitzHerbert to Mrs Hardy, 2 April 1830

Farleigh, Maidstone

Dearest Nanny,

I was delighted to receive your nice long letter, and so were we all to hear from you; you cannot think how often we are all thinking and talking of you and wishing you were here – I have wanted you more than ever lately and you would have been pleased to see us all so happy – we only wanted dear Alleyne to be quite complete . . . but we want you sadly to tell all our jokes to and oh! my dear Nanny you may think how often I have longed for you lately – to coze with you as we have done so often – and now I want you more than ever to sneak into the old nursery corner at your tea time to have a cup of tea with you and a chat to comfort me . . . all the children are quite well and Augusta is so much improved and our dear Grandmama is much better . . . dear Nanny I must give my dear Mamma's messages – in the first place she wishes to thank you for seeing after the things and sending her word so well about them. She and I are always quite impatient to receive your letters, Dear Nanny. My Mamma would like the new closet to be painted white to suit the room and the door the same . . . and she wishes Mr Thos Hardy to set about this immediately . . . Thos Hardy is also to do your chimney in the bedroom and to do it very well and <u>thoroughly</u> and Mamma says you are not to neglect this because it is a job for you – as she will be equally angry if it is not well done as if those for herself were ill done and so you must see that it is nice as my lady says you really deserve a handsome reward for being such a good stewardess to her and my Mamma wishes Dick Marsh and Wm to make a real good path up to the Hennery for the children – and lay it with stone and gravel from the River – the other gravel is so full of lead it wd kill all the fowls. The door of the top room over the study, both of the closet and the room to be painted black as before – and the room to be white washed – we shall be very much obliged to you, dearest Mrs Hardy to see after these orders – and pray write again soon and tell us about everybody and things . . . My little Brothers and Sisters all desire their best love to you and a great many kisses. The children wish to remember them to Mr Hardy and do tell him they shall often come to see him and you when we get home again . . . Now farewell my dear old nurse – write again to your eldest child soon and believe her to remain ever yours gratefully attached, Selina FitzHerbert

Lord FitzHerbert to Mrs Hardy, nd

. . . Miss Augusta is much afraid that they will destroy her <u>Stable Cat</u> for killing some chickens; but begs that I will request you to see Dick Marsh <u>immediately</u> and desire him to feed the cat regularly <u>every day</u> as she thinks that it may be from want of food that she has killed the chickens as she shewed no propensity to destroy them while we were at home and she got regularly fed. She wishes at all events that her life should be spared till a trial of regular feeding should be made

I remain your friend
H FitzHerbert

(DeRO, FitzHerbert, 239m/F8196, F8212)

Servants could also be in effect the carers of elderly employers.

William Lanceley

. . . Her Ladyship had to be carried up and down stairs and wheeled about the rooms, and as time went on she got very feeble, and towards the last would only allow myself and the hall porter to carry her, declaring the other men servants shook her too much. This kept us both in constant attendance. One day she stayed in bed and I took the opportunity to go to the theatre. After I had left the house, Her Ladyship decided to get up and come downstairs. One of the other men had to take my place with the carrying-chair. Unfortunately Her Ladyship could not rest and wanted to go back to bed. When carrying her upstairs, the man slipped or stumbled and Her Ladyship slid out of the chair. Seeing I was not there, she asked for some one to lift her into the chair again. She was a heavy woman, and in trying to lift her back to the chair, she complained that they hurt her. When told I had gone to the theatre she said, 'Bring me some pillows and blankets. I will wait until he returns.'

A curious coincidence happened that night. On my arriving at the theatre, I discovered I had no money except twopence, with which I promptly took a bus and returned to Belgrave Square. On my arrival I was met by the hall porter, who related all that had happened. I at once went to the stairs, where I found Her Ladyship asleep, the maids sitting on either side of her. We placed the chair behind her, the maids holding it. Then striding over her and quietly putting my hands underneath her arms, I lifted her into the chair before she was well awake, and we carried her into her bedroom. . . .

Soon after this, Her Ladyship decided to sleep downstairs. This relieved us all, as it was better in every way. The doctor warned us that the end was approaching and a thinning out of the servants now took place. Hearing of a suitable situation, I applied and got it. I was sorry to go, for the place had been so full of life and sunshine. Shortly after I left, the dear old lady passed away in the arms of her servants. 'Take me in your arms, Margery,' were her last words, then resting like a child in its mother's arms, she passed peacefully away – a fitting end to one who loved her servants and was in turn beloved by them. Her Ladyship often said, 'The greatest blessing in old age is good health and a dear kind servant.'

(Lanceley, *Hall-Boy to House-Steward*, pp. 47–8)

Rosina Harrison found that even personal relationships were formal.

My relationship with Miss Patricia [aged 18] isn't easy for me to describe. We weren't friends, though, if she were asked today, she might well deny this. We weren't even acquaintances. We never exchanged confidences, never discussed people, nothing we said brought us closer; my advice might be asked about clothes or bits of shopping, but my opinions were never sought or given on her music or on the people we met or on anything that was personal to either of us, nor did I expect such attention or miss it at that time. That was the accepted way of things. It was different with Miss Ann; she was younger and as she grew up was more open with me – that is, until she went to finishing school in Switzerland. When she came back her attitude was the same as her sister's. We met again almost as strangers. . . .

(Harrison, *Rose*, p. 20)

In the nineteenth century most employers were very clear about what they expected of their servants in at least one respect – adherence to the Church of England.

Anne, 3rd Duchess of Sutherland, to Mrs Ingram, nd

Stafford House

Mrs Ingram,

. . . I have been rather vexed and surprised to find that both laundry maids are Roman Catholics – a thing I very much dislike as a rule, in the Establishment – I cannot understand the last one at least, having been engaged without my knowing it.

I have now seen a very nice looking young woman who would make a very good head one – if the present one now temporarily at the head (who was second) objects to this one being put over her, I think she had better leave.

I cannot go on with two Roman Catholics, for one because it was the cause of the last one leaving – and I would rather have none.

Yours truly,
A Sutherland

(SRO, Sutherland, D593/R/10/2)

Some employers found the relationship between master and servant difficult.

Edwin Lee worked as 2nd footman with Hon. Frederick George Wynn, Glynliven Park, Caernarvonshire.

Mr Wynn was easy to serve but he had his peculiarities. One that I found irritating and disturbing was that he always spoke to the servants with his back to them. It was almost as if we were some strange creatures that he couldn't bear to look at. It was probably because he felt no kind of affinity with the likes of us and this made him nervous and shy. He would bark when things went wrong but a barking back is not frightening, it needs an angry face to go with it.

(Lee, 'Page Boy's Story', pp. 98–9)

Can we see a change in servant–master relationships over time?

Margaret Powell's grandmother told her about the old days of the nineteenth century, typified by deference and closed villages.

She worked in a large manor house and the man who owned it owned the entire village; all the land for miles around and every cottage were owned by him too and he was very particular indeed about how they were kept. Nobody from outside could come and live in his village. He made sure that nothing and nobody changed. As Grandmother said, this system had its advantages because when the villagers were ill, medicines and food were sent down from the big house. But, she said, even so the villagers weren't grateful. They used to detest having to doff their caps to the squire who they felt was rude and arrogant to them. Still Grandmother reckoned that the villagers then had a better life than when things became freer for the working class. Because then nobody really cared at all.

(Powell, *Climbing the Stairs*, pp. 152–3)

Writing in 1892, John Robinson was very clear that the master–servant relationship was demoralising, and had deteriorated from the eighteenth to the nineteenth centuries.

How infinitely superior was the manly and self-respecting lacquey or major-domo of one hundred years ago to the servile and obsequious servant of modern days! . . .

To methodically perform certain stereotyped duties in a stereotyped manner is in service the highest virtue. . . . Any departure from certain conventional rules is sternly repressed, and yet, if an emergency finds him unprepared to take the initiative, he is sworn at for his incapacity. . . . If in any difficulty he ventures to make a suggestion, he at once evokes a more or less direct reminder of his position. A careful conning of his weekly book and a critical surveillance of the monthly bills convinces him he is not to be trusted. . . . There is nothing more readily makes a rogue of a man than systematic distrust. . . . He argues that he is not to be trusted, therefore there can be no breach of confidence in taking all he can get. He does not care a straw for the wine or the stores, but he learns to take a pleasure in showing that his would-be clever master can be 'done'.

(Robinson, 'Butler's View', pp. 204–7)

Certainly it is difficult to envisage many Victorian masters being as tolerant as his eighteenth-century employer was towards John Macdonald, the footman who had fathered a child on a groom's daughter.

. . . my master went to Glasgow on business. Going through Kilburnie parish, he asked questions, and said: . . . 'Have you not a child in this parish?' 'Yes, sir, in that village before you.' 'Well, you may go and see him: I shall ride gently on.' I went, and saw Amelia and the boy, and, having had something to drink, went after my master.

(Macdonald, *Memoirs*, p. 52)

Sexual abuse of servants by masters is one of the great themes running through the history of domestic service, but one which is frustratingly difficult to document. Neither party would be likely to want to see details consigned to a written record. Only occasionally do servants' autobiographies give glimpses.

In the 1830s and 1840s Christian Watt was a laundry maid in Lord Saltoun's house at Philorth and its 'overflow' Kinglasser, in north Aberdeenshire.

The Fraser sons . . . would try and take on the girls, but we were well prepared. One morning, while giving a hand to make beds at Kinglasser, a Capt. Leslie Melville put his arms around me and embraced me. I dug my claws in his face and with all the force I could I tore for all I was worth, his journey into flirtation land cost him the skin of his nose.

(Fraser, *Christian Watt*, p. 40)

FIGHTING BACK

Servants were not always subservient and were perfectly capable of standing up for themselves.

In the 1830s William Tayler was hardly respectful towards his mistress, but neither was he without affection.

19th. . . . Our old Lady is got quite well, thinks of little else but playing cards and paying visits all the time. I was takeing in breakfast to the drawing room – she was talking about cards and who was good players and who was bad ones and choseing the people she should have to her next party and when it should be. When I went to take the breakfast away, she was fretting because her violets were all withered and had lost their smell. When I went to take lunch up, she was making matches or candlelights. When I took lunch away, she was reading a novel with the Bible laying by her, ready to take up if any body came in. . . . At tea time, she was talking about china, how much was broke in her house and what it would cost to replace it again. I think these were excelent ideas for an old Lady near eighty years of age on a Sunday, but for all this she is not a bad one in the end.

April 22nd . . . Took the young gent to the coach office and sent him off into the country again, which is the best place for such cattle. . . .

May 19th. Got up with a headache and feel stupid all day. Been out with the carriage this afternoon with Miss P. She kept me out longer than I thought she aught to of done, therefore I gave her a little row for it. I hope it will do her good. I served the old lady the same way the other day and it did her a deal of good, and I have no doubt that it will act the same in this case.

(Wise, *William Tayler*, pp. 19, 29, 36)

Rosina Harrison had a long but stormy relationship with Lady Astor.

The moment I began one thing, Lady Astor wanted another. She was quite unpredictable, and always unappreciative. She was sadistic and sarcastic. If I reminded her of something she'd say, 'I never need telling anything twice, thank you, Rose.' She mimicked me, not out of fun but to hurt. She'd change her mind purposely over her clothes, accuse me of not getting things right, and call me a liar if I protested to her. She shouted and rampaged like a fishwife, though without using bad language. . . .

And she'd use my rank to belittle me. 'You're as bad as a housemaid, Rose,' she said to me once.

'You ought to know better than to speak to me like that,' I replied. 'My sister Ann is a housemaid, a good one, and she's a good person. I expect there are a lot of them who are better people than me. You've no right to talk of housemaids as though they are the lowest of the low, you only belittle yourself.'

And she recalled one occasion at the Astors' house in Sandwich when one servant fought back.

We had just gone to bed when there was the sound of a shot, and shortly afterwards I heard Tommy Phipps[4] shouting from downstairs. The whole house turned out in their dressing gowns. Mr Tommy was trembling from head to foot and stuttering and spluttering; eventually we gathered that a man had appeared at his door, demanding his money or his life. He'd given him a pound, which was all he had; the man had taken it from him, fired at him, missed, and run out into the night. It was like a scene from a detective play. The footmen seized whatever weapons they could from the kitchen and rushed outside, the housekeeper fainted, Mr Billy called his dogs and went off with a knife, and his lordship followed with a golf club. . . . Eventually two carloads of police arrived . . . an inspector was left behind to cross-examine us servants. To everyone's amazement, John, the young footman, suddenly burst out that he had been the villain of the piece. . . . It was several days before we were able to put the pieces together. Apparently Tommy Phipps, who was unpopular with the staff anyway, had been getting at John, taking advantage of his position to tease him out of his wits. So John decided to get his own back. He used a toy pistol and planned eventually to reveal his identity. He hadn't expected Mr Tommy to get so scared. His lordship, although he reprimanded John, was also extremely angry with Mr Tommy, and he held him responsible for the whole incident. The police inspector apparently mumbled something about arresting John . . . but his lordship had already tried the case and administered the sentence, so he was quickly silenced. In those days even the police knew their place.

(Harrison, *Rose*, pp. 80, 84, 160–1)

Some servants were rude about their employers behind their backs.

Gordon Grimmett

Mrs Sandford, Hettie, or Hett as her husband called her, or 'That tart from Streatham' as she was known in the servants' hall, was of an indefinable age. She might have been anything from forty to fifty. She had, as the saying was, 'let herself go'. She'd have gone still further if it hadn't been for her corsetier. The lady's maid used to come sweating down to the servants' hall. 'Give me a cup of tea, love, I need it, I've just got a quart into a pint pot!' According to her Hett was over fourteen stone. 'It's a lot of ground for me to cover,' she'd complain.

(Grimmett, 'Lamp Boy's Story', p. 42)

It was unusual but not unknown for servants to complain formally, even to go on strike, not usually about wages but about some other injustice or deficiency.

Lavinia Swainbank, housemaid to a titled family in the country, reached breaking point over breakfast.

. . . a dish of very tainted bacon was served up for breakfast in the Servants' Hall. No one was able to eat it and just made do with bread and jam. However, when it was served up a second morning this was just too much, and we were in a distinctly explosive mood. There was some discussion of what steps should be taken. The one I suggested was decided, if I was willing to be spokeswoman. This was the plan – that a deputation should take the bacon for her Ladyship's inspection. Through the head house-maid we were granted an audience with the august body. With shaking voice and knees I passed the dish of rancid bacon under her nose.

She was as indignant as we were, and said that for some time she had doubted the authenticity of her household accounts as they were enormous, but feeling that the staff were being well catered for had done nothing about it. . . . Two hours later an ex-Cook left by taxi with a mound of luggage and a set of golf clubs!

(Swainbank, p. 226)

At Welbeck during the 1870s the correspondence between the bachelor 5th Duke of Portland, then in his 70s, and his agent William Cripwell reveals a series of minor skirmishes with some of his maids.

Duke of Portland to William Cripwell, 8 August 1873

Welbeck

Sir,

. . . The strike of the maids is rather amusing. It is partly my fault perhaps for having thrown all the Printed Circulars I recd about Women's rights into the Waste Paper basket. I don't doubt we shall have to give way . . .

When I went outside after having glanced over your letter I was under the impression that Mary Gorrell had started for the same pay in all respects as your own Cook . . . I had observed that the tone of her other letter to you looked very much as if she thought we couldn't do without her & that she might dictate her own terms. I have every reason to believe she is an honest and trustworthy servant – for the H. Keeper who came from Mrs C . . . thought extremely well of her – & said she always knew better where to find anything wanted than she did herself. She was subsequently discharged without my being consulted by another H. Keeper who was anything but a trustworthy servant and without a shadow of justifiable cause. She was thereafter returned to the situation and it is not at all unlikely that her head is turned . . . At present she is . . . Head maid acting as Deputy H. Keeper in Mrs Jolly's absence. I myself stopped her scrubbing the floors!! a few years ago.

Same, nd

. . . in looking at your letter again about the maids I see they have never said what increase of B[oar]d Wages they expect. Mary Gorrell asks to have the same as Jane & Co who have not it appears applied for an increase.

As to her being called Mrs Gorrell . . . I query whether she will ever accomplish that end unless she takes another Place where she has no old acquaintances.

If the Queen was to make her a Lady she w[oul]d still be called plain Mary here by her old female servants . . .

Same, nd

It has occurred to me that perhaps it w[oul]d be as well not to give too much an acquiescence to the Maids' demands as they may think they have not asked enough.

. . .

A couple of years later there were more problems caused by the fiery-tempered Mary Gorrell and her niece, also called Mary Gorrell.

William Cripwell to the Duke of Portland, 20 July 1877

> The Old Hall Hotel
> Buxton

My Lord Duke,

. . . Mary Gorrell

I had a long talk with her the last time I was at Welbeck & hoped I had succeeded in 'calming her down', but she is a somewhat unmanageable piece of goods. She complains of John

Harrington's manner towards her and that he did not address her as he might – John was not at Welbeck that day or I should have advised him to <u>overwhelm</u> her with politeness for a time which would perhaps bring her to her senses. From her own showing I believe John had merely delivered your Grace's message about the windows being left open as he received it, but Mary is so 'touchy' when she is in a temper I have no doubt it is difficult to speak to her at all without giving offence.

I think it would be good for the peace of the Household if Mary's niece goes as there has always been a good deal of jealousy about her & I think she probably inherits some of her Aunt's temper . . .

The Duke of Portland to William Cripwell, 22 July 1877

Sir   Mary Gorrell [the niece]

. . . I had always thought very well of the maid both as to manner and temper and hard-working and when I heard she was going I sent to say I wd see her before she went to hear all particulars and help her to a place if I could. She sent back word that she did not expect a h[ead] m[ai]d's place and wanted a 2nd wch sounded very odd and I concluded she had either quarrelled with her aunt – or had taken huff about some orders I had given via John Harrington and she is not the first of the maids by 2 or 3 who has been herself ridiculously sensitive about being found fault with for some insignificant piffle. The only fault in general to be found with the maids is that they do a good deal too much and are often hard working . . . I had a long talk with her but cdn't get her to give the slightest reason for her wanting to go. She only assured me she had had no words with her aunt . . . I at last persuaded her to change her mind & say she wdnt go – Let us hope she won't be spoilt by being so pulled. Both aunt and niece now know they are valued servants but I hope they won't presume upon that . . .

(NA, Portland, DDP6/13/21/248–50, 259, 260, DDP6/13/25/70, 78–81)

DISHONEST SERVANTS

Petty theft must have been a great temptation to many servants, a fact evidenced by witness statements in quarter-session records. In this case from Huntingdon quarter-sessions both culprit and witnesses were servants in a gentry country house.

Huntingdon Quarter Sessions, Midsummer, 1832

> The Deposition of Harriett Strangwood – servant to Thomas Lindsell of Hemingford Grey in the said county, Gentleman, taken on oath this 29th day of June 1832 . . . touching the loss of a shirt by the aforesaid Thomas Lindsell:
>
> Who saith that she is servant to Thomas Lindsell of Hemingford Grey aforesaid and has the Care and Charge of her Master's Linen and she on the 12th day of June instant (St Ives second fair day) saw one of her Master's Shirts worn by the Groom of her Master named John Nicoll – On the same day the same John Nicoll was employed in assisting to wash her Master's Sheep and he fell into the River . . . John Nicoll had changed his Shirt in the Stable . . . the said Shirt is the Property of her said Master and has been in her Custody ever since and was of the value of seven shillings, that she told her Master of the same only last Night.

> Deposition of Charles Earl, servant to the said Thomas Lindsell:
>
> Who saith that his fellow servant Harriett Strangwood having communicated to him . . . that the Groom named John Nicoll had one of her Master's shirts on, and the said John Nicoll having on that day fallen into the River & changed his shirt in the Stable, he told the said Harriett Strangwood he would go with her and look at the Shirt. They accordingly went & he said Harriett Strangwood took the said Shirt out of the Saddle House . . . quite wet.

> Examination of John Nicoll of Hemingford Grey . . . servant to Thomas Lindsell of Hemingford Grey:
>
> Who having heard the Depositions . . . read over to him & being cautioned not to say any thing against himself saith 'that

he brought the said Shirt from Home with Him & bought the Cloth at Cook's the Drapers at Huntingdon'.

(CROH, HCP/1/16 June 1832)

Other examples come from family letters. Here the Bagot family fell prey to an unscrupulous cook.

LN to William, 1st Baron Bagot, 16 June 1789

Norwich

Dear W,

When I left town I told you I had no occasion to trouble you for a loan of any dollars. A very unpleasant circumstance, for the discovery of which I am indebted to the care of my old trusty servant Martin, may make it necessary for me to call upon you both for your assistance and advice. The case is this – all the while we were in town Mrs Bagot regularly settled her weekly housekeeping account – and had receipts from those Tradesmen where we had Bills, every Monday morning – and a fourpenny Receipt in full of all demands when we came away. It now appears that those receipts were all forged by the Cook who marketed for us – and that she never paid the Bills for which she received the money – this woman we had a very good opinion of – she has lived with us only about a twelve month; and happily was never with us in town before – I am now endeavouring by the help of Martin to get at the extent of this distressing business – If it goes no farther than our Housebook the account for the loss will not be to a very great amount, supposing me liable to pay everything over again . . . Those Tradesmen whom we have dealt with for years and who knew our regular mode of proceeding are ill justified in their connivance – But if the claim is good on the part of others whom we never had any account with at all – God knows where it may stop; or how I can ever feel myself at rest – or indeed how anyone who does not go to market himself can ever be safe . . . We have not said a word of it here amongst our own servants as yet – and the Woman is still with us . . . I shall hear more today or tomorrow . . . If anything occurs to you as prudential for me to do under the such circumstances pray suggest it – for the situation is very distressing – What I had best do with the Woman when the scene opens, I don't know . . .

> Let me hear from you – kind love to all
> Yours, dear W, ever most affec^{tely}

(SRO, Bagot, D3259/13/19B)

Ernest King came across dishonest servants.

Have servants been worse than any other class in bending or breaking the Ten Commandments? Actually, the first 'smart boy' I ran into was a smart girl, to put it mildly. She was a French maid in Mrs. de Wichfeld's house in Paris. Just after Mrs. de Wichfeld and her husband left for America I had seen one of the French chambermaids leave the house, not once, but four times, carrying huge brown-paper parcels. It caused me to wonder. Mr. de Wichfeld's valet had asked me to keep an eye on Mr. De W.'s clothes while he was away, to open the doors of his wardrobes when it was sunny to give them an airing. I went to his dressing-room where I knew one wardrobe contained nothing but his shirts and underclothes and one drawer nothing but very expensive pyjamas of medium and light-weight silk. Each pocket was embroidered with a large crown and 'de W' underneath. All were now missing. So also was an enormous bottle of perfume, as big as a pickled-walnut jar, from his dressing-table.

I waited for the girl to go out the following day and then searched her bedroom. Obviously I needed proof positive before making any fuss. I could find nothing. The following day I made another search. Again nothing and then as I was about to leave her room something prompted me to lift her pillow. And there was one pair of the pyjamas, in an exquisite shade of mauve, I remember. The pocket with the monogram had been cut off and the cord from the trousers removed and replaced by elastic, presumably for her own use. There was no sign of the perfume.

Later, I made a further search. Down on my hands and knees I saw below and behind a chest of drawers a trap door in the wall, which allowed workmen to inspect the attic. I opened it, felt around, and on the left side I came across a dozen large medicine bottles. I drew the cork of one and sniffed. It must obviously have been filled from the large bottle taken from Mr. de Wichfeld's room. . . .

(King, *Green Baize Door*, pp. 54–5)

Trust was an important element in the servant–master relationship, as also in dealings between servant and servant. In 1832, William Lewis, the Trentham agent of the Sutherlands, had to deal with an unpleasant situation relating to the Trentham housekeeper, Mrs Dean, who was leaving due to ill health. Correspondence with his superior agent, James Loch, away in London, reveals a slowly dawning disillusionment with a woman he had previously liked.

William Lewis to James Loch, 4 April 1832

Mrs Dean sent for me . . . and seemed in a very great distress and she acknowledged she had not saved a single shilling but is desirous of setting up a little shop in Newcastle to sell groceries and confectionary goods. Lord Stafford has the house lately occupied as a public office in Newcastle Road if you should approve of her going there. I doubt not she would soon get a little business that would maintain her, the location is good. I should be most happy to throw my little influence in her favour for I do consider she has been a very good and faithful servant to Lord and Lady Stafford . . .

Same, 8 April

I received yours of the 6th. I have had conversation with Mrs Dean and told her that you would be happy to serve her but not in the way she wishes. She seems now much bent about going to Newcastle. It would be impossible for me or any one else to say that she will be successful in business but I really think she would have a very fair chance . . . She says she is not in debt to anyone.

Same, 17 May

There has been some very unpleasant reports about Mrs Dean packing up and sending off some heavy packages from the Hall, and I have this day the enclosed letter from Kirkby.[5] This is altogether a most distressing circumstance, if anything is wrong the woman should have so far forgotten herself in the honest discharge of her duty . . .

Same, 22 May

I duly received your very kind and feeling letter relative to Mrs Dean. I really don't know that any circumstance ever gave me more real uneasiness. The reports I was obliged to hear and I was also bound to communicate the same to you . . . she is certainly in great tribulation still. I find from her conversation she does not wish the boxes opened, but only the hampers examined that were returned from Woolleys. But in my opinion for a thorough justification of her conduct she should not hesitate to open every box and parcel she may have. Her present weak state of health and the affair altogether so unlooked for proves very distressing to my feelings.

Same, 29 May

After the examination of Mrs Dean's boxes which displayed a disgraceful scene of robbery yesterday, I was so much agitated and affected that I was really unwell all day. The hampers were examined first and contained some dozens of home made wine such as Gooseberry, Ginger. The boxes being after opened contained nearly a general collection of every article necessary for housekeeping, many of which she claimed as her own property, which however, is doubtful. Mrs Cleaver[6] and I did not feel disposed to dispute with her except as far as the linen went. She has still a great quantity of it of every description apparently recently marked. Several of the hand towels are so marked, but she gave them up as Lady Stafford's property, the 'S' appears recently put on. There is still a very great deficiency in the linen. We received from out of the boxes 10 dinner damask napkins, 7 table covers, 35 chamber towels, 3 pillow cases, 8 waiting napkins, 1 damask table cloth, 9 table cloths for the steward's or housekeeper's room, 2 glass cloths, 3 pair of sheets. She also exhibited from the boxes quantities of tea, sugar, coffee, foreign wine, soap, candles, mops and many new brushes for shoes and house cleaning, all of which she acknowledged to be the property of Lady Stafford. A more barefaced robbery could not possibly be effected. It is dreadful to contemplate such proceeds and to witness such depravity in one who had every confidence placed in her and it was amazing how hardened she appeared. As for the linen she said it was old and she was entitled to it, but Mrs Cleaver told her she had taken the best and left the old. Mrs Cleaver is to be again amongst the linen today and will be able to give you some account of what is deficient. I can opine you I am much pleased at the conduct of Mrs Cleaver in this affair and it is most desirable for her comfort and the peace of the establishment that Mrs Dean be moved from the house instantly. She is quite able to be moved but of course I await your answer. The articles enumerated (except the linen) remain in Mrs Dean's bedroom. Please say how I am to act with them and her. I never was so deceived in a character in my life and it is really enough to drive confidence from being placed in any one. Do let me hear from you as soon as you have seen Lady Stafford, for I feel so very uncomfortable.

Same, 2 June

I duly received yours of the 30 ult. and am glad that my conduct on a late occasion has met with Lord and Lady Stafford's approval. It was necessary for securing back what belonged to the family to have another examination of the boxes and a general look through every drawer in the room, which took place yesterday. I thought proper to send for the husband. He came and went through the unpleasantness with me and behaved himself with much propriety – the articles which we claimed were taken from her and the boxes again packed. I would not allow Mrs Cleaver and one of the Girls to leave her until all was packed and her out of the house. I went to the Inn and bespoke a room for her, it being a wet day. She goes off tomorrow to her friends in the North. I told the husband that

Lord and Lady Stafford could not be expected to do anything for her after her infamous conduct. On our second examination we certainly found many articles missing that we formerly saw and from the arrangements I had made I felt confident nothing would be got away without a connivance with some of the Girls. This deficiency annoyed me much and when the girls were told of it by Mrs Cleaver they all declared their innocence. The woman that attended the wretch, for I can call her nothing else, was also examined and from her we found that she had been sent out of the room and on her return found the room in an intolerable stench from burning such as hair brushes, mops or flannel. Drops of glass had been found in the ashes and the nail of a new mop. Not a doubt remains in my mind but that the vile wretch had committed many articles to the flames. His Lordship may here say that I ought to have taken the boxes away out of her room. But the whole was so bundled up with her own apparel that I felt a delicacy in doing so. I thought I had so arranged so as to prevent any of the articles being conveyed away and all would be found again. But who could have dreamt of such depravity or who could guard against such a Devil . . .

(SRO, Sutherland, D593/K/3/2/12)

NINE

'And a nice bit of fun she is made of' – relationships with servants and family

Though the good nature or otherwise of the employer was critical in setting the foundation for a happy house, most servants were affected in their daily lives more by the attitudes of their co-workers. Some households were clearly well run, with servants helping each other. Elsewhere, servants could create hell for each other. Jealousies and backbiting were rife in the contained atmosphere of the country house, where social relationships were indivisible from work. The degree of integration between these two aspects of life is illustrated by the widespread tradition of calling servants by their Christian name and then their position – for example, Thomas the Sutherlands' footman's references to 'Sarah Dairy' and 'James Porter'.

Menservants in particular might have problems. Some clearly enjoyed their service in a world totally divorced from the reality of their own existence; others seem to have longed for an escape from an ill-fitting and deferential domestication.[1] Release could come in many ways – petty squabbling, youthful horseplay, relationships with women. Homesickness was a common complaint among so many youngsters taken out of their home environment for the first time at an early age – before compulsory schooling perhaps as young as 9 or 10 years old. There must have been many a servant who cried herself to sleep and tales of runaways are fairly numerous, especially among girls.

Sexual relationships between servants were not, of course, supposed to happen, given a vigilant upper management. Admirers from outside were also frowned upon partly for moral reasons but partly also from considerations of domestic economy – a good deal of food could go missing that way. It is clear, however, that servants themselves regarded domestic service as a good marriage market for girls – where better could they meet a variety of eligible young men, more exciting or exotic perhaps than those available from their own village? At least from the Edwardian period onwards there was very little status in service; as one lady's maid put it: 'You were a nobody; marriage was the way out of it.' Yet servants always needed to watch their reputations. Even in the eighteenth century, a manservant could get to the point where no respectable country house would employ him.[2]

If a woman servant did decide to marry, she would leave service – after all, she could not have two full-time jobs. The only exception to this rule was the occasional married housekeeper, but even this was frowned upon. Butlers and other senior male staff were allowed to marry but had to rent or lease a suitable cottage for their family. If this was on the estate where they worked they were in a difficult situation if they wanted to leave or were sacked, as they would lose their home as well as their job. If it was further afield they could end up not seeing their family for years, other than for short breaks.

Keeping in touch with family – whether marital or parental – was important and sometimes difficult. Domestic service as a trade tended to run in families and, as Eric Horne pointed out, it served to scatter brothers and sisters who moved around the country from situation to situation.[3] A conscious effort must have been needed to visit and correspond, although some families would help by allowing the cost of servants' letters to be covered by their own frank. Employers' attitudes varied to 'kitchen visiting' by friends and servants from other houses, but most would allow servants to entertain close family members to a meal or even an overnight stay, as a means of encouraging stable relationships.

RELATIONSHIPS WITH OTHER SERVANTS

In a closed community, friendships with co-workers were important.

Dorothy Fudge

> The other staff were kind to me, and always had an excuse for me if anything went wrong – like the time I went out to talk to Horace one night, after supper. The colonel rang for me and the lady's-maid answered, and said: 'Park is washing her hair, Sir.' 'Well', he said, 'when she comes in, tell her I wish to speak to her.' We were especially asked not to go out after supper.
>
> (Fudge, *Sands of Time*, p. 26)

Eric Horne

> There was a goodly company of us in the servants' hall at night, as the grooms and the undergardeners would come in, and wash up all the silver and glass in the pantries; more for company than anything else, for there was nowhere for them to go for miles, in the evenings. So that by the time we had finished waiting dinner, all the glass and silver would be washed up and put away. All we had to do was adjourn to supper. There was the usual old-fashioned usages observed in the servants' hall, such as drinking the 'Health' every day, etc., also a certain amount of Esprit de Corps among us all. . . . I shall never forget one day. The head laundry-maid took my face between her hands and kissed me before them all, she said she could not resist it. She was a woman of forty, stout and buxom and I a chubby boy of eighteen, though I went as aged twenty. I also went crimson.
>
> (Horne, *What the Butler Winked at*, p. 64)

Among youngsters, there was a lot of horseplay.

Charles Cooper

> All manner of games or tricks were played on one another. If you asked for the butter the plate was passed along upside down; this happened once too often, for it dropped right off, right into the steward's room boy's cup of tea. . . .

> (Cooper, *Town and Country*, p. 57)

Gordon Grimmett

> There was an oil lamp outside [the butler's] room and the stairs up to my bedroom overlooked it. When Bob Huthwaite and I were retiring for the night I bet him he couldn't spit the wick out. Leaning over the bannisters, with my first shot I hit the side of the lamp which exploded with a report like a shotgun. We dashed upstairs but Mr. Brazier was quicker. He flew out of his door, realised what had happened, and who had done it, and he barked at us to report to him the following morning. When we did, he dressed us down and made our lives hell for the rest of the week.

> (Grimmett, 'Lamp Boy's Story', p. 30)

Eric Horne

> One night we arranged to have a game with the under butler . . . we tied a string to the corner of his bedclothes, waited till we thought he had gone to sleep, then we began gently to pull his bedclothes off. But he had not gone to sleep, but had discovered the plot, and was waiting for us with the wooden bar that kept his bed up in the day time. He shot out after us, and laid on with the bar . . . but it was all taken in good part.

> (Horne, *What the Butler Winked at*, pp. 66–7)

But many younger servants suffered the misery of homesickness.

Margaret Thomas

I was rather homesick at first. . . . In my new place the one thing seemed efficiency, it wasn't what you were but how well you did your work. I found it so all the way through: the heads of each department usually engaged their 'unders', one was given no quarter and expected none, if you couldn't do your work, either through ill-health or any other cause, you had to go, there were plenty of people to replace you.

The fourth housemaid, who did nothing but servants' rooms, found me in tears one day, and gave me some advice I have never forgotten. 'Sing at your work,' she said, 'when you feel low.' Often I have mingled my tears with the washing-up water while I sang to keep my spirits up; ever since then I have developed an awful habit of singing whether I felt 'high' or 'low,' usually hymns which have the best rhythm for working.

(Thomas, 'Green Baize Door', p. 84)

Dorothy Fudge was an under-nurse at Hucknall, near Nottingham, aged 17 when she decided to run away.

It was so boring that, about the third week, I got up early one morning and cycled out to find someone I could hire, to fetch me and my luggage the following day. . . . He came with a horse and trap and I was ready, bicycle and all. We arrived at the station and the porter came and took my cycle off the cart and put it on the train, which was in, and away it went with my bike – but not me or my luggage. The porter said: 'Don't worry, my dear. You go on the next train and you'll find the bike waiting for you when you change at Birmingham.'

It was there when I arrived, so all was well, except I discovered that I only had enough money to take me to Bath. At Bath I told a porter my story, and asked him to ring the station master at Sherborne, telling him I would pay my fare as soon as I was home and could ask my father for the money. Mr Lazenby, the station master, knew me well enough, and replied: 'Yes, of course, send her on. I know her quite well and it will be alright.'

By the time we were approaching Sherborne I had been

travelling for eleven hours, and was very tired, and so when I looked out of the window and saw our dear house at Castleton, I was very glad. And there were my father and two brothers standing close to the railway line! I thought: I wonder who they're expecting? Then I waved to them and they saw me – and off came my father's cap and he threw it up in the air in excitement! (I had no idea they knew I had run away, but they had received a telegram in the morning from my employer to say I had left and they knew not where.) When I arrived at the station, there were my mother and aunt, looking frightened as they hardly dared hope to see me. But I increased their fright by running straight past them – there were no toilets on the trains in those days!

(Fudge, *Sands of Time*, pp. 19–21)

Enclosed communities like country houses must have been prey to squabbles, as illustrated by this letter from the farm steward at Trentham to the housekeeper.

John Reid to Mrs Ingram, 11 August 1875

Trentham Farm
Dear Mrs Ingram,

I am in receipt of your note and the contents has rather astonished me – now will you be good enough to say who is in the habit of carrying off the Laundry coals at the same time I hope you will kindly give me your authority for saying so – The last Coals carted to the Laundry was put into the Cellar the next day after their arrival consequently they could not be carried away – we have had plenty of Coals in the Farm yard and had no need to take the Laundry Coals – if you will allow me to give you an advice don't be too ready to believe the Laundry people in the matter if they chance to burn too many Coals tis very easy to transfer the blame to others. You threaten to complain to Mr. Menzies. You can do so if you see proper and I will be prepared to explain matters to him when he speaks to me on the subject – tis very easy to write scolding letters but you should be quite sure of the right party before you do so.

Madam, I am yours etc John Reid

(SRO, Sutherland, D593/R/10/7)

Thomas the footman

Sept 19 . . . the still room maid asked me to break some sugar for her & I said that I would as soon as dinner was over. So as soon as we had wiped up . . . I went into the still room and began to break. Charly directly came & looked about & sat himself down by the fire but did not say anything. Presently the bell rang, he says: 'that is the bell to clear the room' So away he went. I went directly after him. When we had brought the things down into the pantry he catches up a tray & takes it into the still room & began to break sugar I went into the Kitchen & got a little cherry tart off Julia & went into the pantry again. Charly comes in. I says you have took my job of me in breaking sugar & he says that is none of your work. It is mine I did it last night & you have no business there at all. O very well says I, I did not profer myself . . .

Today at dinnertime there being a little animosity between Charly and Charlotte so while we were at dinner they had a few words one with the other while all the people were at dinner, foolish people. Charles I think is too bad for he is always talking about other people behind their backs.

Sept 20 . . . At night when it was time to light up I went into the lamp place to fetch a lamp for the pantry. Charles always requires 4 of the same sort and there being but 4 left I took one of them. Charly said I should not have it. I said I would & took it. He followed me to the pantry but he did not get it. Presently he came again I had it in my hand he caught hold of it & I let it go. I then called him a stupid blockhead. He did not speak but went sulkily away . . .

Thomas was still a young man and very impressionable where women were concerned. M (Martha) was a long-standing girlfriend whom he'd met while in service with the Wilbrahams in Cheshire. She now worked in London and he was still taking her out but rather begrudgingly, for there were other attractions.

2nd Jan At ¼ before 6 we started for Drury Lane theatre there was some little said where we should go I said into the Pit and the others said into the 2/- Gallery and in the gallery we went there was four of us, M, Elizabeth and John Nott. I paid for M and myself there was a pantomime and another piece called Wm Tell, I didn't think much of it there was a great deal of fun but to make short of it I don't like plays and it is not to please myself that I go to them . . . we came out I got a Hackney coach and came to WH and had a little supper and then made my exit first lending M 10/- till she gets her wages it has cost me tonight 4/- going into the theatre 2/- Hackney coach and 1/- for drink in all 7/- . . .

1st April I went to call on M and found her at home . . . she seemd very much put out because I could not stay a little while but I did not say much I did not stay many minutes

4th April . . . I brought Anne Lakin a new watch today . . . paid £5 15 6 for it and a very pretty watch it was . . .

23rd April I promised to go with Sarah to day to Chiswick but coming on to rain prevented us from going so we are to go on Thursday . . .

25 th April Got up and got my work done and got my dinners done and a little before 2 we started for Chiswick it was a beautiful day and we had such a pleasant walk we cross'd over the ferry and got there by a ½ past 3 had tea and then the house keeper showed me the best rooms and then we had a walk round the grounds and very fine they were . . . we went in the house again and then came home by the ferry. We got home about 10 Anne L finds herself very much offended because she was not asked to go, and a nice bit of fun she is made of. She has been crying about something.

2nd May . . . my first place was the Watchmakers with Ann's watch

15th *May* after tea I went to see M where I stayed some time . . . It was bothering me about coming down to Westhill some Sunday but I would rather she would go somewhere else for I am sure I don't want her here . . .

29th *May* . . . I went to see M and I took her one bouquet . . .

2nd *June* I was expecting M and C till 1 o'clock when they were not come I had almost given them up but before half past they were here. They had dinner in the hall after dinner we had a walk through the grounds the afternoon was rather cold we went through the gardens and got each of them a nosegay, got into the Laundry by 5 they went into there for tea but I did not, a little before 8 they started I went with them to the Telegraph just as we got there it began to rain we stayed there about 15 minutes and then set out for Putney bridge and got them into the omnibus and then came home I got home a little before 9. I have not spent a very pleasant day the first place I did not want her come down at all but I did not tell her so I treated her as distant as I possibly could saying I treated her civily.

9th *June* after tea I went with Anne and Sarah's sister round the grounds got her a nosegay etc got home about 8 and about ½ past she started for London, Anne and me went with her to Putney and saw her safe on the Omnibus we got back home from Putney about 10 and then we went to hear the birds sing in the woods . . .

(Thomas, 'Journal', SRO D4177/1–2)

Ernest King at the Llewellyns

There was another reason for my wishing to leave – the second housemaid. The lady had become rather too possessive. She used to give me a kick under the table, enough to break my shin-bone, in the servants' hall if ever I said 'Good morning' to any of the other girls. It was when she took her holiday that I took the opportunity to give in my notice. She was due to return one evening and I left at midday on the same day. It was a lesson to me. Never again did I allow my affections to wander in any house where I worked.

(King, *Green Baize Door*, p. 22)

Sexual relationships between servants were not supposed to happen.

Gordon Grimmett

An example of the kind of restraint we were expected to exercise had happened some time before I had joined, but was still talked about. A nursery maid and the groom of the chambers announced their intention of getting married. The house was in an uproar, both above and below stairs. How could they have met, let alone have been together for the length of time that acquaintanceship could ripen into affection?

A full-scale enquiry was launched. The children eventually gave the game away; the couple's tryst had been the nursery sink. . . . They had to leave, of course, heaven knows what the children might have seen and heard.

There was no question but that servants were owned body and soul. In service in London things were much the same. A maidservant who had 'followers' didn't stay very long.

(Grimmett, 'Lamp Boy's Story', p. 30)

Eileen Balderson

Once, when I had been to the pictures with Hilda, we returned to the house to be confronted with a scene as exciting as anything we had seen in a film. There had been a burglary. The police were taking finger prints and we were told to search our belongings and report if anything was missing. The next day all who had been in the house at the time of the unpleasant occurrence were questioned. By that evening it became obvious who the burglar was. . . .

A young footman, William, who was a nice, quiet lad became very fond of Grace, the second housemaid. No doubt she flirted with him, but his feelings for her were more than just that. She took up with a young man in the village called Cyril. Poor

William became so incensed with jealousy that he decided, I suppose, to get his own back for the unhappiness this caused him, and stole a wrist watch given to her by Cyril.

He staged a burglary. One evening, when there were only a few staff on duty, and little chance of being caught in the act, he went to her room and took the watch. Grace went to turn down the beds in the staff quarters and was shocked to find one room ransacked, and her own room, next door, locked on the inside.

She rushed downstairs to tell William, who was washing glasses and silver in the butler's pantry. With a great pretence of concern, he went upstairs. By looking out of the window of the adjoining room, he could see Grace's window wide open. To the accompaniment of her pleas to be careful, he climbed out of the neighbouring window and went gingerly along a ledge and into Grace's room which was in even greater disorder than next door. He unlocked the door, went downstairs and, as the butler was off duty, told the master there had been a burglary.

A plaster cast was made of a footprint in the wet earth of the shrubbery and it fitted William's muddy shoes in his bedroom. After taking the watch he had jumped out of Grace's window on to the flat roof of a passage leading to the servants' hall and then down to the shrubbery. The last I saw of poor William was when he was taken away by the police.

When she worked for the Keppels at Grove Lodge, Windsor, Eileen herself had a relationship which ended unhappily.

When George Higgs and I were going out together we had to be very discreet. We used to meet away from Grove Lodge and on our return from an outing I usually went in first while he had a drink in the village, arriving back at the house later.

Our half days were spent walking in the Great Park, and once we walked to Eton to see the college. In the evening we indulged in my passion, the pictures.

Sundays were spent either at Virginia Water or visiting his widowed mother and younger sister at Yateley, near Camberley. . . . George decided to leave Grove Lodge since keeping our friendship a secret was rather a strain. He took a butler's post in Eaton Square.

So I began to travel to London each half day to meet George there. I had my eye on that flat over the garage in Eaton Place Mews. This had always been occupied by the married butler in the past. We hoped, one day, to be the new tenants. I remember looking over it one afternoon, full of plans for the future, but it was not to be. . . .

Eileen went to Scotland with the Keppels for the shooting season.

My happiness was clouded about two weeks before the end of the season. I had, of course, written regularly, to George in Scotland, and always looked forward to his letters. Alas, one morning I received a letter saying he wished to end our relationship. . . .

I wanted to run away and hide. I soaked his letters in tears, and was very miserable, sniffing as I got through my work. . . .

(Balderson, *Backstairs Life*, pp. 63–4, 70–1)

While he was hall boy at Little Missenden Abbey George Washington got into trouble.

Another [consolation] was Doris, the little housemaid whose life was nearly as wretched as mine. Her father ran a pub, the Black Horse, at nearby Lacy Green and whenever we could snatch an hour or two off we would cycle over there for tea. I suppose in an innocent way we became fond of each other, but our relationship was not allowed to blossom.

The head housemaid, whom I looked on as an old spinster though she was probably only about twenty-five, took a shine to me, only I didn't realise it at the time. I did think it a bit fishy when she kept calling me up to her bedroom to give me orders and that she always seemed to be in various stages of undress, pretending that she was changing. She also seemed to be pawing me when she talked to me. I took no notice; if I thought about it at all I put it down to a sort of motherly feeling for me, but I suppose she felt my growing friendship with Doris was putting her nose out of joint.

One morning I overslept and Doris, noticing my absence, ran up to my room to wake me. As she was leaving she bumped into the head housemaid who went up like a volcano and accused us of having spent the night together. Nothing we could say would quieten her and the long and short of it was that I was sent for by Mrs Ronald, called a filthy fornicator and told to pack my things and get out of the house immediately.

It wasn't pleasant for me to explain what had happened when I got home. I think it would have been simpler if I had been guilty, at least then I could have made a clean breast of it and started from there; as it was, although my word was accepted, it was done in a half-hearted sort of way as though there was no smoke without fire and I felt my behaviour was watched not only by my family but by the villagers who had girls of a seducible age, while friends of my own sex seemed uncertain whether to admire me or despise me.

(Washington, 'Hall Boy's Story', p. 178)

Servants were also discouraged from having admirers, or 'followers', from outside.

This was a cause of stress between Ruth Barrow, a servant in Leicestershire, and her sweetheart, John Spendlove, who worked in Gretton. The two were highly respectable, staunch Nonconformists who later went on to marry, and their courtship is marked over 100 letters, many of them written in cross writing.

Ruth Barrow to John Spendlove, 12 December 1847

Leicester

Dear John.

According to your wish I will try to send you an answer. And I hope you will allow me to say I cannot think of seeing you as you pass through Lr as I am sure if I do I shall be obliged to leave where I am now, and this I have no wish to do at present. I think therefore that you will not wish it. You perhaps will think it strange but I cannot get out without asking, and then they would want to know where I was going so that I should be obliged to deceive them for they are very jealous. But for you to talk of making a trial of such a trifle I am quite surprised . . .

Later Ruth asked him to come to Leicester to the October fair at the same time as her sister, giving her an excuse to get out of the house.

(NRO, Spendlove, Sp G 355)

The disapproval vented upon 'followers' was not simply a moral one. Food and drink could be lavished on them and some servants certainly made free with their employer's hospitality.

Mrs Bateman, for example, had a cook who had been feeding a man friend in the kitchen every Sunday for weeks. She wrote to her son, a lawyer in the Middle Temple, describing the events and asking for advice.

Mrs Bateman to Thos Bateman, 24 January 1838

Guilsborough

My Dear Tom,

. . . When I wrote to you last I think I told you we heard of a man coming every Sunday – he made his appearance again – I having given her notice on Monday 15th – last Sunday the 21st the cold made me stay from Ch: . . . soon after all had gone to Ch: Don bark'd just so I felt some one had just come in – I ran up to the garret stair window, saw her talking to a man who walk'd up with her to the kitchen, went in and shut the door – I went down into the kitchen – look'd at him for a moment – and asked if he wanted Mr Bateman – he said no he did not want Mr. Bateman, he came to speak to the Cook – I ask'd him what his name was – she call'd out he is my Brother – at the same instant he spoke and said his name was Failby – she said you mean Tyrrel – I look'd surprised and said how very strange that this man does not know his own name . . . and then I asked her if he was the same man that was with her last Sunday – she said yes – then I said I do not believe you are her Brother and the sooner you leave this House the better . . . The Cook scream'd very loud that she wd go with him – I said she shd not but he said she should come out and speak to him, upon wh she ran out of the scullery door and he went out at the other door – I sent Lyne out after some time to tell her to come in and him to give his name and leave the premises – he said he should go soon – but wd not tell his name . . .

I never went into the kitchen on Monday, but ordered Mary and Ann to get the dinner – saying I did not choose to speak to her – Papa came in from Kibworth late and after dinner we told him – when he sent for Lyne and made him tell how often the man had been here and that he had had all his meals for the fourteen Sundays. He then sent for Mary and Ann and with a good deal of trouble made them say the same – and ask'd them whether they did not confess themselves guilty of a Breach of trust in seeing that man regularly fed . . . Mary very reluctantly said she did not know or something like it – I think she may have prevented the others from telling – he gave the two maids a very good lecture – and then sent a message by Lyne to the Cook to desire she wd be quite off before 12 the next day – and she might apply to the Magistrate's for her wages next Saturday when he would pay her what they ordered – but the next morning he was ill with a cold – and I thought it would save trouble so I persuaded him to let me pay her up to the day she went – she said she had agreed for a months wages or warning – I said here is the money up to this time in my hand and if you choose to take it you will sign the receipt wh I laid before her – she then signed it and I paid her in the presence of three witnesses – I then told her that Mr Bateman would consider of what steps would be taken in consequence of her hiding the man in the house various times, giving him food, refusing as she did to the last to tell his name and for slipping back the lock of the scullery door . . . the next morning I sent for Robin to put on Padlocks – to shew her that in future it shd be made safe.

Now is there anything we can do to the woman, we think of finding out the man's name – who I believe is Cooper or Mason of Long Buckby . . . it is strange the servants all persist in saying they never once heard his name – I said so to Mrs Booth and it struck her that he is a married man – at any rate there is something bad as I told Cook wh makes her wish to hide it . . . . I shd like to have a line from you on Saturday to tell me what I ought to have done in this case, whether anything ought now to be done . . . if he shd prove to be a married man Papa says he will send a person over to Lamport to tell her friends of it . . .

Will my having paid her off prevent our punishing her in any way if Papa wishes it . . .

Give my kind love to aunt and Jos and believe me your loving Mother

MB

(NRO, Bateman, ZA1253)

MARRIAGE

Women servants usually left work on marriage. Butlers could marry, but the more lowly footmen were expected to be single. For this reason, Gordon Grimmett used to meet his future wife in secret.

Pop had a job in the house as floral decorator and this meant that she was responsible for all the plants and flowers in the rooms at Cliveden. It was considered a superior position as it brought her into contact with the family, and close to Lady Astor who took a personal interest in the flower decoration. . . . And therefore it wasn't surprising that at first Pop took scant notice of the glances and occasional wisecracks of a second footman.

We first met properly at a dance at a nearby village. I may have been no Fred Astaire but comparison with some of the other men there made me a near relation, so I might say without conceit that I swept Pop off her feet. She loved dancing as I did and it gave expression to the gaiety, fun and mischievousness that were so much a part of her. From that night on we sought each other's company. . . . In a way we were 'star crossed' lovers. We knew that no one would approve of our relationship – not Pop's family, because of her father's position, not Mr Lee, because 'that sort of nonsense' was bound to interfere with the smooth running of the house, and certainly not Lady Astor. So our meetings were conducted with stealth and were in a way all the more valued because of that. Just a touch of hands as we passed each other in a corridor was a thrill and sensation to be remembered, and if our work brought us together for just a few moments it was as if the world stood still. We plotted and planned our surreptitious meetings in whispers or with the passing of silly little notes, and when those times came we would wander hand in hand, speechless and bewildered by the wonder of it all. We danced, of course, always choosing places where we hoped we would be unobserved. We walked the fields and parklands around Cliveden and saw the country-side in a new light together. We rowed and swam in the Thames.

. . . We would meet at the boathouse. Old Joe Brooks, the ferryman and boatman, was a simple soul given more to grumbling to himself than talking and unlikely, even if he suspected our secret meetings, of telling anyone about them. He was, however, very fond of his bed so that the chances of getting him up from it to ferry us back on our return journeys were light. We didn't find this out until I'd had to swim the river a couple of times to get the ferry and to retrieve Pop, which not only cooled my ardour but offended my dignity, for no man cuts much of a figure in dripping wet underpants, shivering cold and covered in goose pimples.

We eventually decided to borrow a boat each time and leave it out of sight downstream. This worked well in good weather, but there came one terrible night when a storm had blown up. When we got to the river the current was in full spate. We were already late so there was nothing for it but to take a chance. It nearly cost us our lives, for despite my pulling on the oars like a long-shoreman we were carried downstream and began shipping water as the boat turned sideways into the current. When I thought we were finished a wave flung us towards the quieter waters near the bank and although we were a mile downstream of the boathouse we were safe. Our night wasn't over, we had the job of dragging the boat against the stream back to its moorings, stumbling along the bank and often having to wade into the water, with the screeching of disturbed birds and the red eyes of the water rats adding to the discomfort of soaking clothes and mud-coated legs. . . .

I, of course, was sacked, but Pop came away with me, the Gods smiled on us, we married and almost immediately I found employment as a floor manager in one of the Lyons Corner Houses, and despite some occasional hard struggles I think I can

say we have both enjoyed our lives together, and have made a
success of our marriage.

(Grimmett, 'Lamp Boy's Story', pp. 79–82)

During the course of footman William Tayler's journal it is clear that not
only was he married, but his wife lived nearby and gave birth to a child.
Indeed, he recorded the christening. Even in his diary, however, the
relationship was mentioned cryptically – going to church or going for a
run sometimes meaning he was visiting his wife.

15th. This being Sunday of course I went to church – or rather,
I took a little walk elsewhere.

12th. This is Sunday; went to church *of course.*

8th. I don't like this being kept in from going out on their
account because I cannot have the face to go out in the evening
on my own account.

Sept 30th. . . . Having a particular *friend* unwell I jenerally go to
see her twice a day, that is, before dinner and before supper.

Oct 4th . . . I jeneraly go twice a day to see my sick friend; she is
better, I am happy to say . . .

Nov 5th I have had a holiday and have been to a christening, but
to whos I do not say. Spent a very pleasant day. . . .

(Wise, *William Tayler*, pp. 12, 18, 22, 52–5)

There was usually no obstacle to outdoor servants marrying, though
accommodation might be a problem. At Welbeck Abbey, however, the
Duke of Portland, himself a bachelor, had strict rules, which emerge in a
letter to his steward about the third coachman, William Hancock.

The Duke of Portland to William Cripwell, nd

. . . I have said nothing to him about his marriage and don't
intend to but I sh'd like to know where he mar'd and where he
is now living. If he was not to all appearances so good . . . a
servant – my natural answer to give to his application for a

house w'd be 'so far from giving you a house you ought to expect that we sh'd give you your discharge as has invariably been the case with any man wanting to marry and sh'd still more so be when one actually marries without leave.'

. . . we had better not be in a hurry to make any change but wait till we can see someone able . . .

(NA, Portland, DDP6/13/25/37)

FAMILY

Maintaining family ties must have taken some effort, given restricted time off. Many young servants spent their holiday going home to their parents.

Though away in London for most of the year, Thomas the footman kept in touch with his family in Cheshire, writing to them and buying them presents.

14th Aug . . . and having promised to buy my sister Rachel a doll I put on my plain cloths and went to the Pantheon one for sister Rachel and one for Eliz Ball 6/- and a small book of pretty pictures with reading cost 1/6 and then for Charly a book and two other small books altogether 3/- . . .

On a short stay at Trentham in Staffordshire he invited his brother to see the house.

31st Aug I am expecting my brother William or some of them to come and see me today.

1st Sept . . . I made sure Wm would have come to see me to day but he did not come . . .

2nd Sept After our dinner and we had nearly finished Lunch I went into the servants hall to see if any body was come from Cheshire and who should I find there but Brother Wm, he was just come in from the Railway he said that he had been from home and did not get my letter till Saturday . . . I did not go out with him this afternoon me being in waiting . . . I got to bed very early about ¼ past 12 . . . I promised William to get up very early in the morning and to show him round the grounds

3rd Sept The night porter called me this morning about 5, I got up at ½ past and started to go on the pleasure grounds and went to the boat house and found the boats unlocked so we took one and went out on the water for an hour we came back and went into the gardens and the foreman showed us through the gardens and we got in by 8. After breakfast I showed him through the house . . . William started for the Railway at 11 . . .

(Thomas, 'Journal', SRO D4177/1–2)

Married men kept in touch with their families by letter, as did this manservant in the service of Captain White, of Crenmere, near Blackmore, Hampshire.

John McEvely to his wife, 1 October 1885

Crenmere

My dear Wife and Children,

I received your kind letter this morning and am sorry to hear that you have got such a bad cold. I am sorry to tell you that I cannot come home until Monday as his sons is coming on Sunday and he wants me to fetch them from the station in the morning and take them back at night, he wants me to remain at 10 shillings a week and my Board but I told him I could not do it, Miss White is very good and I please her She tells me to stick up for my wages until her Brother comes and she is sure that they won't let me go the old man is a miserable old chap, he wants men to work over again for their pension but I am not going to do it I hope the children is not hungry for I cannot get any money to send them, write as soon as you receive this and let me know if my papers has come yet, tell davy that I shall bring him the grapes and some aples and I am very much obliged to him for his letter . . . give my love to the Children with lots of Kisses, I remain your

Affectionate Husband,
J McEvely

(HRO, Rogers, 152M88/46)

Of course the contrast between servant's home and workplace must have been extreme.

George Washington recalled one stillroom maid, Maisy, who asked him home to visit her family in Brynmawr, a small Welsh mining town.

We caught a train from Paddington to Newport where her father met us and together we went up the Welsh valleys, through Ebbw Vale to Brynmawr. Maisy had six young brothers and sisters and two grown-up sisters, all living in a small miner's cottage. The thing that struck me immediately was its austerity and cleanliness. We had toast Friday night for supper, bread and margarine for breakfast and when Saturday lunch was served it was a plate of chips and nothing else. When Maisy and I went for a walk over the pit tips in the afternoon she said, 'Are you hungry?'

'Not half,' I replied. Then she explained that her father had silicosis and had been laid off from the mine, and was living on relief money.

'We're no worse off than most people though,' she said, 'there's been no regular work round here for years.' This then, I thought, accounted for the look of hopelessness on the faces of the men and women that I'd noticed.

'Never mind, love,' I said, 'I've got quite a bit of money with me, we'll give them a treat, we'll buy them a joint for Sunday lunch.' They of course called it dinner. We went into the town to the butchers and I asked for a leg of lamb.

He looked at me incredulously. 'I haven't got a leg of lamb, in fact I haven't seen a leg of lamb for God knows how long.' But he added hastily, 'I can get you one by Monday.'

I ordered it. 'What can you let us have now?' I asked.

'I've only got some scrag-end of beef, how much do you want, a quarter of a pound?'

When I asked for 2 lb he nearly fainted. His reaction was nothing to the reception we got from Maisy's mother. When we put it on the kitchen table in front of her she sat down on the chair just looking at it, with tears pouring down her cheeks.

'What on earth will she do when she sees that leg of lamb?' I later asked Maisy.

She did the same, and when her father saw the joint on the table he went down on his knees and prayed, and we and the rest of the family joined him. Never since then have I complained of being hungry or under-fed. . . .

Regularly when we were back in London we'd send some food parcels. I felt no shame now from scrounging anything from the kitchen, and if the birds or the animals at the zoo got fewer cakes and buns than before I felt it was in a good cause.

(Washington, 'Hall Boy's Story', pp. 186–7)

For many women, domestic service was a life-long career, for others a useful staging post in their progress towards achieving their own family. For some it was a bit of both, a safety net and protection against the trials and tribulations of life.

Sarah Neal went into service as lady's maid at Uppark in West Sussex in September 1850.

Aug 1852 This being a convenient distance from home I frequently go in to see dr Mother, Father . . .

Had very sad letters from home, frequently going home to see my dr Mother. I hope with God's blessing she will again be restored to me. A mother's love what can exceed it, I feel at times unhappy being away from her when I know she needs me at home when she is poorly. I hope God will forgive me and direct me how to act.

Sarah left Uppark in the spring of 1853 to nurse her mother. In August of that year her father died, followed on 5 November by her mother. But Sarah had already met Joseph Wells, a gardener at Uppark, whom she married on 22 November of that same year. The couple had three sons, and one daughter who died young. Sarah was 44 when the youngest son, Herbert, was born. Joseph, Sarah's husband, proved unable to provide adequately for his family either as a gardener or later as a semi-professional cricket coach and shop keeper. In 1880, aged 58, Sarah was forced by her husband's ill health and insolvency to return to service – as housekeeper at Uppark, serving the same mistress as before. Her diary records her worries – about money, her own health, sons Frank, Freddy and Bertie, and the difficult relationships with the other servants at

Uppark. By 1892 she was 70 years old, a pathetic figure, increasingly deaf and easily irritated, far from an efficient housekeeper, given to gossiping and passing on imaginary tales to her mistress.

1892

Jan 30 Busy all day – Wrote to Mrs Holmes hoping she will come and suit. What a worry this house is!!

Feb 26 Busy all day indoors. Felt so unsettled now, I wish I could get elsewhere.

Feb 27 Busy as usual all day. Did not move out. No peace with servants here.

Feb 29 Dairy woman most disagreeable. What a party!

March 26 I do not feel comfortable such strange things one sees and hears!

April 23 What there is to put up with in this house.

April 25 Began the house cleaning. My feet so tender. What can it be!

May 28 Could not get out very busy as usual. Unpleasant comment from the Cook who seems to act very queer.

June 2 Only to the Dairy. What a parcel of women I am surrounded with!

June 4 I went to the Dairy. What a passionate woman. I never can think what the end is to it all.

June 23 Did not go out . . . been greatly worried about servants.

July 25 . . . how I wish I had a home out of this worry.

Aug 2 Numerous disagreeables, what tempers to contend with.

Aug 4 12 years today I came here and left Beverley. What anxious years they have been to me. What rude insulting people I have had to live with and it is worse <u>now</u>.

Aug 12 Worried with Head Dairy maids tales.

Aug 13 Did not move out, busy all day, as usual. Named to Miss F. the tales in circulation.[4]

Aug 29 Frank came to tea, cool as usual, not a word that is kind, Bertie cross letter. What trouble they are to me forgetting their duty.

Sept 2 That horrid woman vexed me again. Oh how hard to be obliged to stay in such a place!

Sept 16 Worried with the Cook leaving, how unsettled this house is.

Oct 1 I felt so much my deafness.

Oct 27 No walk how dull in these under ground rooms!

Nov 8 Oh, I hope a quiet house to end my days in.

Nov 15 Sent Bertie by Rail Brace of Pheasants, wrote to Frank, sent a leg of mutton.

Nov 28 Miss F. always finding fault.

Dec 2 Unpacked stores, so tired. No thought of me if tired or not.

Dec 6 Today the Duke of Connaught arrived, Oh such fuss and work. How I wish I was out of it, what ignorant people as a rule servants are!

Dec 8 How tired I am worn out with worry.

Dec 26 Busy all day preparing and waiting on company, felt so tired, having a severe cold & cough. Thankful to get to bed.

In January 1893 Sarah was finally given a month's notice. She left Uppark having found no other place and clearly in great distress of mind.

May 8 Felt very anxious about a situation.

May 15 No bright news, what shall we do for a living, please God send me work to do.

July 6 I hope if please God I may soon hear of some place to suit me. I fear my deafness . . . Please God I could get some little house where I could be earning my living.

But there is a happy ending to this story, for the Bertie she refers to became better known as H.G. Wells and by 1893 he was already in the process of establishing himself as a writer and could afford to arrange a home for her.[5] Sarah Wells died in 1905, aged 83.

(WSRO, Add Mss. 41,235, 41,237)

TEN

'If I must die in the workhouse, I must' – health, old age and death

Health care was one of the real advantages of working for a great country estate. Traditionally the aristocratic household looked after their servants' health needs, especially when the servant was aged and had been with them a long time. Dunham Massey, a household with a long tradition of patriarchal care for its employees, spent in 1822 more on medical bills for the servants and craftsmen working in the house than for the family. This was despite the fact that the family members were treated by an expensive doctor, while the servants were prescribed for by an apothecary from Altrincham.[1]

Servants of the landed estates enjoyed yet another advantage regarding health care. In the nineteenth century, most members of the landed gentry and aristocracy made subscriptions and charitable donations to their local dispensary or hospital. This entitled them to free medical care for a set number of people, to whom they could issue tickets when needed. These were, of course, not for the use of their families but for poorer people. In this respect servants were regarded as family, and employers were expected to pay for servants' treatments themselves. But servants' families were a different matter and could benefit.

When the time came that they could no longer work, old,

long-serving servants were often well treated by their aristocratic employers – in terms of either a pension or accommodation in an estate cottage or alms house. Servants might even achieve the ultimate acceptance of a place in the family graveyard: the Cecil graveyard at Hatfield contains only three people who were not family – two nurses and a housekeeper.[2] But such comforts and assurances were available as a reward only for those who gave long and faithful service. Pensions as a whole were unusual. Country-house servants were well paid and expected to save for their old age. Younger servants or employees of the *nouveau riche* would usually find themselves dismissed out of hand when they became chronically ill. Even the old patriarchal estates found themselves on the receiving end of letters from elderly servants begging for money or work, some of them in very great penury. So numerous were destitute elderly servants, indeed, that a national Servants' Benevolent Institution was founded in 1846.[3]

Senior servants such as stewards justifiably regarded themselves as gentlemen and many owned the appurtenances of gentility, disposing of them accordingly in their wills. Instructions for investments and charitable endowments are by no means rare in such circumstances, the servant learning from his master and often using the same lawyer to draw up the will. In some households even more junior staff became relatively wealthy, especially where estates kept up the practice of leasing property for several lives to servants. Even single women who had spent their entire career in service could do well enough to leave what for a working man would be substantial wealth, making dispositions for charities and even leaving legacies to their employer's families.

Yet it is perhaps too easy to paint a rosy picture. Servants who left wills must represent a tiny fraction of the many thousands working in service. Eric Horne for one left a much more jaundiced and probably realistic view of the rewards of a lifetime in service.

HEALTH

At Welbeck Abbey, the 5th Duke of Portland seems to have spared no expense over his servants' health. In 1877 one of his kitchen maids, Mary Lenthall, became 'run down' and anaemic. Having received the doctor's report, for which he paid, he debated the best thing to do with his agent, W. Cripwell. Cripwell himself had been sent at the Duke's insistence and expense to the spa at Buxton for a rest-cure.

B.B. Thurgar to the Duke of Portland, 6 July 1877

> . . . Enclosed is a doctor's letter. Mary Lenthall is suffering from anaemia & has had a fortnight's holiday & three week's rest – she has been undergoing the treatment of steel & is still taking it. She requires however a change to the sea side, in order to get her blood & general health to a fixed standard to enable her to better fulfil her duties for the coming autumn.
>
> > B.B. Thurgar
> > For W. Neale FRCP, MRCS

The Duke of Portland to W. Cripwell, nd

> ### Mary Lenthall (in the kitchen)
> Sir,
> I enclose you the med's reports – it was the first I had heard of the illness – I didn't know what 'anaemia' is in common English – but I can easily imagine the nature of the complaint so frequent with such a young woman as she, steel is the principal remedy and what occurs to me is that <u>perhaps</u> Buxton may be better than the sea side if as I think I have heard there is <u>now</u> a steel spring at Buxton which is much recommended . . .
>
> Perhaps if you could show Thurgar's report to some med he wd know at once whether Buxton or the sea side wd be the preferable remedy.

W. Cripwell to the Duke of Portland, 20 July 1877

The Old Hall Hotel
Buxton

My Lord Duke,

. . . <u>Mary Lenthall</u>

. . . W. Shipton says the iron spring here is very weak and unless the girl has rheumatism he does not think Buxton would be of much use and that the sea-side would be much better, in fact any where for a change.

Mrs Cripwell [says] they have had several similar cases in the Village Hospital at Mansfield Woodhouse and they have soon come round with the change and proper treatment . . . and we have such a first rate nurse who has been trained with Miss Nightingale's nurses at St Thomas Hospital and has been head nurse at Swansea 7 years and appears to thoroughly understand her business. All the beds are occupied and we are now getting more as we have ample space.

From Duke of Portland to W. Cripwell, 22 July 1877

Sir

<u>Mary Lenthall</u>

Perhaps she will dislike the Village hospital even if there is room for her which seems doubtful. Scarboro' or some watering Place wd be more amenable.

(NA, Portland, DDP6/13/25/68, 67, 70, 81)

This was very different from the reception met with by another ex-servant, Mary Brook, who had been housemaid to Jemima, the Marchioness of Grey. She seems not to have been on good terms with other senior servants of the family and on her mistress's death in 1797 she was dismissed, without being left anything in the will. In poor health, she contacted the Marchioness's daughter Amabel, the new Baroness Lucas, to ask for help.

Mary Brook to the Hon Lady Lucas, nd, c. 1798

After most submissively Intreating pardon for Daring to take this liberty with a person of your Ladyships' Distinction – Mary Brook housemaid to the late Marchioness of Gray . . . To state my case to Your Ladyship . . . as the Marchioness particular Desire to retain Mrs Boad, Mrs Boads very ill state of health and the great aversion which her Ladyship had to new faces made it necessary for me very often to act in a Double Capacity and by long continuing to overexert myself my health . . . eversince I left St James Square have been so Indifferent that I find it very difficult to obtain bread in the hard line which I am destined to earn it. Shoud therefore be very thankfull for some employment in the family at lest till my health is established . . .

> Your Ladyship's most Hble Supplyant
> Mary Brook

No offer was forthcoming, but Mary did manage to get employment with the Earl of Moira. But her health was such that her position in the new household was precarious. So her sister Elizabeth tried again, writing to the Lucases' housekeeper, Mrs Brazier.

Elizabeth Brook to Mrs Brazier, nd

Madam, As you knowd how my sister were situated before she went into the Earl of Moireas family I am by her Desire to Inform you her health has been so very Indifferent that she have found much Difficulty to stay so long in that place – for more than three weeks she has been unable to do her work and as she is a person that have rendered the family but little service and the housekeeper is tired of alowing so much help, she is fearful of being discharged as soon as she is able to travel.

. . . I please myself with the hopes that I shall find access to their Ladyships through the channel of your humanity and should I be so fortunate the favour will be most gratefully remembered as my sister have no other friend in this world but myself . . . its not in my power to supply her wants . . .

> Mad^m
> Y^r H^ble ser
> Eliz Brook

This letter seems to have offended Mrs Brazier. Nothing daunted, Elizabeth wrote to Baroness Lucas herself, explaining that Mary was indeed going to have to leave the Earl of Moira's establishment due to ill health.

Elizabeth Brook to the Hon Lady Lucas, nd

> . . . Mrs Brazier was much offended. She deemed the contents both improper and impertinent and said she coud not help my sisters being disappointed that Lady Grey did not leave her anything. I gave Mrs B to know that w[h]ere no hopes of that kind was grounded no disappointment could be felt and I am assured if it shoud be her hard lot even to feel the keen pain of pinching want she will sink beneath the sad burden, still revering the memory of her much respected Lady . . .
>
> With the greatest humility, I beg pardon for trespassing on your Ladyship's patience
>
> Eliz. Brook

Nothing is recorded of the outcome.

(BLARS, Lucas, L30/11/36/1–3)

One hundred years later, at Blechingley in Surrey, a 20-year-old Lilian Westall also found country-house service just too much for her physically.

> The food was good here, but the work very hard. All the cooking was done on a huge range; I had to clean this range with black-lead, and the great copper preserving pans I burnished inside and out so that they gleamed golden. The great kitchen had to be scrubbed daily, and it had to be spotless. I had one evening off a week, and one day off a month. I didn't dislike it here, but this sort of work needed the stamina of an ox, and years of semi-starvation meant I hadn't this sort of strength. I left after about three months.

(Westall, 'Good Old Days', p. 217)

If both family and servants were prepared to make allowances, some servants could lead an active working life despite a severe disability.

Charles Dean remembered an under-butler at Badminton in the 1930s.

Jimmy Weedon, the under butler at Badminton, was one of the great characters in my life in service. His duties were ill defined, and he seemed to do a bit of everything. Perhaps this was because he had come to the house some forty years before as telegraph boy. It was of course in the days before the telephone, and he'd been sent from London to take and transmit messages in morse code. When the phone was installed Jimmy was out of a job, but as he didn't want to leave he was allowed to stay on as a general dog's body. He was lamp boy, odd man, steward's room boy, footman and butler rolled into one. He had no pride of office, but a deal of pride in his work. When I arrived he was three parts blind but had a fantastic sense of place and touch; to watch him carrying food on a butler's tray fitted to his stomach, from the kitchen to the dining-room, was a sight to wonder at. He'd leave the kitchen, pacing his way to the stairs, up eight, turn right, down four then to the green baize door, push it open, so many steps across the octagonal hall and into the servery, moving at one hell of a pace so that the food arrived hot. One day trying to be helpful I opened the baize door to let him through; he was lost. 'You stupid bugger, what did you do that for? Now I don't know where I am, guide me to the dining-room.'

(Dean, 'Boot Boy's Story', pp. 142–3)

On the other hand, domestic service could put an intolerable burden on young children if they were mentally unstable.

Entry in Apothecary's Day Book, Stafford Asylum, 1818–19

Ann Bayley. This is a Pauper Patient, a single woman from Newcastle, who has been insane about 12 years; her insanity having been occasioned in consequence of a fright, a felloe servants having come to her at night, wrapped in a sheet with that intention; she appears to be nearly in a state of fatuity . . . she is nearly idiotic but very manageable.

(SRO, Stafford Asylum, D550/65)

Servants' ill health had repercussions on their fellow workers. It was they who had to look after an invalid.

Lady Elizabeth Dryden, widow of Sir John Turner Dryden of Canons Ashby, was told of the progress of one of her servants by William Peacock, bailiff of Canons Ashby.

William Peacock to Lady Elizabeth Dryden, 31 January 1804

Canons Ashby

Honoured Lady,

This is to inform your Ladyship . . . James was not well on Friday night when in bed. He thought it to be the cramp, on Saturday he walked into the Best Garden by himself & his lame knee fauld & he fell down. Ricd smith was at work there & with his assistance got up . . . & then Smith came to the House for further assistance & on the Evening sent for Mr Page & he sent him something to take & he complained of a pain on his left side. I seen James on Sunday & he still complained of the pain in his side but he could walk about – when I came to Ashby on Tuesday afternoon I found him very bad with a complaint in his Bowels. Mr Page had given him something to go through him but had not had any effect, he was setting in an arm chair but could not stand & by times is very weavering in his Talk. His Bed is brought down into the Hall, he is very helpless. Capel & Hawten's wife set up last night & Mary & Richd Smith set up tonight, he appears as if he could not get the better of this.

I am

Your

Ladyship

Most obedient

& most humble serv^t

Wm Peacock

I stopd at Ashby all night. James has had but an indifferent night, Dos'd a little by times, he has had a passage this morning & has answered the designed effect. Young Mr Page has been at

Ashby this morning, he says James is very Bad, has had a stroke of the palsy & his legs swell, he is very helpless . . .

Same, 7 February 1804

I was sorry to give your Ladyship so sudden a surprise about James but his illness was alarming to all hear – one of Mr Ward's sons went for James Brother who came on Friday & as there was a Better return of James illness on Sunday morning his Brother left him & he still continued better on Monday he set up some time & with assistance led him across the Room. There has been two people sett up every night from Sunday week, Capel, Rd Smith, Hawten & Richd Ashby & Mary & Hawten's wife every other night – & Mrs Mumford has but little rest. James is so very heavy & helpless that there has always been Two or Three people to help & assist him night & Day – & has your Ladyship is so kind as to order all care & Assistance to make him Easy that if James continues getting better & has no return it is hoped he will in a short time be able to do with less Assistance. The boy Richd Smith has slept at Ashby some nights & James calls out for Drink very often . . .

Same, 28 February 1804

. . . James situation is a very melancholy one if he continues in the state he is now in. Two people have had him across the room & Himself has at the same time a stirup leather under his foot to lift his left leg along. Mr Page wish'd them to move him often, he has more use of his right leg than he had & eats any thing that he has a mind to, Drinks some ale, some gin & some Brandy. I believe Mr Page advised him to live pretty well, his left leg has lately swell'd more I have told Mrs Mumford that after a little time it must be considered of a plan to go on with as Capel must do all James used to do as to feeding the Horses & Deer & if James finds he is not likely to get about again he will probably procure a person himself to attend him as it appears there can be no prospect of his ever being fit for service. Your Ladyship thinks his Wages should cease on the first of the next month as there will want an additional Labourer . . .

Same, 6 March 1804

. . . James continues much the same his left leg rather more swell'd he has got one Hemings from Morton who has been in Gentlemens service & he is a very steady young active man to attend him . . .

Same, 13 March 1804

. . . James is so much better as to be able to walk with Cruches and the man to assist him by times a little from the Servants Hall to the Best Garden Door for this 4 or 5 days past & sometimes twice a day & yesterday went as far as the Shepheard in the park with cruches himself . . .

Same, 27 March 1804

. . . James continues getting better . . .

(NRO, Dryden, D (CA) 360)

In the winter of 1837, William Tayler had a whole household to care for, struck down by influenza.

10th. All the people in the house are ill with the influenza. The old Lady and two of the boys and one of the maids are ill in bed now, therefore we that are well have plenty to do to wait on the others. I cannot hardly leave the house in consequence, obliged to remain at home all this day, amused myself with drawing and reading. This evening the old lady thought herself worse; went for the doctor . . . the patient is better and I am just going to bed.

15th. The old Lady, I am sory to say, gets worse, I am afraid we shall soon lose her. The cook is very ill too; she keeps her bed. A gentleman called, a nephew of the old Lady's, expecting to get a dinner but I told him everybody was ill in the house but me, which news very soon started him of, to my satisfaction.

16th. Got up at half past seven; done my usual work. The old Lady and the cook both very ill in bed. The housemaid gone home to bury her Mother, the Ladys maid very ill but obliged to keep about – myself and Miss P. are the only two that has not had it. We expect to be caught hold of very soon. The Influenza was never known to be so bad as it is now . . . I am obliged to stay within to help the sick. This is what I don't like as I like to get a run everyday when I can.

On another occasion William was hardly sympathetic towards the lady's maid, afflicted by motion sickness.

29th Last summer, when we were coming home from Canterbury, she actually spewed all the way, a distance of sixty miles and not less time than eight hours. The people stared as we passed through the towns and villages as she couldent stop even then. It amused me very much to see how the country people stood stareing with their mouthes half open and half shut to see her pumping over the side of the carriage and me sitting by, quite unconserned, gnawing a piece of cake or some sand-wiches or something or other, as her sickness did not spoil my apatite. It was very bad for her but I couldent do her any good as it was the motion of the carriage that caused her illness. I gave her something to drink every time we changed horses but no sooner than it was down than it came up again, and so the road from Canterbury to London was pretty well perfumed with Brandy, Rum, Shrub, wine and such stuff. She very soon recovered after she got home and was all the better for it after.

(Wise, *William Tayler*, pp. 11–12, 15, 59)

Albert Thomas remembered the hospital ticket system of his youth, when he used to visit his sister, a parlourmaid with an elderly lady.

If any of us were ill she would always give us what in those days was called a Dispensary ticket. Being a regular subscriber to the Hospital funds she was allowed so many of these tickets a year, which were used to obtain medical treatment for all people who were too poor to pay for a doctor. Altogether, a dozen of us qualified for this privilege – thanks to this lady's generosity – and there were nearly always one or other of us attending the Dispensary. We had to go up once a week to see the doctor, sit in a large room and take our turn, for which we sometimes had to wait as long as three hours. When our turn eventually did arrive the doctor would examine us and perhaps change our medicine. This would entail returning home for another bottle. . . . On returning to the dispensary once more, we again had to wait our turn. . . . The queer thing in those days was that there was only a tiny spot of medicine in the bottom of the bottle, which was then filled with water, and it nearly always tasted of peppermint.

(Thomas, *Wait and See*, p. 12)

OLD AGE AND RETIREMENT

Tryphosa Box was housekeeper to Amabel, Baroness Lucas, and was rewarded for her long service by an annuity. She settled in a cottage where at one point she was in dispute with her neighbours over common rights. Lady Lucas helped her resolve the problem and here Tryphosa writes to her Ladyship to make arrangements for the payment of the annuity and to report that all is well.

Tryphosa Box to Lady Lucas, 29 October 1809

Silcoe

Box presents her Duty if your Ladyship thinks proper to pay the annuity to Mr Edwards, bookkeeper in town, Mr Edwards will pay me at Silcoe, the inclosed is a Direction he wrote him selfe – Mr Edwards is very obliging to me, will do aney thing to Serve me – I am happy to say they are all very Sivil, at present . . . I hope never to trouble your Ladyship aney more – I live in good youmer with all nabours & at present am very happy & comfortable, through your goodeness . . .

I beg leve to subscribe myself
Your Dutifull Servant
Tryphosa Box

(BLARS, Lucas, L30/11/32/2)

Noel Streatfeild recalled her own Nannie's old age and death.

Servants who remained with one family became part of it. . . . At grandfather's in the old nurseries lived the nurse who had brought my father and his nine brothers and sisters up. We came under her charge, when a baby was born at home we called her Grand-nannie. . . .

When my father and his brothers and sisters grew up many of the boys took jobs abroad, and when they came home on leave, almost before they had greeted their parents, they were up the stairs and flinging their arms round old Nannie's neck. . . .

Nannie lived to be a great age, and when she died, by good fortune my father and his seven brothers were in England. Although my grandparents' house was quite a way from the church, they would not allow their Nannie's body to travel on a hearse, but instead they whom she had carried in her arms, carried her to her grave on their shoulders. After her death a Will was found; in it she left her lifetime's savings in trust for any of her nurslings, or their children, or grandchildren, who might be in need.

(Streatfeild, *Day Before Yesterday*, pp. 77–8)

The Sutherlands had a long tradition of caring for their faithful old servants.

Anne, the Duchess of Sutherland to Mrs Ingram, housekeeper, n.d.

Stafford House, St. James

Dear Mrs Ingram,

I think it would do poor Louise (my old maid) good to have a little change with rest and good food, at Trentham. Will you therefore expect her there on Saturday and tell Brewster to send for her at 4.

As she may not go up high stairs will you let her have what was Penson's room in the wing – you know I dare say that she left Princess Christian because of being unable to attend on her, from a bad fall out of a railway carriage by which her back and leg were much hurt, and she is still quite low.

Yours truly,
A. Sutherland

Here the Duke of Sutherland's agent at Trentham writes to the senior land agent about a lower-placed servant.

William Lewis to James Loch, 22 November 1830

Wolverhampton

Dear Sir,

I am very sorry to name you that Mrs Tungate is very unwell and desires me to inform you that she considers herself quite incapable of continuing to do the work, Baking & Brewing as it is really too much for her, as she has been a long and faithful servant to the family I hope you and Lord Gower will be disposed to allow her some thing to retire comfortably and to some cottage. I know she has saved a little but not enough to keep her, she has failed much of late and will not live many years. I am perhaps saying more than I am authorized but I know her worth and I sincerely trust that something will be done to make her comfortable during life. I have had a good many opportunities of judging of her upright good conduct.

I am Dear Sir
Your most ob[t]
William Lewis

Fifty years later, the successor and descendant of James Loch wrote to the housekeeper at Trentham about another servant.

George Loch to Mrs Ingram, 23 October 1880

Uppark

Dear Mrs Ingram,

I have spoken to the Duke of Sutherland – he consents to allow the old Laundry maid 6/- a week. He suggests that perhaps it might be a good plan for her to go into the almshouse, in case a vacancy were to occur.

I am writing to Mr. Menzies to pay the pension.
Yours sincerely,
George Loch

(SRO, Sutherland, D593/R/10/2, D593/K/3/2/10, D593/R/10/3)

But many servants and their dependants were reduced to begging for help.

Isabella MacKenzie to Anne, 3rd Duchess of Sutherland, 18 October 1888

Morefield
Cromartie Estate
Lochbroom

Your Grace

I have considerable delicacy in addressing your Grace but I am now a poor widow and circumstances compel me to do so.

My husband, the late John Mackenzie was at one time your Grace's father's piper and was a tenant on your Grace's property until his death in July 1887. It is because thus my husband served in your Grace's family that I take upon myself to appeal to your Grace at this time for help. My son who is living with me, recently lost his herring nets and although he has a new boat he cannot go to sea for want of nets.

Would your Grace kindly give a little help to purchase nets and I need hardly say that my son if he should at all succeed at the fishing will refund any money that may be lent to the estate.

Hoping your Grace will pardon this letter,
I am your Grace's humble servant,
Isabella MacKenzie

James Fowler to same, 19 September 1888

8 McDonalds Haugh
Inverness

Your Grace the Duchess of Sutherland,

I pray your Grace will pardon me for using this liberty but it is the uttermost distress and necessity that obliges me to do so. I, the bearer of this, James Fowler, who has been on the road as Coachman 54 years and now 82 years of age and unable to do any thing for the last 5 years with roumatic and catrack on the eyes, I was with Late Duke in his service 4 years. I was there the time your Grace married and the next season if your Grace remembers I came up to Tarbet and Strathfether to visit the tenantry and heave had my dear wife confined to bed for the last 12 month and now she has departed this life and I have nothing to defray the expence of her funeral. We were 51 together. If your Grace would please give a little assistance I hope God will reward you.

> I shall wait your grace's answer,
> I am your Graces most humble and ob^t.
> James Fowler

Jane Jordon to same, 30 April 1888

> Womens Hall
> St Pancras Infirmary
> London, NW

Her Grace the Duchess of Sutherland

Honoured Madam,
I trust your Grace will pardon the liberty I am taking in writing as I am not known to your Grace, but was well known to her Grace the late Duchess of Sutherland at Windsor when I was Head Nurse to Lady Bertha Clifton, then Lady in Waiting to the Queen when her Grace was Mistress of the Robes – Lady Bertha, later Baroness de Ruthgen and her niece the late lamented Duchess of Norfolk, both these ladies have been the kindest friends to me, and I can't tell you how much I miss both these kind and charitable ladies – some months back I lost all I possessed by Fire, and as a long illness followed I had to take refuge in this Infirmary. I am still a good nurse and needlewoman, and am anxious to leave this place now I am better and try to get some light occupation outside, for after holding a good position tis very hard to be in a place of this kind, but I am quite destitute of means having lost all I had. I enclose a piece of work as a sample for your Grace to see, I have done a little in this place just to enable me to get a little extra support to get up my strength. If your Grace will help me a little in any form I shall feel very grateful – years back I lived in Torquay with my uncle and aunt Mr & Mrs Tapper, very old and

respected inhabitants and tradespeople of Torquay but they with all the rest of my family have now died out –

I trust your Grace will pardon this intrusion.

I am your Grace's Humble Servant
Jane Jordon

(SRO, Sutherland, D593/P/28/13)

WILLS

Servants' wills reflect a wide variety of wealth and ownership of goods.

Extract from the last will and testament of William Stoddard, coachman to the Salvin family of Croxdale Hall, who died in 1750

In the name of God Amen I William Stoddard, late Coachman at Croxdale in the Chappelory of Croxdale in the Parish of St Oswald in the County of Durham, being very Infirm of body but of Sound Mind and Memory, Do make this My Last Will and Testament in Manner Following First I Give my Soul to God: and My Body to the Earth to be Buryed in a Privet and Dessent Mannure and as to such worldly Goods as it has Pleased God to Bless me with I Give and Despose of as Follows:

Imprimis: I Give to Ann Palmour as a Gratefull Acqnowlagement for the Trubelle an Pains She has Taken with Me My Silvir Wire Buckals. Itm: I Give to Ralph Cragg Junr for the Truble and Pains he has Taken with Me Half a Crown. Itm: I Give to Mr Warham Mr Maire Mr Watterton Mr Bamber Mr Ashmall Mr Hankin Mr Rafer & Mr Whilson, Half a Crown Each and as to all the Rest or Residue of My Personall Estate or worldly Goods what so ever after My Just Debts, Funerall Expence and What further may be Contracted be paid I Give and bequeath unto My Sunn James Stoddard whom I Heare Make and Declare my Sole Executor of this My last will and Teastament . . . Dated the Eight Day of June One Thousand Seven Hundred & Fifty . . .

Inventory of the belongings of William Stoddard, taken 8 June 1750

Itm: A Note for 20£
A Silver Watch Makers name Gorge Thornbourg, London, inside numb^d 635
One Pare Silvir Buckals Tow Pare Silvir Sleave Buttons
Nine Sharts & Nine Stocks
One wide Cote, a Strate Cote wastcot and Buck Skin Briches
Tow Looking Glases one at Croxdale & at Durham
A Table at Durham
One Pare of Bouts & Tow Pare of Soled Shows
A Shagg Rean Case with Three Razers a Pare of Spers
A Shaggrean Case & Hone
Silvir Stock Buckall

Receipt dated 22 December 1750

Reced . . . by me James Stoddard . . . from Bryan Salvin Esq. The sum of Twenty Pounds being so much of my late fathers Effects as was at the time of his Decease in the hands of the said Bryan Salvin on his promissory note. I rayceved the same by the hands of John Maire of Grays Inn Esq.

(DRO, Salvin, D/Sa/F/151)

Extracts from the last will and testament of George Cooke, house steward at Dunham Massey, who died 1791. Will dated 9 November 1790

And first I desire to be privately buried in a morning . . . I also give and devise unto my friend Isaac Worthington of Altrincham . . . Gentleman,[4] and my nephew John Hodgkinson the younger of Liverpool . . . Book-keeper, all that my freehold Messuage Burgage and Tenement . . . being in Altrincham . . . now in the possession of Josiah Garner the elder as tenant to me, and also all that my leasehold messuage and tenement . . . now in the possession of Thomas Rowlinson and John Royle[5] as tenants to me and which I hold by Lease for lives granted to me by the Right Honourable George Harry Earl of Stamford,[6] and also all that my other messuage and tenement . . . now in the possession of John Howard and Ann Farnworth as tenants to me . . . And I do declare that I have given and

222

devised the said respective freehold and leasehold hereditaments and premises unto the said Isaac Worthington and John Hodgkinson . . . upon trust and to the intent and purpose that they . . . shall make sale . . . of all the said respective . . . premises . . .

And I give and devise unto the said Isaac Worthington and John Hodgkinson the sum of four hundred pounds . . . upon trust . . . that they do place the said sum . . . out at Interest and . . . shall . . . dispose of the yearly Interest Income . . . into the proper hands of my Sister Frances Saunders . . .

And I also give and devise unto the said Isaac Worthington and John Hodgkinson . . . the further sum of four hundred pounds . . . upon trust . . . that they do place the said sum . . . out at Interest and . . . shall . . . dispose of the yearly Interest Income . . . into the proper hands of my Sister Martha Hodgkinson . . .

And I also give and bequeath to the following persons the several Legacies following, that is to say, To my Brother Augustine Cooke the sum of three hundred pounds and my wearing apparel, silver watch, rasor case with the five rasors therein, one penknife, one pair of scissors, one large hone, and my money scales and weights in the shagreen case. To Mary Cooke wife of my said brother . . . the sum of twenty pounds . . . To my Sister Ellen Garner the sum of One Hundred pounds . . . To the children of my late niece Mary Bradshaw the sum of one hundred pounds apiece . . . To Jane the daughter of my late Brother Samuel Cooke the sum of three hundred pounds . . . To the children of my said sister Frances Saunders the sum of two hundred pounds apiece . . . To the children of my said Sister Martha Hodgkinson the sum of two hundred pounds apiece . . . To the two daughters of my said Brother Augustine Cooke the sum of three hundred pounds apiece . . .

To the right honourable George Harry Earl of Stamford the sum of one hundred pounds and my mare Tabinet . . . To the honourable Booth Grey the sum of one hundred pounds and half of my silver waiter given to me by him and the honourable John Grey and eight volumes of Ellis's modern husbandry . . . To the said John Grey the other half of my said silver waiter, my picture of the late dear Earl of Warrington, my picture of old Driver, my amberheaded Cane, my Gun made by Barker of Wigan, my shot Belt, my large quarto volume of the late reverend Mr. Lancaster's work on the revelation of Saint John and my large quarto volume of the complete farmer . . . To Sir Henry Mainwaring Baronet the sum of one hundred pounds, my silver Gill with arms engraved thereon, my large money scales and weights in a mahogany case, my late dear wife's gold ring and my silver seal with arms engraved thereon with red ground . . .

And it is my desire that the Dunham Family and Sir Henry Mainwaring will accept of their respective legacies as token of my gratitude for the many favors they have been pleased to confer on me . . .

To my said Nephew John Hodgkinson the further sum of twenty pounds, my two hand whips, my measuring chain and my Money weights and scales in a mahogany Case made by Gibson . . .

To my Servant Hannah Leather the sum of one hundred pounds . . . To the servants of the said Earl of Stamford residing at Dunham Massey in the Winter Season and usually stiled the Dunham Servants and who shall be living in the said Earl's service at my decease the sum of two guineas each . . .

And I give and bequeath all my books, pamphlets and manuscripts and my silver plate not by me herein before disposed of unto my said Brother Augustine, my said sisters Frances Saunders, Martha Hodgkinson and Ellen Garner and my said Nephew John Hodgkinson to be divided amongst them as equally in point of value as the said Isaac Worthington and John Foster can divide the same. And I give and bequeath all my household goods and furniture of what nature or kind soever unto my said Brother . . . and my said Sisters to be divided amongst them . . .

(CRO, WS 1791, George Cooke)

Extracts from the will of John Cutler, brewer, Dunham Massey, Cheshire, who died 1830. Will dated 29 December 1829

And I give and bequeath unto my wife Betty . . . all the household goods and furniture plate linen and china of which I shall or may be possessed of at the time of my decease . . .

Also I give and bequeath all that my leasehold cottage . . . with the garden and appurtenances thereto belonging situate in Dunham Massey . . . which is now in the occupation of William Lingard[7] as Tenant thereof to me, and held by virtue of a Lease for three lives granted by the Earl of Stamford and Warrington, unto my said wife . . . And I give devise and bequeath all those my freehold messuages, cottages or dwelling houses with the buildings lands and appurtenances thereto belonging situate . . . in the parish of Old Swinford in the county of Worcester . . . which are now in the occupation of William Perrins as Tenant thereof to me unto my friends Harry Staples of Lymm in the County of Chester, Gentleman, and Thomas Griffith of Liverpool in the County of Lancaster, Liquor Merchant . . . upon trust that they . . . shall from time to time during the natural life of my said wife permit and suffer her to receive and take the Rents, Issues and profits of the said hereditaments and premises as the same shall become due, for her own sole use. . . .

On 13 April 1830 executors swore Cutler's personal estate was worth not more than £600.

(CRO, WS 1830, John Cutler)

Extracts from the will of William Trenholm, servant, of Whittlebury, Northampton. Will dated 22 March 1838

. . . And my Will is that my Wife shall have all my books and my Will is further that Ann Turlington Wife of William Turlington of Brixworth in the said county of Northampton immediately after my death shall take and sell my watch, Flute and Wearing apparel also my best Boots and Shoes and the proceeds of such sale to be paid over to my said wife Ann Trenholm for her own use . . .

On 17 November 1838 executor swore the estate was worth under £200.

(NRO, Northampton wills, William Trenholm, 1838)

The wills of female servants are more unusual, as they were likely to own fewer goods and property than men. However, a woman servant who had remained single and without children might well make a will.

Extracts from the will of Elizabeth Morris, servant, of Northampton. Will dated 11 December 1843

> I give and bequeath unto my friend Elizabeth Linnell my clothes chest to and for her own use and benefit and I give and bequeath unto her all my clothes and wearing apparel whatsoever trusting that she will distribute them among my nieces . . . I give and bequeath my money and all other my personal estate whatsoever unto William Tomalin of Northampton, gentleman . . . upon trust to pay my debts funeral and testamentary expences thereout and to place the residue thereof out at Interest and pay such Interest as it shall become due unto my Brother William Morris of Frisby, Leicestershire . . .

On 2 June 1847, executor swore the estate was worth not more than £200.

(NRO, Northampton wills, Elizabeth Morris, 1843)

A few female servants died wealthy, leaving charitable endowments more usually seen in the wills of well-to-do men.

Extracts from the last will and testament of Margaret Parke, spinster and servant of Bryan Salvin of Croxdale, Durham. Will dated 1734.

> . . . In the first place I Give and Bequeath unto my Sister Elizabeth Morrison of Hexham in the County of Northumberland Widow, One Hundred Pounds. I also Give and Bequeath unto the three Daughters of my late Brother, Hugh Parke of Rye Hill deceased, unto each of them Ten Pounds apiece, and unto Elizabeth Parke Widow & Relict of my said late Brother Hugh Parke, Five pounds to buy her Mourning. I also Give and Bequeath unto Margaret, Daughter of my late Brother Henry Parke deceased Ten Pounds. I also Give and Bequeath unto the Three Sons of my above said Sister Elizabeth Morrison

as followeth . . . unto James Morrison & Gilbert Morrison . . . unto each of them Ten Pounds apiece & unto William Morrison . . . Twenty Pounds. I also Give and Bequeath unto my Cousin Barbara Hall of Newcastle upon Tine Spinster Five Pounds. And whereas Mrs Jane Haggerston, whom I formerly served, was Pleased to Give me One Hundred Pounds, now out of my Gratitude to her, I Desire she will accept of a Legacy of One Hundred Pounds . . . And I Desire my Present Master Bryan Salvin of Croxdale aforesaid Esquire to Allow me to Give and Bequeath . . . unto his eldest Son & Heir Apparent, One Mourning Ring and unto each of his other Children Ten Pounds apiece. And I Give my best Wearing Apparel & Linnen unto my said Sister Elizabeth Morrison, & my Neice Mary, Wife of John Hardwick of Hexham in the County of Northumberland, Esquire. And as to my meaner Wearing Apparel, I Desire it may be Disposed of to & amongst such of the Servants of my said Master Bryan Salvin, & in True Proportion, as he shall think Proper. And I do hereby Appoint & Appropriate the summ of Twenty Pounds for my Funeral Expences & to be Given unto the Poor at or about the time of my Interment in such Manner & Proportion as my Executor herein after named shall think Proper. And lastly all the rest of my Estate whatsoever, as well real as Personal (my Debts, Legacies & Funeral Expences being first Paid & Discharged) I Give Devise & Bequeath unto my said Master Bryan Salvin of Croxdale Esquire, whom I do hereby make constitute and appoint sole Executor of this my last Will and Testament . . . this First day of June in the year of our Lord One Thousand Seavon Hundred & Thirty Four . . .

Codicil dated a few months later

Whereas I Margaret Parke . . . have in my last Will & Testament . . . Appointed my Present Master Bryan Salvin . . . sole Executor . . . I now do hereby Desire he will Please to Undertake . . . to Perform the underwritten Requests I thought Proper not to Express in my said last Will & Testament[8] . . . that as soon as Conveniently may be after my Decease there may be Given unto each of the Priests who now are . . . Resident at the following Places, Five Shillings apiece, to wit, Berrington, Haggerston, Ellingham, Callaley, Biddleston, Thropton, Newcastle upon Tine

& Gateshead House. And the like summ of Five Shillings apiece to each of the Priests who now are . . . Resident in the County Palatine of Durham, not already herein specifyd, except the Priest who shall assist me on my Death Bed, to whom I Desire a Guinea may be Given. I also Desire my said Master Bryan Salvin . . . may from time to time, for Ever, put out . . . Thirty Pounds out of the Yearly Produce of which I Desire Eight Priests may each for ever have Half a Crown apiece given them to say each of them a Mass for my Soul, on the Anniversary of that Day on which it shall Please Almighty God to call me out of this World.

And the remaining Yearly Produce of the said Thirty Pounds I Desire may each year for ever be Distributed to & amongst such Poor Catholics as my said Master Bryan Salvin . . . shall think Proper . . . And a Desire a Debt of Six Pounds due to me from my Neice Mary Wife of John Hardwick of Hexham . . . may be forgiven her. And as to the summ of One Hundred Pounds . . . Given and Bequeathed to Mrs Jane Haggerston, I Desire my said Master Bryan Salvin Esq. may yearly & every year during the lifetime of the said Mrs Jane Haggerston pay . . . to the said Mrs Jane Haggerston the Interest thereof for her own Proper use. And after the Decease of the said Mrs Jane Haggerston I Desire the said One Hundred Pounds may be Given unto the Monastery of English Nuns at Pont Oise . . . upon Condition that the said Monastery of English Nuns at Pont Oise . . . shall Cause or Procure each year for ever Ten Masses to be said for the Repose of my Soul & of the Soul of the sd. Mrs Jane Haggerston . . .

As evidence that Margaret's desires were carried out, the Salvin Papers include a series of receipts for payments of interest to Mrs Haggerston and other payments to the English nuns at Pont Oise, which continue well into the 1750s.

(DRO, Salvin, D/Sa/F 144)

Single women, unlike married women, were allowed to own an interest in property in their own right and this too might necessitate the making of a will.

Extracts from the last will and testament of Elizabeth Byrom, kitchen maid at Dunham Massey, who died 1819. Will dated 16 November 1815

First I give and bequeath unto my niece Martha Thomason . . . the Bed with the Bolster and Pillow used therewith, the whitewood Box standing in my Bedchamber, the Chest of Mahogany Drawers . . . my mahogany Tea Board and Tea Table, my Tea Spoons, and Tea Tongs and Brass Pestle and Mortar, two of my Brass candlesticks and all my Chinaware. And I also give and bequeath unto my sister Phoebe all the rest of my household goods, furniture, wearing apparel . . . and also the sum of thirty three pounds and fourteen shillings now in the hands of Messieurs Worthington Harrop and Nicholls of Altrincham . . . together with all interest which shall be due in respect thereof at the time of my decease . . .

And I give and bequeath unto Isaac Ridgway of Brown Edge within Lymm . . . yeoman, and my nephew Samuel Thomason of Thelwall . . . farmer . . . the sum of two pounds apiece for the trouble they may have in the execution of the trusts and executorship with which they are hereinafter invested.

And I give and devise unto my said niece Martha Thomason . . . one annuity of eight pounds of lawful money to be payable out of my leasehold estate situate . . . in High Legh.

And subject to the said annuity . . . I give and bequeath my said leasehold estate unto my said sister Phoebe Thomason

On 8 January 1820 the executors swore the personal estate was under the value of £300.

(CRO, WS 1820, Elizabeth Byrom)

Wills, of course, can give a distorted picture of the whole. Generally, the servant who died wealthy was an exception, and this was true even of country-house servants.

Eric Horne summed up his experience

Had I been three inches taller, a six-foot man, I could easily have got to the very top of the tree. . . . Though I have never had to borrow a penny in my life, I cannot say I am much

229

better off than when I began in gentleman's service . . . if a man has a family and wife to keep, and house rent to pay, there is not much left out of a wage of seventy or eighty pounds a year, finding his own clothes. If a servant is an honest man . . . he will be worse off at the end of thirty years' service than when he began. He may, if he is a single man all his life, manage to keep out of the workhouse at the end, but he would have to be lucky, and have found good situations. Perhaps one in a hundred butlers gets a sort of pension, enough to keep him out of the workhouse . . . if I must die in the workhouse, I must.

(Horne, *What the Butler Winked at*, pp. 280–1)

Notes

Introduction

1. For discussions on working-class autobiography and literacy see, for example, John Burnett, ed., *Useful Toil: Autobiographies of Working People from the 1820s to the 1920s*, Allen Lane, 1974 and David Vincent, *Bread, Knowledge and Freedom: a Study of Nineteenth-century Working-class Autobiography*, Europa, 1981.
2. For this and for a comprehensive bibliography of works on country-house service see Jessica Gerard, *Country House Life: Family and Servants, 1815–1914*, Blackwells, 1994, p. 6.
3. 'A Daily Journal or Memorandum Book' by Thomas, Footman in the service of the 2nd Duke of Sutherland, 1838–9, SRO, D4177/1–2. The diary does not give the writer's surname and therefore he is referred to throughout as 'Thomas the footman'.
4. For urban service see Tim Meldrum, *Domestic Service and Gender, 1660–1750: Life and work in the London Household*, Longman, 2000.
5. Gerard, *Country House Life*, p. 162.
6. See Pamela Sambrook, *A Country House at Work: Three Centuries of Dunham Massey*, National Trust, 2003, pp, 57–74.
7. NRO, Fitzwilliam of Milton, F(M)C.
8. DeRO, FitzHerberts of Tissington, 239M/F8196 et alia.
9. SRO, Sutherland Ms, D593/P/28/13.
10. Published in Frank Victor Dawes, *Not in Front of the Servants*, 1973, Century 1989, pp. 22–3.
11. NRO, Spendlove of Gretton, Sp G 354 et alia.
12. DeRO, Harpur Crewe of Calke, D2375M 242/16/5 et alia.
13. See for example Peter Brears, *The Compleat Housekeeper: a household in Queen Anne times*, Wakefield Historical Publications, 2000.
14. National Trust, Stamford Estates Office, Altrincham, Cheshire, Journal of WT.
15. Dorothy Wise, ed., *Diary of William Tayler, Footman, 1837*, St Marylebone Society, 1987.
16. Thomas, 'Journal', SRO, D4177/1–2.

17. Annie Norman's Diary, 1914, DeRO, D5161/1.
18. Liz Stanley, ed., *The Diaries of Hannah Cullwick*, Virago, 1984; Harriet Messenger's Diary (1880s), SHC, 498/6/2; and Sarah Wells's Diary, WSRO, Add. Mss. 41, 235 and 237.
19. See John Burnett, David Vincent and David Mayall, eds, *The Autobiography of the Working Class: an annotated and critical bibliography*, 3 vols, New York University Press, 1984, 1987, 1989.
20. Rosina Harrison, *Gentlemen's Gentlemen: my friends in service*, Arlington Books, 1976 and *Rose: My Life in Service*, Futura, 1976.
21. WCRO, Mordaunt, Cr 1368, vol. 4/62.
22. Wise, *William Tayler*, p. 54.
23. NRO, Fitzwilliam of Milton, F(M)G 1039; Mrs Wrigley, 'A Plate-Layer's Wife' in *Life as we have known it*, ed. Margaret Llewelyn Davies, 1931, Virago, 1977, p. 59.
24. Annie Norman's Diary, 1914, DeRO, D5161/1.
25. BRO, Lucas Papers L30/11/36/1–3.

Chapter One

1. E.g. Mrs Penelope Sternes to her mother Lady Mordaunt, 22 September 1728, WCRO, Mordaunt, CR 1368, vol. 2/31.
2. See CRO, Huddlestones of Sawston, 488/C3/DG.
3. Harrison, *Rose*, p. 36.
4. Ernest King, *The Green Baize Door*, William Kimber, 1963, p. 19.
5. See Gerard, *Country House Life*, p. 181.
6. Census returns for Tittensor, 1841.

Chapter Two

1. For an analysis of wage rates see Gerard, *Country House Life*, pp. 200–4.
2. Mr Barry, later Sir Charles Barry, at that time employed in rebuilding Trentham Hall.

Chapter Three

1. Frederick Gorst, *Of Carriages and Kings*, Allen, 1956, pp. 129–31.
2. Burnett, *Useful Toil*, p. 149.
3. Gorst, *Carriages and Kings*, p. 128.
4. Pamela Sambrook, 'Strategies for Survival: the Servant Problem in the first half of the twentieth century' in *The Twentieth Century Great House*, ed. Malcolm Airs, Oxford University Department for Continuing Education, 2002, pp. 23–34.

Chapter Five

1. Margaret Thomas, 'Behind the Green Baize Door', from *The Day before Yesterday*, ed. Noel Streatfeild, Collins, 1956, p. 94.
2. Chaumer: separate building for servants. Hanging lum: a chimney hood over the fireplace.
3. Loons: lads.

Chapter Six

1. For board wages and other arrangements about servant meals see C. Anne Wilson, 'Keeping Hospitality and Board Wages: Servants' Feeding Arrangements from the Middle Ages to the Nineteenth Century' in Wilson, ed., *Food for the Community: Special diets for Special Groups*, Edinburgh University Press, 1993.
2. See Pamela Sambrook, *Country House Brewing in England, 1500–1900*, Hambledon, 1996.
3. Egg hot or nog: a drink of beer, eggs, sugar and nutmeg.
4. Scimmerlads: dumplings cooked with vegetables.
5. Brose: made from oatmeal and boiling water.
6. Cairnbulg quinie: a girl from Cairnbulg, i.e. a day labourer.
7. Mrs Galleazzie was the Sutherlands' London housekeeper.
8. This refers to the practice of serving beer in a table-top barrel which was wheeled down the centre of the table so that everyone could fill their horn cup in their turn.
9. A hogshead contained 54 gallons.

Chapter Seven

1. Ernest King, *Green Baize Door*, p. 51.
2. Charles W. Cooper, *Town and Country or Forty Years in Private Service with the Aristocracy*, Lovat Dickson, London, 1937, p. 198.
3. Gordon Grimmett, 'The Lamp Boy's Story' in Rosina Harrison, ed., *Gentlemen's Gentlemen*, 1976, p. 36.
4. 'Lion' was the traditional name of a series of house mastiffs at Dunham Massey, guard dogs whose care probably fell to the footmen.
5. Philip Osgood was the butler from 1819. He obviously had a house on the estate at Enville.
6. David Seamman was head coachman.
7. John Davenport was the son of the Farm Steward at Dunham Massey.
8. The gamekeepers were paid for killing rats and other vermin, a tally of tails kept as a record on which to base payment, which could amount to several pounds in a year. Here they seem to have treated the rest of the staff to a party.
9. Mrs Jones was the lodge-keeper at Dunham Massey.

10. Mme Rousseau was the Duchess of Sutherland's personal laundry maid and older than the French nursery maid.
11. Mrs Perry was the woman who came in to do the laundry.
12. Bill was Annie's brother and a soldier in the Yorkshire Regiment.
13. The footmen's dormitory at West Hill was over the servants' hall and big enough to accommodate dances.
14. Mrs Adams was the housekeeper at West Hill.
15. Mr Wright was the Duke of Sutherland's secretary.

Chapter Eight

1. See Jill Barber, '"Stolen Goods": the Sexual Harassment of Female Servants in West Wales during the Nineteenth Century', *Rural History*, vol. 4, no. 2, October 1993.
2. Sambrook, *Country House at Work*, p. 196.
3. Lady Alexandra's parents, the 3rd Duke and Duchess of Sutherland, were estranged and the latter set up home at Sutherland Towers, Torquay. See Denis Stuart, *Dear Duchess: Millicent Duchess of Sutherland, 1867–1955*, Victor Gollancz, 1982, p. 43.
4. Tommy Phipps was Lady Astor's nephew and Joyce Grenfell's brother.
5. Mrs Kirkby was the Lilleshall housekeeper.
6. Mrs Cleaver was the replacement housekeeper.

Chapter Nine

1. Eric Horne, *What the Butler Winked at*, Werner Laurie, 1923, p. 83.
2. For example, John Macdonald, *The Memoirs of an Eighteenth-Century Footman, 1790*, Century, 1985, p. 57.
3. Horne, *What the Butler Winked at*, p. 58.
4. Miss Fetherstonhaugh, spinster younger sister to that more famous Miss Frances Bullock, housemaid, who married Sir Harry Fetherstonhaugh. She was Sarah Neal/Wells' mistress who took the name of Fetherstonhaugh in the 1870s.
5. See H.G. Wells, *Experiment in Autobiography, vol. 1*, 1934, Faber & Faber, 1984 – 'Except that she was honest, my mother was perhaps the worst housekeeper that was ever thought of', p. 110.

Chapter Ten

1. Pamela Sambrook, *A Country House at Work*, p. 90.
2. Adeline Hartcup, *Below Stairs in the Great Country Houses*, Sidgwick and Jackson, 1980, p. 111.
3. An Old Servant, *Domestic Servant*, Constable, 1917, p. 45.
4. Isaac Worthington was a leading solicitor in nearby Altrincham and also the Dunham land agent.

5. John Royle was a gamekeeper on the Dunham estate.
6. George Harry Grey, the 5th Earl of Stamford, Cooke's employer.
7. William Lingard was a labourer on the home farm at Dunham.
8. Probably because she was making legacies to Roman Catholics.

Sources and Select Bibliography

SOURCES

Archival Collections
Bagot Ms, Staffordshire Record Office
Bateman Ms, Northamptonshire Record Office
Cheshire Wills, Cheshire Record Office
Dryden of Canons Ashby, Northamptonshire Record Office
Dyott Ms, Staffordshire Record Office
Effingham Ms, Surrey History Centre
FitzHerberts of Tissington Ms, Derbyshire Record Office
Fitzwilliam of Milton Ms, Northamptonshire Record Office
Goodwood Ms, West Sussex Record Office
Harpur Crewe of Calke Ms, Derbyshire Record Office
Heathcote of Hursley Ms, Hampshire Record Office
Hodgkins Ms, Durham Record Office
Huddlestones of Sawston Ms, Cambridgeshire County Record Office, Cambridge
Huntingdon Quarter Sessions, Cambridgeshire County Record Office, Huntingdon
Jervise of Herriard Ms, Hampshire Record Office
Lancaster Ms, Kelmarsh Hall
Lane Fox Ms, Leeds Central Library
Leicester-Warren of Tabley Ms, Cheshire Record Office
Londonderry Estate Archives, Durham Record Office
Lucas Ms, Bedfordshire and Luton Archives and Records Service
Mordaunt Ms, Warwickshire County Record Office
Newdigate Ms, Warwickshire County Record Office
Northampton Wills, Northampton Record Office
Orlebar Ms, Bedfordshire and Luton Archives and Records Service
Packe Ms, Leicestershire Record Office
Portland Ms, Nottinghamshire Archives
Rogers of Titchfield and Warsash Ms, Hampshire Record Office
Salvin Estate Archives, Durham Record Office
Shrewsbury Ms, Staffordshire Record Office

Spendlove of Gretton Ms, Northamptonshire Record Office
Stafford Family Ms, Staffordshire Record Office
Stafford Asylum, Staffordshire Record Office
Stamford Ms, Enville Archive, Enville Hall
——, John Rylands Library, University of Manchester
Stevens of Bradfield Ms, Berkshire Record Office
Strathmore Estate Archives, Durham Record Office
Sutherland Ms, Staffordshire Record Office
Turvile Constable-Maxwell Ms, Leicestershire Record Office
Whitbread Ms, Bedfordshire and Luton Archives and Records Service
Wimpole Ms, Cambridgeshire County Record Office, Cambridge

Autobiography

Balderson, Eileen, with Douglas Goodlad, *Backstairs Life in a Country House*, David & Charles, 1982

Cooper, Charles W., *Town and Country or Forty Years in Private Service with the Aristocracy*, Lovat Dickson, 1937

Dean, Charles, 'The Boot Boy's Story', in *Gentlemen's Gentlemen: my friends in service*, ed. Rosina Harrison, Arlington Books, 1976

Fraser, David, ed., *The Christian Watt Papers*, Paul Harris, 1983

Fudge, Dorothy, *Sands of Time*, Word and Action, 1981

Gibbs, Rose, *In Service: Rose Gibbs Remembers*, Archives for Bassingbourn and Comberton Village Colleges, 1981

Gorst, Frederick, *Of Carriages and Kings*, Allen, 1956

Grimmett, Gordon, 'The Lamp Boy's Story', in *Gentlemen's Gentlemen: my friends in service*, ed. Rosina Harrison, Arlington Books, 1976

Harrison, Rosina, *Rose: My Life in Service*, 1975, Futura 1976

Horne, Eric, *What the Butler Winked at*, Werner Laurie, 1923

James, John, *The Memoirs of a House Steward*, Bury, Holt & Co., 1949

King, Ernest, *The Green Baize Door*, William Kimber, 1963

Lanceley, William, *From Hall-Boy to House-Steward*, Edward Arnold, 1925

Layton, Mrs, 'Memories of seventy years', in *Life as we have known it*, ed. Margaret Llewelyn Davies, 1931, Virago, 1977

Lee, Edwin, 'The Page Boy's Story', in *Gentlemen's Gentlemen: my friends in service*, ed. Rosina Harrison, Arlington Books, 1976

Macdonald, John, *The Memoirs of an Eighteenth-Century Footman, 1790*, Century Publishing, 1985

Powell, Margaret, *Climbing the Stairs*, Peter Davies, 1969

Rennie, Jean, *Every Other Sunday: the Autobiography of a Kitchenmaid*, Arthur Barker, 1955

Sedgwick, Sarah, 'Other People's Children', in *The Day before Yesterday*, ed. Noel Streatfeild, Collins, 1956

Stanbridge, Ethel, 'Below Stairs in Bedfordshire', *Bedfordshire Record Society*, 17, 1911

Swainbank, Lavinia, unpublished autobiography, extracts published in John Burnett, ed., *Useful Toil: Autobiographies of Working People from the 1820s to the 1920s*, Allen Lane, 1974, pp. 220–6

Thomas, Albert, *Wait and See*, Michael Joseph, 1944

Thomas, Margaret, 'Behind the Green Baize Door', in *The Day before Yesterday*, ed. Noel Streatfeild, Collins, 1956

Washington, George, 'The Hall Boy's Story' in *Gentlemen's Gentlemen: my friends in service*, ed. Rosina Harrison, Arlington Books, 1976

Westall, Lilian, 'The Good Old Days', unpublished autobiography, extracts published in John Burnett, ed., *Useful Toil: Autobiographies of Working People from the 1820s to the 1920s*, Allen Lane, 1974, pp. 214–20

Wrigley, Mrs, 'A Plate-Layer's Wife', in *Life as we have known it*, ed. Margaret Llewelyn Davies, 1931, Virago, 1977

Collected Autobiography

Burnett, John, ed., *Useful Toil: Autobiographies of Working People from the 1820s to the 1920s*, Allen Lane, 1974

Davies, Margaret Llewelyn, ed., *Life as we have known it*, 1931, Virago, 1977

Harrison, Rosina, ed., *Gentlemen's Gentlemen: my friends in service*, Arlington Books, 1976

Streatfeild, Noel, *The Day Before Yesterday*, Collins, 1956

Diaries (published)

Stanley, Liz, ed., *The Diaries of Hannah Cullwick*, Virago, 1984

Wise, Dorothy, ed., *Diary of William Tayler, Footman, 1837*, St Marylebone Society, 1987

Diaries (unpublished)

Messenger, Harriet, 'Diary', 1884–94, SHC, 498/6/2

Norman, Annie's Diary, 1914, DRO, D5161/1

Thomas, 'A Daily Journal or Memorandum Book' by Thomas, Footman in the service of the 2nd Duke of Sutherland, 1838–9, SRO D4177/1–2)

Torry, William, 'Memorandum Book', unpublished manuscript, National Trust, Altrincham

Wells, Sarah, 'Diary', University of Illinois Library at Urbana-Champaign, copy in WSR, Add Mss. 41, 235–41, 237

Others

Dawes, Frank Victor, *Not in Front of the Servants*, 1973, Century, 1989

Robinson, John, 'A Butler's View of Man-Service', *The Nineteenth Century: a monthly Review*, vol. XXXI, Jan.–July 1892, quoted in John Burnett, ed., *Useful Toil, Autobiographies of Working People from the 1820s to the 1920s*, Allen Lane, 1974

Stevens, Christine, 'In Service at St Fagans Castle', *Medel*, no. 3, 1986

SELECT BIBLIOGRAPHY

Place of publication is London unless otherwise stated.

Barber, Jill, '"Stolen Goods": the Sexual Harassment of Female Servants in West Wales during the Nineteenth Century', *Rural History*, vol. 4, no. 2, October 1993

Brears, Peter, *The Compleat Housekeeper: a household in Queen Anne times*, Wakefield, Wakefield Historical Publications, 2000

Burnett, John, Vincent, David and Mayall, David, eds, *The Autobiography of the Working Class: an annotated and critical bibliography*, 3 vols, New York, New York University Press, 1984, 1987, 1989

Dawes, Frank Victor, *Not in Front of the Servants*, 1973, Century, 1989

Foster, Charles F., *Seven Households: Life in Cheshire and Lancashire, 1582 to 1774*, Northwich, Arley Hall Press, 2002

Gerard, Jessica, *Country House Life: Family and Servants, 1815–1914*, Oxford, Blackwells, 1994

Hartcup, Adeline, *Below Stairs in the Great Country Houses*, Sidgwick and Jackson, 1980

Hecht, Joseph Jean, *The Domestic Servant in Eighteenth-Century England*, Routledge and Kegan Paul, 1956, reprinted 1980

Horn, Pamela, *The Rise and Fall of the Victorian Servant*, 1975, Stroud, Alan Sutton, 1986

——, *Life Below Stairs in the 20th Century*, Stroud, Sutton Publishing, 2001

Hughes, Kathryn, *The Victorian Governess*, Hambledon Press, 1993

Meldrum, Tim, *Domestic Service and Gender, 1660–1750: Life and work in the London Household*, Longman, 2000

Sambrook, Pamela, *Country House Brewing in England, 1500–1900*, Hambledon Press, 1996

——, *The Country House Servant*, Stroud, Sutton Publishing in association with the National Trust, 1999

——, 'Strategies for Survival: the Servant Problem in the first half of the twentieth century', in *The Twentieth Century Great House*, ed. Malcolm Airs, Oxford University Department for Continuing Education, 2002

——, *A Country House at Work: Three Centuries of Dunham Massey*, National Trust, 2003

Turner, E.S., *What the Butler Saw*, Michael Joseph, 1962

Vincent, David, *Bread, Knowledge and Freedom: a Study of Nineteenth-century Working-class Autobiography*, Europa, 1981

Wells, H.G., *Experiment in Autobiography, vol. 1*, 1934, Faber & Faber, 1984

Wilson, C. Anne, 'Keeping Hospitality and Board Wages: Servants' Feeding Arrangements from the Middle Ages to the Nineteenth Century', in Wilson, ed., *Food for the Community: Special Diets for Special Groups*, Edinburgh University Press, 1993

Index

General Index

Name Index